BUILDING
BRILLIANT
SCHOOLS

WHAT G.R.E.A.T.
LEADERS DO DIFFERENTLY

INTERNATIONAL BESTSELLER

DR. ANDY PARKER

Praise for Building Brilliant Schools

Dr. Andy's description of a Brilliant school is what ALL schools should look like. His thoughts offer a refreshing examination of what Expectations really are or should be in schools.

— **Lt. Col. Nick Overby**, Educational and
Military Leader, ret. United States Army

This book nearly catapulted me out of my chair when I read that tenacity is paramount to reaching students and to increasing student achievement. I literally shouted, "Yes!" Sometimes, in the education business, you just have to "endeavor to persevere," and Dr. Andy explains that tenacity is key to reaching students and to increasing student achievement.

— **Dr. Sandra Reed,** Superintendent,
Bay St. Louis-Waveland Schools

The parallels presented between achievement and academic success, as well as subsequent professional accomplishments, are so profound and logical that they provided a "let there be light moment" and truly impressed upon me the need for a celebration of achievement no matter how small it may be.

— **Jamie Williams**, Leadership Coach and former
School Principal, Jackson County Schools

One of the things I absolutely adore about Dr. Andy Parker's G.R.E.A.T. Leadership Philosophy is that he begins by reminding practitioners of the importance of gratitude in day-to-day life. As someone who has focused extensively on gratitude in both my personal and professional roles for at least a decade, I will admit I did not expect to be challenged by this section of the book. But Dr. Andy managed to inspire and challenge me when he pushed beyond the why of gratitude, outlining concrete steps that we can take as school leaders to bring the practice of gratitude to school life. He clearly articulates how to bring practices of gratitude to students, teachers, and other leaders through the book, making it a valuable tool for anyone who wants to take the application of gratitude to the next level. This book truly has the potential to transform schools—and in turn, the lives of students and families.

— Dr. Monique Harrison Henderson,
Author, Educator, and Leader

*Andy captures the essence of what G.R.E.A.T leaders do differently! "Brilliant" schools don't happen unless leaders are hyper-focused on the pillars described in this book.
I was particularly taken by Dr. Andy's focus on tenacity. Improving student outcomes and building a brilliant school culture is hard work . . . and the work is not linear. You make progress one day, and you have a setback the next—the work can be discouraging. The very best leaders are tenacious. They behave in a way that inspires others to keep moving forward. They create growth mindsets. And, they despise and seek to abolish an "I can't" attitude. Dr. Andy's focus on tenacity provides school leaders with a roadmap for success.*

— Dr. Hank Bounds, former Mississippi State Superintendent of Education and President of the University of Nebraska

Andy's powerful take on the integral role of the Relationship Pillar in building G.R.E.A.T. schools is both insightful and compelling. His experience and passion as a servant leader jump off of the pages throughout this section. You will find yourself teary-eyed, challenged, and inspired throughout. Ultimately, you will be a more self-aware, relationship-focused leader on your way to impacting students' lives in a way you could have never imagined before.

— **Clay Corley**, Superintendent, Desoto Parish Schools

With his quote "It [achievement] is deeper than letter grades on a report card or the scores on the state test," Dr. Parker reminds us that even in this age of accountability, we must remember that the goal of education is to create college and career-ready students who are prepared to be contributing citizens. The process of achievement and the ability to transfer the process will illuminate the path for students to become such. The goal, therefore, is not the state test; the goal is the mission. The state test is a checkpoint on the journey.

— **Patty Cooper**, Chief Academic Officer,
Pass Christian Schools

Dr. Parker's book, Building Brilliant Schools, *walks school leaders through what it takes to lead in our schools today. It begins with the power of gratitude and how being grateful leads to great leadership. This is a must-read for all individuals wishing to improve their leadership and lead their schools to brilliance.*

— **Kim Campbell**, Author, Speaker, and School
Leader, Hopkins Middle School

Building Brilliant Schools: What G.R.E.A.T. Leaders Do Differently is a very organized, personal, and easy to read text. While reading, I felt as if I were in the room speaking directly to the author. In particular, the pillar on Achievement spoke to both high performing and lower performing school and district leaders, as learning is the process of growing the muscle in all brains. As a veteran superintendent in a high-poverty district, the research provided in this chapter spoke to my purpose, progress, and struggle to achieve, when there are so many obstacles before us. This book is practical, witty, and heartfelt. I enjoyed it and look forward to sharing it with the leaders in my district and my professional colleagues.

— Dr. Shannon Vincent-Raymond,
Superintendent, Moss Point School District

Building Brilliant Schools is the prescription for every human who ever dared to embrace young people's hearts and minds and to make the world a better place. Imagine having in your possession the key to consistency, genuineness, and motivation for students. Picture being the kind of leader who has the brightest torch with an infinite supply of fuel to illuminate the path, share the light, and lead your team to the splendor of success.
Bound in the pages of Building Brilliant Schools, readers will find extraordinary truths, compelling anecdotes, and thought-provoking questions for educators who wish to grow and develop positive beliefs and a lifestyle of grace, gratitude, and greatness. Dr. Andy's theme champions the incredible influence we, as educators and leaders, wield in our communities. He speaks clearly, kindly, and directly and his wisdom about building school culture is evident on every page. Dive headlong into the waters of this incredible book and be a beam of light for others.

— Cythina Lofton, Educational Leader

In Building Brillant Schools, *Dr. Parker underscores the importance of having positive relationships with oneself and others as a pillar in building a Brillant School. Not having this pillar makes it impossible to build an institution of learning that's enjoyed by students, staff, and parents.*

— Dr. William Merritt, Chief of Staff,
Jackson Public Schools

Every positive result likely began with a thought and then the expectation that it would happen. Dr. Andy does a brilliant job of messaging that expectations are critical to academic and personal growth. He examines expectations from a leader's perspective, and his writing is relevant and filled with examples that add depth and relatability. Every leader who wants to achieve success in an academic setting should read this book!

— Tanisha Washington, Director of Educational
Services, Bailey Education Group

BUILDING BRILLIANT SCHOOLS

What G.R.E.A.T. Leaders Do Differently

Dr. Andy Parker

GLOBAL WELLNESS MEDIA
STRATEGIC EDGE INNOVATIONS PUBLISHING
LOS ANGELES, TORONTO, MONTREAL

For permission requests, send an email to drandy@drandyparker.com

First Edition. Published by:
Global Wellness Media
Strategic Edge Innovations Publishing
340 S Lemon Ave #2027
Walnut, California 91789-2706
(866) 467-9090
StrategicEdgeInnovations.com

Publisher's Note: The views expressed in this work are solely those of the authors and do not necessarily reflect the views of the publisher, and the publisher hereby disclaims any responsibilities for them.

Editor: Marjorie Frank
Book Design: Global Wellness Media

Building Brilliant Schools / Dr. Andy Parker. -- 1st ed.
ISBN: 978-1-7363047-7-8 (Kindle)
ISBN: 978-1-7363047-8-5 (Paperback)

Dedications

This book is dedicated to my two parents, David and Rebecca Parker. Their high expectations and loving support served as buoys for my personal and professional preparation and growth.

The book is also dedicated to those students and fellow educators along my journey who have inspired me to work harder and smarter, love my career every day, have fun, and challenge my thinking so that my leadership serves ALL students positively. Thank you!

Acknowledgements

Special thanks go to Jodi Arndt and Marj Frank for their help in making this book a reality. Both served as invaluable thought partners and editors to make my vision for this book come to life. I also want to acknowledge my husband, Ranzy Montet, for checking in with me, loving me, and pushing me throughout this process.

Special thanks also go to the following educators who continued to prod me about my progress on this book, reminded me of the brilliant stories that we shared, and served as special markers in my life as an educator and leader: Barbara Hooks, Sydney Carol Murphey, Dr. Carla Evers, Remona Hicks, Paula Bilbo, Cynthia Lofton, and Dr. Toy Watts.

Table of Contents

THE FOURTH PILLAR OF A BRILLIANT SCHOOL

ACHIEVEMENT

THE FIFTH PILLAR OF A BRILLIANT SCHOOL

TENACITY

THE CULTURE OF A BRILLIANT SCHOOL

Let There Be Light!

I want to be part of a school where kids want to be, where parents want their kids to be, where teachers, leaders, and other staff members want to be—and that parents and community members want to brag about! It's a place where all members leave each day knowing that they were trusted to do and pushed to do what they are capable of doing—where everyone ends the school day wanting to come back. I call this a *brilliant school.*

About the Light in Brilliant Schools

I use the word **brilliant** to refer to schools that serve as beacons of light for students, families, school staff, and the communities that they serve. **Brilliance** is associated with *light, shining, illumination, radiance, color, sunshine, dazzle, talent, smartness, sharpness, cleverness, wisdom, innovation,* and *creativity.* It is in a school described with these terms that I see students happily flourishing and learning; feeling safety, equality, belonging, and connection; and performing at their absolute best.

Every student IS a light, even if you see her hovering under the protection of a hoodie or him hiding quietly in the shadows of others. G.R.E.A.T. leaders and staff members in a brilliant school **look for the brilliance that shines in each student**. We use practices and build relationships that **turn on the switch** and **set students ablaze**. Our teachers and our dynamic school climate **ignite** students' imaginations and **illuminate** possibilities. In the atmosphere of trust, safety, equality, and acceptance, students discover the **radiance within themselves**. They're not afraid to **glow**! Just look at the faces of students who achieve even more than they thought they could—or of students who

1

discover that they belong and have repeated assurance of that. **You'll see them gleam**.

In such a school, **teachers, leaders, and support staff shine,** too. There's **light** burning in each colleague. Working collaboratively to **cast rays** on the capabilities and contributions of each other and of students, all of you can produce **fireworks**! And all members of the brilliant school community **illuminate** each other's value, ideas, talents, and growth. Yes, it is the **dazzling light**—of trusting relationships, gratitude, challenge, respect, and learning milestones— that make growth possible. Students' parents and families, too, are touched by the **beams**. What **radiance** you'll see shining from parents who watch their children enjoying inclusion, trust, respect, and academic achievements!

Most of us also think of ***brilliance*** in the sense of being smart. With high expectations (equally) for all students and with the belief (accompanied by action) that all students can get smarter, we see **sunbursts** of intellectual growth, mastery, competence, academic tenacity, and academic self-efficacy. And as we continue to work in the context of a growth mindset and gratitude for one another, the **radiance** grows and spreads.

When I use the term ***brilliant schools*** throughout this book, I'm also speaking of schools that are steeped in academic tenacity, growth, and "smarts." I use it in the sense of planning and operating a *smart school*. This is a school where we use our brains and hearts and whole beings— everything we know and can learn about gaining, processing, and using knowledge and about academic, social, and personal wellbeing—to make successful things happen for every student. The leaders and staff continually listen to one another, to parents, and to students, gathering data, making evidence-based decisions, and tenaciously working hard and working smart.

I want every educator, staff member, student, and student's family member that I know—and don't know—to be part of a **brilliant school**!

2

About This Book

What's in It?

When I sit down to identify characteristics of a brilliant school, I find it quite easy to describe the kind of school that I feel and believe is great for students, students' families, teachers, support staff, and leaders. (I admit that the list is a long one!) Would that be easy for you, also? Maybe you'd like to take a few minutes right now to make your own list before you go forward with reading this book. Or do this jointly with colleagues or the entire school staff. It will be a great reference for you to revisit often (and maybe revise) as you read and use this book.

So, you've made a list. But getting a brilliant school is something else! As I've pondered what it is that creates and sustains this kind of school, I've found that certain themes keep arising. Looking closely at the desired attributes of a school, I noticed that each was based on underpinnings—assumptions about what needed to exist to establish and support that particular attribute. The underpinnings began to fall into the following categories that, out of my experience, made sense to me. All of them, I realized, were far deeper and broader than just concepts. Each one required belief, vision, and action.

$\quad$ **G**ratitude—noticing, understanding, and actively appreciating people and situations

$\quad$ **R**elationships—the real, trusting, and reliable connections with others

$\quad$ **E**xpectations—the assumptions, intentions, and possibilities we project to each other

$\quad$ **A**chievement—what we believe and how we act to help each other attain at best levels

$\quad$ **T**enacity—how we keep trying, working, adapting, and hoping—without giving up

The more I've delved into the qualities and attributes of what I believe to be *a brilliant school,* I've found that these five underpinning elements (and the beliefs and actions that flow from them) entwine to build a strong, reliable foundation for a school. This is why I've called them **pillars**. When you've researched what it takes to build successful schools (as any leader undoubtedly has), you've likely found other themes or structures. I've chosen these particular ones because I've experienced them first-hand. I've seen how these pillars, together, can transform struggling schools into thriving, engaging, student-centered, equitable places of learning and can also turn fairly successful schools into brilliantly successful schools.

Thus, each section of *Building Brilliant Schools: What G.R.E.A.T. Leaders Do Differently,* describes a time-tested, research-based, key underpinning for a school. The chapters in each pillar address:

- **The Definition**—A clear explanation of what the named pillar means in the context of a school setting
- **The Research**—Some key studies and findings that explore and support the qualities of the pillar and affirm it as a key part of a brilliant school's groundwork
- **The Benefits**—A research-based overview of the gains and contributions (to students and educators) that result from the focus on that pillar
- **Getting Results**—Concrete steps and actions, as well as beliefs and attitudes, to build that pillar and advance the positive outcomes that are possible

Who's the Audience?

The book's title mentions leaders. Yes! This is for school principals, assistant principals, headmasters, and such. It's also for district superintendents and others who coach and manage principals. But we know that principals and superintendents are not the only leaders in schools. Hopefully not, in this age of knowledge about the importance of shared leadership! Department heads, literacy coaches, curriculum directors, team leaders, committee heads, coaches, and every teacher who strives to enlighten and motivate young minds—all fill leadership roles. So, the book is good reading and powerful support for all educators. Parents and school board members will also benefit from the discussions in this book. These chapters focus mostly on the application of the ideas and strategies at a K-12 level, but the information is relevant to pre-school and university practitioners as well.

How Can I Best Use the Book?

The book was designed with the pillars arranged in the G. R. E. A. T. order and with frequent connections to show how the elements and strengths of the five pillars work together. Chapters are arranged logically, consistently addressing the categories shown above. The last chapter in each pillar—the "How Great Leaders Get Results" chapter—describes ready-to-use practices, attitudes, and beliefs, and inspires leaders, staff, and students to create more along the same veins.

You may choose to read the book straight through, grasping the "building" of a brilliant school—pillar by pillar. But it can also be used "reference-style" by leaders, teachers, or college teachers and students: each pillar can stand alone and serve as a guide to educators working on that particular pillar for school improvement.

This book is also a great tool for professional development settings (for leaders, teachers, other staff members, or parents). A leader can use a single pillar, chapter, part of a chapter, specific strategy, quote, or a key idea as the centerpiece for a session or series of sessions.

As you explore this book, you'll notice other ways to use it. They are unlimited! If you are one of the thousands of teachers, leaders, parents, or school board members with the awesome responsibility of building schools that inspire students to flourish, believe in themselves and their peers, and reach goals they never thought imaginable, then— this book Is for YOU!

The First Pillar of a
Brilliant School

Gratitude

In ordinary life, we hardly realize that we receive a great deal more than we give, and that it is only with gratitude that life becomes rich.

—Dietrich Bonhoeffer, 20th Century
Theologian and Anti-Nazi Activist

Growing up in Mississippi, I remember how the expressions "please" and "thank you" peppered everyday interactions between my Mama and the mailman or the waitress at our local diner. I noticed that those seemingly simple words led to smiles and moments of connection. When an acquaintance of my parents would give me a piece of candy or some other coveted token, my mother or father would prompt me: "What are you supposed to say?" I'd respond, "thank you" to the generous adult, and feeling a sense of satisfaction, I'd run off to enjoy the prize.

*At the time, it's unlikely that I gave any thought to the importance of these interactions. Maybe I saw them as habits of a polite, well-mannered upbringing. (After all, this was the South!) Perhaps I watched and listened to my parents' social cues and picked them up just like the toys that dotted the front yard. While "please," "thank you," and "yes ma'am" or "yes sir" frequently tumbled out of my mouth, I didn't necessarily **feel** grateful when I said those things. The outward practice of gratitude was being **ingrained** in me. Yet I hadn't consciously **incorporated** it into an attitude. The quote that opened this section of the book (see the previous page) was certainly true for me: I hardly realized the power of gratitude.*

As an adult, I was more aware that I had blessings granted by others, and I did occasionally express gratitude. Still, even well into adulthood, I had not grasped anything close to Bonhoeffer's words. But then on August 29, 2005, Hurricane Katrina changed life as I knew it and transformed my understanding of gratitude.

Late on the evening of August 29, after the fury of the catastrophic storm had passed, I returned to my home. I found a neighborhood forever altered, water still standing twelve to fourteen feet high in homes, people calling out to their neighbors from their attic windows that they were okay, and a decade of my planning and hard work drowned—floating in the murky bayou water that had once been a source of fun and happiness for my family and friends.

With one storm, priorities were turned upside down; people (those fortunate enough to survive) were turned inside out. What had been significant became insignificant. Loss often serves as the mirror one needs to reexamine life. Katrina was that mirror. In the face of adversity and the absence of the structure that gave us safety, we had to look for security and strength in places other than material goods and circumstances. We had to look to our inner strengths. But we also had to look to each other. We had to face the hard fact that we needed help.

Standing on my street, I stared at broad, blank spaces where homes and belongings were missing and at battered structures of what remained. As strange as it may seem, the surreal scene propelled me to gratitude. While for years I had performed the rituals ordinarily associated with a grateful heart—I had not **known** *or* **felt from within myself** *a warm, deep appreciation for kindness or gifts I received. Just as the devastating material loss deluged me, I had my first down-to-the-bone wave of true gratitude.*

In the days that followed August 29, the American Red Cross became a fixture in our neighborhood. They set up in the parking lot of the local Kmart to distribute water and food supplies. In the human line that snaked through that vacant parking lot dotted with abandoned cars, the atmosphere was hot, humid, and eerily quiet. I stood in hushed silence with the fifty or so people. Like me, they were in shock and need of sustenance as they began to clean up and make sense of the warlike zone around them.

Dazed, I watched the volunteer workers and listened to their kind, uplifting words. I felt grateful that people had come so quickly after the storm to help out, to give water and food, to provide dry clothes, and to assure us that we would be okay. These folks, getting no visible material rewards in return, actively cared. They looked us in the eyes, saw and asked what we needed, and treated us with dignity. In many cases, they had left their homes and families to step into a mess. Unpaid, they worked tirelessly.

Over the next days, weeks, and months, I noticed innumerable small and not-so-small acts of human kindness all around me. Strangers became neighbors, local and national church groups cleaned and cleared what was once our home; volunteers kept showing up— serving food and necessities. And, again and again, I was humbled to tears. I couldn't miss the effects of these acts: the generosity and kind human touches did for me and my neighbors what we could not do for ourselves. And this warm benevolence inspired us to do what we did not think we could do—begin to breathe again, to live again, to hope again. I am continuously grateful to these selfless volunteers because their actions changed me. The seeds of gratitude planted in me as a child sprouted and flourished, renewing my awareness and practice of gratitude.

The effects of my repeated thankfulness for small and large blessings accumulated into a new mindset. I felt positive. The realization that this was not some form of skewed optimism spread through me. There were no rose-colored glasses to shade images of the daily harsh realities. Yet gratitude overshadowed anxiety. **It gave me hope.** It renewed excitement about life and the future.

I found myself awed by this discovery. As I reflected on this inner change—my own new mindset—I was flooded with ideas and questions:

- How does gratitude get deep into one's soul and become part of a mindset?
- It's probably a given that people are thankful when they get help and relief in the face of crisis or tragedy; but how can I be grateful outside of a setting wherein I'm being rescued?
- How can I put my discoveries about gratitude to use right away? Where could I begin?
- How can I share the power of this with others?
- What could the practice of gratitude do in a school setting?
- Could gratitude, perhaps, transform my school community?
- Can we teach gratitude to students or school staff? What would the outcomes be?

Standing in lines in that Kmart parking lot, I had plenty of time to ponder these questions. Before long, I found myself committed to exploring and formulating ways to incorporate gratitude into the lives of the members of my school community.

Chapter 1

What Is Gratitude?

Gratitude is a currency that we can mint for ourselves,
and spend without fear of bankruptcy.
—Fred DeWitt Van Amburgh, Author, Publisher, Lecturer

There are many variations in the definition of gratitude. A few are: the quality of being thankful, the state of being thankful, a readiness to show appreciation for kindness, a readiness to return kindness, expressing appreciation, and acting with appreciation. In approaching the topic of gratitude here, I've borrowed two definitions as starting points. Then, other facets of gratitude have filtered into my definition as I've watched gratitude grow and translate into actions in real-life situations.

Gratitude: A Working Definition

For this book and our work with gratitude in schools, I'll combine two definitions of gratitude explained by three gratitude researchers.

Gratitude: *a two-step cognitive process*
(a) *recognizing that one has obtained a positive outcome*, and
(b) *recognizing that there is an external source for this positive outcome* (Emmons & McCullough, 2003, p. 378).

Gratitude: *an act of giving back out of acknowledgment for what we received* (Howells, 2013, p. 1).

Some definitions include the idea that gratitude is the **emotion** people experience when they recognize the outcome and source of a gift (Bono et al., 2015). Others, such as Kerry Howells, quoted above, include **action** as a part of gratitude—thankfulness given visibly and freely without concern about how the receiver will respond. Others have expanded the understanding of gratitude to apply to situations where a particular person or set of persons is not identifiable as the external source. For example, we can be grateful for such things as situations, elements of nature, poetry, homes, pets, friendships, favorite activities, personal talents or skills, or anything that brings us joy or satisfaction— whether or not another person or being is involved. We can even be grateful for tough situations we've weathered or painful experiences that have helped us grow. A definition of gratitude might then include that it is a thankful response to life circumstances; that is, the ability to notice and savor the many features of one's life.

Long before I read the definition of gratitude articulated by Emmons and McCullough, I had come to understand their concept. Notice this phrase in their definition: "cognitive process." This implies conscious awareness and thoughtfulness. I believe that in the past I would have defined gratitude as a feeling. But during my Katrina experience, I **consciously** recognized "positive outcomes" from "external sources"— acts of kindness and care, contributions of hard physical labor, gifts of material essentials, of grueling work, of sweat, and of sacrifice.

Beyond identifying the gifts and the sources, I paid more attention to the feelings I was having around gratitude. I recognized and examined my appreciation for and acceptance of these outcomes, as awkward and humbling as that acceptance felt at times. I

The components of gratitude include the cognitive understanding, the emotional response, and the action that flows from those.

got better and better at identifying the multiple sources of goodness that very much stood outside of myself. I was grateful for life, grateful to see the faces of neighbors, and grateful to be sharing my grief with others in the same situation. Every single thing that I **did have** in my possession became a treasure. I found myself grateful for shoes, for a blue sky or a breeze, or even for cooling rain splashing on me as I stood in line waiting for food.

Eventually, I experienced the natural outcome of recognizing and feeling gratitude—the act of giving back. In sum, the components of a gratitude definition encompass the cognitive understanding, the emotional response, and the action that flows from those.

Chapter 2

Why Gratitude?

Gratitude is a powerful catalyst for happiness.
It's the spark that lights a fire of joy in your soul.

—Amy Collette, author of The Gratitude Connection

What does gratitude have to do with building brilliant schools? Plenty! For several decades the scientific community, as well as the general public, has developed a keen interest in the concept of gratitude—what it means, how it's expressed, its connection to happiness, what difference it makes for personal and group well-being, and how to develop it. There is a growing awareness in our culture of the power of gratitude, along with an expanding body of research to verify it. This has led practitioners in many fields, including education, to take note of the benefits and possibilities for improving the quality of life and learning in many settings.

More and more, schools are applying understandings of gratitude to their learning communities. And the folks in these schools are seeing results. I'm one of those folks. Everything that's been learned about gratitude has direct implications for schools. I've spent over 30 years in education, much of it helping turn schools from underperforming to excelling. In that time, I have repeatedly witnessed the truth that gratitude is a key cornerstone of all of the values and actions that create successful change.

Benefits of Gratitude —————————————————————————

In a landmark study by gratitude researchers Robert Emmons and Michael McCullough (2003), participants kept regular records of their "blessings" (things for which they were grateful) once a week over a 9-week period or daily over a 13-day period. In addition, they regularly rated their moods, physical systems, exercise time, appraisals of their lives as a whole, and reactions to social support. In comparison to a control group, results showed that participants who kept these records were more optimistic about the near future, felt better about their lives as a whole, spent more time exercising, and had fewer complaints about their physical health. In addition, they were more likely to offer help or emotional support to others.

The "Count Your Blessings" study was only one of dozens of efforts to investigate the ramifications of gratitude. In the past few decades, other researchers have found similar and expanded benefits resulting from gratitude practices. Many individual and social or cultural factors (e.g., personality traits, gender, social groups, parenting, religion, level of materialism) do lead to variations in the outcomes. Yet research has consistently shown that people of many ages who regularly practice gratitude, in comparison to those who don't regularly practice gratitude, report more positive outlooks on life, stronger and healthier relationship bonds, greater optimism, a higher sense of connectedness to others, increased overall physical and psychological well-being, better attention to their health, and increased happiness. Those practicing gratitude also report or show greater job satisfaction and general life satisfaction; decreased depression; heightened generosity; improved ability to cope with stress, anxiety, grief, and adversity; and higher energy, hope, and optimism (Allen, 2018; Bono & Emmons, 2010; Bono & Sender, 2018; Chowdhury, 2020; Emmons & McCullough, 2003; Greater Good Science Center, 2020; Hill et al., 2013; McCullough et al., 2002).

In a pair of studies, Charlotte van Oyen Witliet and her colleagues at Hope College (2019) investigated gratitude as a predictor of hope and happiness. The first study revealed that gratitude (the appreciation of a gift received) exceeded forgivingness, patience, and self-control in predicting hope and happiness. The second study found that participants who took part in a gratitude-related writing intervention (wherein they gratefully remembered a meaningful positive outcome from the past) showed bolstered scores on measures of current hope and happiness.

Benefits of Gratitude for Youth

Recently, interest in the connections between gratitude and the well-being of youth has blossomed. Research increasingly includes examinations of gratitude interventions with children and adolescents in schools and other settings. Findings in this area have strong implications for the role of gratitude in the positive development of young people. Emerging evidence shows benefits correlated to

> *Daily gratitude boosters will function like a vaccine against impulsiveness and enhance self-control.*
>
> –David DeSteno, Northeastern University Professor and Gratitude Researcher

gratitude in youth (in contrast to their less grateful peers or classmates). Among these are higher levels of

- Social integration and friendships
- Prosocial behavior (and decreases in antisocial behavior)
- Motivation to use abilities and strengths to help others
- Building strong and satisfying connections to others
- Valuing connections to people
- Self-respect and self-satisfaction
- Self-regulation
- Sense of purpose
- Generosity
- Empathy and patience
- Hope and resilience

- Trust
- Positive mood (positive affect)
- Interest in helping others
- Overall psychological well-being
- General life satisfaction
  (Bartlett et al., 2012; Bono et al., 2017; Bono & Sender, 2018; Dickens & DeSteno, 2016; Emmons & McCullough, 2003; Froh & Bono, 2011; Froh, Bono, & Emmons, 2010; Froh et al., 2014; Howells, 2007, 2009, 2013, 2014; McCanlies et al., 2018; Pedersen & Lieberman, 2017).

Other research has found that gratitude in young people reduces levels of aggression and other antisocial behaviors and also diminishes cheating, combats materialism, buffers students from stress and depression, and supports resilience (Bono, G. et al., 2017; Bono & Sender, 2018; DeSteno, Duong, Lim, & Kates, 2019; Froh et al., 2011; Wood et al., 2009).

Benefits of Gratitude for Young People in Schools ———

It's quite obvious that all of the positive impacts listed above would also contribute to more satisfying and successful social, emotional, and academic experiences for students at school. Some other findings are even more directly related to students' school lives. In a school setting, students who can feel and express appreciation for benefits in their lives (in comparison to students who show less gratitude) show higher levels of

- Interest in school.
- School connectedness and sense of well-being at school.
- Academic success (including higher GPAs for adolescents.)
- Strong social ties at school.
- Absorption (full engagement in learning activities.)
- Social-emotional learning skills.

- Ability to set and pursue meaningful, intrinsic goals.
- Self-regulation in school activities.
- Motivations oriented positively toward others.
- Kind and helpful behavior.
- Prosocial relationships with other students.
  (Appleton et al., 2008; Bono et al., 2017; Froh & Bono, 2011; Froh, Bono, & Emmons, 2010; Froh et al., 2011; McKibben, 2013; Pederson & Lieberman, 2017; Polak & McCullough, 2006)

> *Gratitude helps students feel safe and connected, make friends, and perform better in school.*

This is compelling information—knowing that gratitude helps students feel safe and connected, make friends, perform better in school, and establish a foundation for thriving! It's enough to inspire every educator to take seriously the power of gratitude. And furthermore, it's a good reason to explore the possibilities for increasing the number and depth of gratitude experiences for all of our students.

Benefits of Gratitude for School Staff

The benefits of gratitude are not limited to the students. Practicing gratitude diminishes resentment and negativity. It leads to greater appreciation on the part of staff members for students, colleagues, parents, and for their own opportunities to teach. It enables educators to better handle the stresses and pressures of their work, raises job satisfaction, increases resilience, and improves effectiveness (Howells, 2007, 2009, 2013).

The more a teacher (or leader, or any adult staff member) practices gratitude, the more it will become a part of who he or she is, and the more it will be visible to students and colleagues. When a school is filled with grateful leaders, teachers, support staff members, and students—we breed an atmosphere of togetherness and trust. In a 2010 review of gratitude interventions, researchers Jeffrey Froh and Giacomo Bono note,

> Social exchange is necessary for most organizations in society to function properly. The positive emotions of leaders (e.g., principals, teachers) predict the performance for their entire group (George, 1995). Grateful principals may beget grateful teachers, who beget grateful students; grateful teachers and grateful students may outperform their less grateful counterparts. Indeed, evidence suggests that gratitude promotes social cohesion, relational and job satisfaction, and even organizational functioning (Emmons, 2003). Appreciation interventions indicate that many people—in organizational, educational, and health care settings—benefit from experiences of gratitude (Childre & Cryer, 2000).

Be mindful of this: In the "begetting chain" (described above), grateful students, in return, beget grateful teachers. And grateful teachers beget grateful administrators. Gratitude growth is not a top-down process. It spreads and reaches back and forth from all of us in a school culture.

Gratitude gets results. It does. It increases engagement and satisfaction. Not only have I read the research—I have witnessed this firsthand in classrooms, hallways, and faculty lounges. I've seen it work with my

> *The more practice you give your brain at feeling and expressing gratitude, the more it adapts to this mind-set.*
>
> –Robert Emmons,
> Gratitude Researcher

colleagues. It works for me. When I am engaged and satisfied, I work. I relate more authentically and supportively with others. The effects of creating a gratitude-centered environment have both short- and long-term benefits—even if you start small. For instance, teachers report the most effective gratitude practices to be some that are fairly simple to implement. These include greeting students, smiling more often, thanking students and colleagues, and teaching with a sense of appreciation for the subject matter and opportunity to teach.

Gratitude Interventions

Much of the gratitude study has measured the already-existing levels of gratitude in participants and moved to then find out what characteristics and behaviors correlated or resulted from gratitude. But what about those who started with lower levels of gratitude? Could interventions change that? And, no matter what the initial gratitude attitude, can we help **everyone** grow in understanding, expressing (acting on), and benefitting from gratitude? In time, researchers were eager to answer these questions. Several have delved into the questions to find out if specific interventions could teach or increase gratitude.

The good news is that there are many successes with gratitude interventions. Studies involving young people in intentional, age-appropriate gratitude practices show that parents, teachers, and other adults **can help** to build gratitude in young people. Children, even as young as early elementary grades, expressed and showed (behaviorally) more gratitude, and were observably happier. Gratitude interventions for a few weeks or a few times a week boosted gratitude, positive attitudes about school, and overall well-being in children and adolescents (Bono & Sender, 2018; Emmons & McCullough, 2003; Froh et al., 2009; Froh & Bono, 2014; Froh et al., 2008; Huebner et al., 2000).

Here's more good news: **gratitude interventions have long-lasting effects**. In a gratitude-intervention study at Indiana University, researchers led by Prathik Kini described "profound" and "long-lasting" neural effects suggesting that "the more practice you give your brain at feeling and expressing gratitude, the more it adapts to this mindset—you could even think of your brain as having a sort of gratitude "muscle" that can be exercised and strengthened" (Jarrett, 2016, para. 6). Other researchers have found similar long-lasting neural effects of gratitude (Brown & Wong, 2017; Kini et al., 2015; McCraty & Childre, 2004; Wood et al., 2009; Zahn et al., 2009).

Studies using interventions with young people have also found indications that intentional gratitude tasks are self-perpetuating. The social, psychological, and academic effects were still evident when revisited weeks or months after the initial "experiments." (Bono & Sender, 2017; Emmons & MuCullough, 2003; Froh, Bono, & Emmons, 2010; Jarrett, 2016; Seligman et al., 2005). It lasts! The more often gratitude is experienced, acknowledged, and expressed—the more grateful the students become.

> *Gratitude is not only the greatest of virtues but the parent of all others.*
>
> –Marcus Tullius Cicero, Roman Scholar and Statesman

24

Chapter 3

How Can We Prime the Brain for Gratitude?

A Yes Brain is one that is open and resilient in the world, and a No Brain is one that is shut down and reactive in the world.

—Dr. Tina Payne Bryson, co-author of The Yes Brain

You may remember that my working definition of gratitude is based on the concept of gratitude as a cognitive process. This means that it is something you examine and think about. You look inside to identify what you've received and the source from which it came. You also attend to and name the feelings that arise in connection with that gift. As you grow that skill, you may begin to notice this thinking/examining process in others. This process primes the brain (opens the mind and paves the way) for feeling, understanding, and expressing gratitude. It's a process called *mindsight*.

The term *mindsight* was coined by Dr. Daniel Siegel, clinical professor of psychiatry at UCLA School of Medicine, founding co-director of the Mindful Awareness Research Center at UCLA, and author of numerous books including, *The Yes Brain*. On his website, Siegel (2020) defines *mindsight* as

> . . . our human capacity to perceive the mind of the self and others. It is a powerful lens through which we can understand our inner lives with more clarity, integrate the brain, and enhance our relationships with others. Mindsight is a kind of

25

focused attention that allows us to see the internal workings of our own minds. It helps us get ourselves off of the autopilot of ingrained behaviors and habitual responses. It lets us "name and tame" the emotions we are experiencing, rather than being overwhelmed by them. (para. 1).

I've included the topic of mindsight in this chapter because it has been such an important part of my discoveries about gratitude and about how it blossoms and deepens. I've found that the skills of mindsight and their connections to Yes-Brain thinking are inseparable from the growth of gratitude. The mindsight concept struck my heart because it named the experience that brought me to my own gratitude "revolution." Katrina forced me to attend to my inner life and the inner workings of others. The focused attention that is mindsight allowed me to see the inner workings of my mind. It shook me out of the autopilot of my habitual behaviors and put me in touch with the gratitude I was feeling! It enabled me to understand so many facets of gratitude. Without that process, I'm not sure I would have been able to learn about and fully practice gratitude. Siegel says, "Simply labeling a difficult emotional experience allows you to take the reins back, if only briefly" (cited in Ablett, 2019, para. 3).

Two Brain States

Dr. Siegel explains that our physiology has an intimate relationship with our feelings, and when we are aware of the interior signals of the body, we are more likely to exhibit empathy and self-regulation—two abilities needed to be productive, successful members of any society. In researching this connection and seeking to help people develop this lens to perceive their minds (that is, to use mindsight), he describes two brain states.

I'll describe (in a simplified version) his findings and views on this topic. They are deeply rooted in understandings of neuroscience. For deeper understanding, consult the sources in this pillar's resource list for Dr. Siegel and the neuroscience of gratitude.

The No Brain is a reactive, non-receptive state—a state people experience during conditions of threat. In Siegel's research (2017), he asked people to listen to a series of "no" messages and identify sensations related to them. These sensations included tightness, constriction, anger, fear, sadness, shame, resistance, defiance, powerlessness, or a feeling of shutting down—along with heaviness in the chest and an urge to run away. When I think of children in such a state, I can see, right away, how they can't possibly be trusting, open to learning, or connected with others. That is enough for me to know that an atmosphere of No-Brain messaging is not conducive to building a culture where kids can learn and thrive (or find it easier to get in touch with gratitude).

> *The No Brain shuts kids down—to learning and to connection with other people.*
>
> –Dr. Dan Siegel, Co-author of *The Yes Brain*

The Yes Brain is receptive. The Yes-Brain state, according to Dr. Siegel, (2017) is one that cultivates curiosity and resilience. If someone sends a "yes" message to another who is in a Yes-Brain state, the receiver is more open to the message and more likely to benefit from it. A Yes Brain opens us up to social engagement so that we can hear from others. It relaxes our fixed state of beliefs and routines, helping us consider the validity of other points of view. In that same exercise mentioned above, Dr. Siegel asked participants to list the words and feelings associated when they hear

> *The Yes Brain is open, flexible. It encourages kids to explore and be resilient.*
>
> –Dr. Dan Siegel, Co-author of *The Yes Brain*

"yes" messages. In striking contrast to "no" messages, "yes" messages were associated with sensations described as caring, warmth, possibilities, hopefulness, kindness, acceptance, connection, motivation, and encouragement.

In his work, Dr. Siegel promotes what he calls a Yes-Brain strategy for working with children and adolescents. The foundations of the approach are to help kids with these:

> **Balance**: riding and experiencing waves of feelings without being reactive
>
> **Resilience**: learning to recognize when they lean toward a No-Brain state and modifying back to a Yes-Brain state
>
> **Insight**: building mindsight skills to sense inner lives
>
> **Empathy**: tuning into others' emotional states, taking the perspective of others, and feeling concern or joy for others' suffering or wellbeing (2017)

Now to me, that's the foundation for a school culture that is supportive of students and the adults who serve them!

Putting the Yes-Brain Attitude into Practice ————

As I began practicing gratitude for my students, their parents, and my staff members, I became aware of another shift in my mindset. I found myself in less of an evaluative and punitive mindset. The gratitude mode had shifted me toward looking for ways to say "yes" to folks—including students—who had ideas on how things could look or be different at the school. I was open to considering policy revisions on such topics as hoodie-wearing and cell phone use. This would not have happened before. In my administrative role, I had simply executed the rules and consequences as they were written; I did not look for ways to say "yes" or even rethink a stance. My discovery of the Yes-Brain benefits immediately intermingled with and nourished my practice of gratitude. Each of these developing habits fed the other.

Beyond the changes in myself, I realized how critical are the skills of perceiving our inner lives and those of others to gratitude work in the school. I saw how a culture of Yes-Brain attitudes can boost our efforts at social-emotional learning for students. I saw that for students to be open to gratitude practices, they need to be given more "yes" messages. They need help developing their own Yes Brains. Then they will truly be able to savor gifts that life gives them, to name gratitude when they see and feel it, to express it, and to act on it in ways that forward care and kindness to others.

Here are some ways to move forward to prime brains for gratitude in your school:

YES-Brain Boosters for Adults

All members of the school community will be most ready to practice and spread gratitude when the setting is awash in a "yes" mindset. Remember that a Yes Brain is a receptive, hopeful, and curious brain. "Yes" messages open people to connection, possibilities, and gratitude. Leaders, take some time to nourish a Yes-Brain mindset in yourself and with your colleagues.

A shift in mindset isn't automatic or easy. Anyone who has ever tried to change a long-standing habit knows that to do so, you need to change your thoughts. Be aware that this change may face some resistance. Unfortunately, many of us have been conditioned from an early age to operate with a lot of "no" thoughts or responses. Many educators, trained in a climate of "If you give kids an inch, they'll take a mile," bring protective or resistant attitudes to their schools. "No" may hold the predominant space in our brains: *NO, that idea is too complicated for our staff. NO, we can't find planning time in the schedule. NO, we don't want noisy classrooms. NO, we can't let Julie do a different assignment than one given to Jason. NO, students can't be trusted to make choices about what they will learn.*

It's exhausting just thinking about how much energy is exerted when in a constant reactive state! Be aware of the possibilities of opposition.

Be patient. But watch for the relief folks will find as they ease out of the wearisome No-Brain state.

The transition to a "yes" culture in which gratitude can flourish takes desire, direction, and trust.

DESIRE: Let's assume that you have the desire. Let's assume you're weary of the stress of "no" thinking. Let's assume that you believe that a "yes" orientation will lead you, your staff, and your students to the supportive, connected school climate described earlier in this chapter. If so, join with your staff and commit to boosting your Yes Brains. State your intention out loud. Write it down. Join hands and agree that it will be a goal.

DIRECTION: While I desired a more positive school culture, one of the most difficult changes I ever made as a school administrator was shifting my mindset from "no" (keeping order and organization by watching out for what to avoid, discourage, or stop) to a structured, disciplined culture of "yes" (not a permissive culture, but one with an attitude to try, go forward, and trust—rather than inhibit).

- First, I had to start with myself. To set a direction for gratitude work in my school, I began looking for ways to say "yes" to students. I kept reminding myself: It's only with a "yes" mindset that we can invite students to be a part of something larger than themselves and to build in them the intrinsic desire to do so. My message to you is, start with yourself!

- Challenge yourself to hesitate every time your mind says "no" to something. (Do this before you open your mouth and say "no"! Think about how you can change the "no" to "yes." Or, if you can't say "yes" to that idea, to what part or what variation of it can you give a "yes" response?)

- Make a list of thoughts, actions, or responses that you regularly do, or have recently done, that come out of a No-Brain state. Replace these with an equal number of thoughts, actions, or responses that come from a Yes-Brain stance.

- Next, I recognized that building strategies and procedures for a "yes" orientation would only work well if we were co-creating the systems together. I knew I needed students and staff ready, willing, and able to support the steps in our direction: destination gratitude! I realized that only when all parties were involved in any plans or policies, would they be invested and receptive to changes. So, don't start on new plans and policies without saying to staff and students, "Yes, you are part of this; your ideas are needed."

- Work together at making a "yes" culture a starting point for building a climate of gratitude. Get students and staff in on making lists of ways to say "yes." Identify things that generate "no" responses. Share them with each other. Examine them. Figure out how to turn "no" instincts into "yes" instincts. Set your "yes" direction for gratitude work (or any other venture) jointly. Then your plan will flow from relationships and mutual excitement. Involve other members of the school community in setting goals and processes for your gratitude work. Seek and use ideas from them all.

TRUST: Trust plays an important part in shifting from the No-Brain state to the Yes-Brain state. It is a foundation for the change to occur. Paul J. Zak (2017a), neuroscience researcher and the author of *Trust Factor*, claims that workers in settings where they experience high trust adopt a growth mindset. They perform higher and show more job satisfaction, collaborate better with their colleagues, and stay with their jobs longer than people working in low-trust situations. Zak's studies also found that people who felt trusted at work were happier with their lives, suffered less stress, felt supportive of the goals of their organization, and improved in their relationships with one another. They were also more likely to behave in trustworthy ways themselves.

In setting a new direction toward a gratitude-centered school culture, intentionally cultivate trust. As the administrator,

- Treat staff members as responsible adults.
- Share leadership and decision-making.
- Enable staff and students to contribute and craft their ideas.
- Celebrate milestones, successes, good practices.
- Learn from students, parents, and staff members.
- Let them know what you've learned from them.
- Let them know that you trust them.
- Nourish social connections of students and staff.
- Say "yes" as often as possible.
- Say "thank you" a lot.

Yes-Brain Boosters for Students

Students will be able to embrace and demonstrate gratitude much more readily if attention is given to exercising those Yes Brains! For our students to have the benefits of a Yes-Brain state (feelings of safety and calm and a balanced receptiveness to their inner world and interactions with others), we educators need to be aware of ways we can nurture the Yes Brain.

Here are some suggestions, based on Dr. Siegel's foundations of a Yes-Brain approach (2017):

- Teach students the skills of mindsight—recognizing what is in their minds and the minds of others. Help students learn about the nature of their inner emotional lives. This is a process where they reflect on and talk about an inner experience, giving them a chance to have a perspective on emotions. Students can SIFT through their minds or someone else's mind by identifying and talking about (S) sensations they feel (or sense from others) about a situation: (I) images or pictures that come to their minds, (F) feelings they are experiencing or sensing from others, and (T) thoughts that are part of an emotional experience. It is only with identifying, acknowledging, and accepting what they find in themselves that persons can handle, let go of, or transform the experiences (Siegel, 2013).

> *Mindsight lets us 'name and tame' the emotions we are experiencing, rather than being overwhelmed by them.*
>
> –Dr. Dan Seigel, Author of *Mindsight: The New Science of Personal Transformation*

- Emphasize the importance of fully experiencing feelings (not running away or repressing them) as they learn to accept them, and find ways to "weather" them without being overtaken. Students, even young ones, can learn to identify when they are lapsing into a No-Brain state—where they feel scared, uptight, nervous, disconnected, or ready to fight, freeze, or run away. Help students identify and practice ways to accept and "ride" the feelings without letting the feelings take over.

- Talk with students about real-life situations that are sure to arise. They can brainstorm and role-play ways to react to or ride out feelings. As children become more aware of their inner lives, they will be more able to regulate their behavior better and be more empathetic toward others. Their insights will prepare them to better choose healthy reactions to future situations.

- Teachers and other educators can learn to be alert for signs of students who are in No-Brain states or heading that way. Introduce students to practices and skills of resilience. This means altering one's mindset to a Yes-Brain state that is receptive to their thoughts and feelings and aware of what is going on.

Make empathy a regular part of conversations. Even young children can "get" the concept of being sensitive to the joy, hurt, disappointments, or confusion of someone else. They can "get" the concept that all human beings share these kinds of feelings and thoughts and the idea of trying to see something from another person's point of view.

Chapter 4

How Do G.R.E.A.T. Leaders Get Results with Gratitude?

Piglet noticed that even though he had a Very Small Heart, it could hold a rather large amount of Gratitude.
—from *Winnie-the-Pooh*, A.A. Milne

Ignited by the "gratitude tsunami" that hit me after Hurricane Katrina, many of my questions, thoughts, and schemes turned toward infusing gratitude into the culture of schools. Or more profoundly perhaps— thoughts turned to "How can we make gratitude a **pillar** of school culture?" But when I thought of school experiences, scenarios of gratitude did not rush into my mind. Quite honestly, I had to push aside images from my own student days (symmetrical rows of desks, cold textures of tiled classrooms, the grittiness of a brick façade, stark moat of blisteringly hot blacktop around the building, students' voices unwelcomed, teachers and teachers' desks center stage, unappealing textbooks, lots of memorization, lots of worksheets, and lots and lots of rules never to be bent or broken). Even scouring over many of the years when I was the teacher or administrator, I could call up no images of gratitude discussions or intentionally-taught gratitude practices. Gratitude certainly was not one of the top characteristics on the list when colleagues focused on school culture.

Gratitude might not be the first component that comes to mind when we seek to identify the pillars upon which to build our school culture. That's likely because we educators weren't trained, told, or coached in teacher prep programs or in our own school experience to rely on gratitude. Through many of the years that I worked with school improvement efforts, researchers were already looking for outcomes of gratitude in youth. Many were wondering if lessons and other interventions could increase gratitude. They were discovering and sharing striking results. I just had not discovered these findings! In addition, the connections between gratitude and school culture that had been discovered were not yet widely disseminated and embraced.

Nevertheless, out of my own Katrina experience, I asked such questions as

- *How could we embrace gratitude work in ways that bring its benefits to our students and staff?*
- *How could we make this long-lasting in our school?*
- *What can I do as the leader?*
- *What can teachers and other staff members do?*

And I began (fast and feverishly) researching gratitude, its practices, and its effects. Even as I was learning, I started putting my convictions into practice right away.

The research (see Chapter 2), born out by the writings and experiences of many educators, gives us clues as answers to my questions. It offers a wealth of understandings and practices for moving ahead with gratitude. Based on those clues, along with my experiences, here are some suggestions and bits of advice for administrators and other leaders. Leaders can use and share these ideas with school staff, students, and parents.

Keep These Discoveries in Mind

- Intentional practices of gratitude (by children and adults) yield a multitude of benefits—all of them positive forces in the work we do in schools.

- Interventions (such as lessons, practices) **do work** to increase genuine gratitude.
- Gratitude is best taught by those who visibly practice it themselves.
- Gratitude is a feeling and an attitude. But it is not those alone. **Gratitude is an action.** Don't ever lose sight of the **action** part of gratitude.
- The development of mindsight and of a Yes-Brain opens one up to embracing, experiencing, and expressing gratitude.
- Gratitude is shown to support all the other pillars of a brilliant school—relationships, high expectations, achievement, and academic tenacity.
- Gratitude broadens and builds as it is examined and practiced. It changes the brain. The more you practice it, the more you experience it. The more you experience it, the more you want to act on it.

Start With These Steps

While I continued to learn about gratitude, I initiated these practices as soon as school began at the high school where I was principal. Get started on them yourself.

Start showing gratitude. As the leader—before giving any talks on gratitude or holding any meetings, discussions, or workshops to promote the benefits of gratitude—deliberately and frequently practice it. Don't advertise that you're doing it; just do it! As your staff and students learn more about gratitude, they'll realize that they've been watching it at work. Here are some of the ways I started showing my gratitude that first year of Katrina and have continued ever since:

1. Gratitude for Students: I modeled gratitude to my students during assemblies and in my communications with them each day. I regularly let them know that I was grateful to be their principal.

2. Gratitude for Teachers: I modeled gratitude for my teachers in after-school meetings, in daily announcements, and in personal contacts. I regularly let them know that I was grateful to be their colleague and friend.

3. Gratitude for Parents: I modeled gratitude for all parents and family members in school-to-home communications and in person. I regularly let them know that I was grateful to have them in the school community and grateful to be their kids' principal.

4. Expectations: I incorporated gratitude and positivity into my expectations of students. I gave such messages as:
   - *I am so grateful to have such a responsible group of young people like my student body. What a lucky principal I am!*
   - *I expect you to always model responsibility. Here's what that looks like to me:*
     - *I expect you to stop and help a fellow Tiger who may have dropped his or her books or who needs help in some other way. (Note: At our school, the Tiger was the school mascot and our identity-- We were all Tigers!)*
     - *I expect you to tell an adult the minute you see something suspicious or something that violates our norms of responsibility.*

5. Gratitude Jar: I set up a gratitude jar in the main office. I invited students and staff to drop entries into the jar—naming a person (friend, classmate, teacher, custodian, etc.) for whom they were grateful and briefly explaining why. Then, we would pull some of the entries each day and read them over the intercom during afternoon announcements. (You can do something similar with gratitude notes to others, gratitude grams, or instant digital gratitude messages.)

6. Yearly Theme: I organized each school year around a positive theme that incorporated gratitude. This theme was supported by graphics throughout the school. For example,

- One of the first themes was "One Degree More." It focused on pushing students to give one degree more in their relationships with friends and teachers, in their academic performance, and in their extracurricular groups.
- We kicked off the theme during the first assembly of the year.
- For this one, we used a video about water boiling at 212°F, showing how that one-degree difference from 211°F gets a different result.
- Then, we built a tagline into morning and afternoon announcements that reminded students to give one degree more. We used it in our data chats and behavior conferences with students; the theme gave us something on which to build momentum for improvement.
- Our gratitude practice allowed us to reflect on our classmates and teachers for whom we were grateful. Students could include expressing gratitude for those who in some way helped them give *one degree more*!

And here are other steps to initiate early in the school year:

Define it together. What does gratitude mean and include? With the whole staff, reflect and discuss it thoroughly. Don't leave students out of the process. Listen to (and incorporate) students' definitions. Discuss, demonstrate, draw, and describe the definition. As you move forward, your plans can be built on your own group's understanding and statement of what gratitude is.

Revisit definitions. Continually revisit, revise, and expand the definition. Be sure that students and adults know that, as they practice gratitude and watch it in action, they will learn new things about what gratitude is. Be willing to adapt your definition. Expand discussions of the definition to descriptions of what gratitude looks like in action.

Believe in gratitude. Expose members of your school community to as much information as you can about how gratitude works. Share research. Encourage staff members to read and explore further. Share research findings with students (explained appropriately for their ages). Adults who take part in gratitude work with students will do it better if they wholeheartedly embrace the idea that time spent on gratitude is worthwhile, and if they

> *Where there is gratitude there cannot be resentment, and vice versa.*
>
> –Kerry Howells,
> Gratitude Researcher

understand the benefits. Do your best to garner everyone's commitment to being an eager part of the gratitude work. If some aren't ready to be "all in," ask them to participate in gratitude practices enthusiastically anyway for several weeks. (They will likely become converts!)

Plan together. As you make plans for gratitude work in the school, draw input from all parties about what to do. Do come armed with information about what has worked in other places, what is learned from research, and such. But hear all the suggestions from all the voices (including students). **Together**, decide what to try. When you're ready to kick off any practice or program, enlist a wide range of stakeholders to join in.

Make staff dialogue part of the plan. From the very beginning, provide time and settings for staff members to learn, grow, share, and evaluate together. Teams or grade-level groups (or the whole staff) can share ideas about and experiences of gratitude to support one another in their gratitude growth. They can try out new strategies and share with colleagues their successes or challenges in doing the work with their students.

Include These Actions Throughout the Year ──────

Model gratitude. Model gratitude. Model gratitude. This was one of the "beginning" steps for leaders. But I'll say it again because it must continue every day of every school year. Gratitude is best taught by those who visibly practice it. All adults in the school must understand that the strongest way to promote, teach, and nourish gratitude for students is to model it for them. Preach and practice this philosophy prolifically and passionately. All adults must be aware, at all times, that the students are watching and listening. Students will notice and mimic your actions. Let students see the adults genuinely showing gratitude toward each other, parents and school visitors, and students. Teachers, discuss your own gratitude experiences with your students. Ask them for feedback. Let them know that the adults learn gratitude lessons from students, too. And, by the way, **every gratitude exercise that students are asked to do—teachers and other staff members should do it too!**

> *Gratitude is best taught by those who visibly practice it.*

Reinforce kindness and personal value. You don't need a formal program to do this. Just encourage all adults in the school to reinforce kind acts and attribute value to everyone. To show gratitude and affirm value, make it a habit to give kudos, thanks, and shout-outs to let people know their kindnesses are noticed.

Plan clear, intentional, systematic approaches. Don't let practices be helter-skelter, intermittent, or half-hearted. Decide what you will do to introduce, teach, practice, reinforce, and keep track of gratitude actions within the school community. This need not be the same for every grade level, but plans need to be purposeful and workable.

Talk (a lot) with students about gratitude (not just **talk to them** about gratitude). Along with specific gratitude plans or practices, make the language of gratitude a normal topic at school. Engage in conversations about gratitude. Ask students about people, experiences, events, situations, and attributes for which (or whom) they are grateful. Ask guiding questions that help them identify specific attributes or actions that led to their gratitude, e.g., *precisely what is it for which you are grateful? Did someone help to make that happen? What did that* *person do?* Help students recognize benefactors and beneficial acts that they might not yet have noticed. This broadens their abilities to perceive all kinds of gifts and to express their gratitude broadly.

Teach students and staff about the Yes Brain and No Brain. Focus discussions and show examples of what happens when people transfer from the "no" to the "yes" thinking. Make this a regular part of the conversation. Have students and colleagues share examples and notice when they make the transfer themselves. Look back at Chapter 3 for those practices that boost the Yes Brain for students and the adults in the school community!

Talk about the emotions connected to gratitude. Ask students to talk about why they feel grateful (i.e., how the gift or action benefitted them). Talk about the complicated feelings that may be in the mix—indebtedness, phoniness (suspicions about the benefactor's sincerity or motivations), humility, joy, surprise, shyness, helplessness (and how to let people help you without feeling helpless or worthless). Identify people who help get you through hard times and how it feels to be with people who know your darkest or toughest stuff. Realize that facets of expressing and receiving gratitude are uncomfortable for some people. Don't press for public expressions if it is scary or stressful for someone. Don't read journal entries, notes, gratitude grams, or gratitude letters without a student's or colleague's permission. Try to make the expression of gratitude as non-threatening as possible for all students and staff members.

Integrate gratitude work into existing programs. Instead of creating a "gratitude program," mix gratitude observations, comments, stories, and recognition into what you already do. Use moments in advisory classes or homerooms. Take advantage of reading, writing, and thinking activities that you already do; include a gratitude moment or theme into some of them. Find ways to combine brief gratitude expressions with your subject area. Watch for moments to teach a bit about gratitude concerning a topic or situation that arises.

Don't forget students' families. Too often, we think about including parents only at the beginning of a new plan or program. Keep parents in the gratitude loop. First, vow that parents will be met with expressions of gratitude whenever they visit or contact the school. Beyond that, keep them informed about gratitude work with the students. Use gratitude practices that include home involvement. Ask parents for feedback about what they see and hear from their children and about what they experience in school-home communications.

Compare gratitude with materialism. In an age-appropriate manner, engage students in conversations about gratitude experiences in comparison with the experience of materialism—wanting and getting "things." They can compare and contrast the feelings they have when someone gives or does something that they did not request or expect with the feelings of getting material things that they've begged for. Also, talk about the value of each experience—getting a "gift" that you did not intentionally seek or earn but received out of good intentions of someone else or good fortune—and getting material possessions (particularly if they are things you don't need). By the way, research has found that gratefulness in youth is a high predictor of such positive attributes as life satisfaction, social integration, engagement, and school achievement

> *Materialism and gratitude are like oil and water. Gratitude is psychologically fulfilling and things are not.*
>
> –Giacomo Bono,
> Gratitude Researcher

while materialism is a lower predictor of those attributes (Froh et al., 2011).

Keep gratitude practices meaningful and enjoyable. It can be easy to make "be grateful" into a rote practice. Carefully avoid taking the heart out of gratitude or letting it lose its meaning and importance. Keep the practices timely, genuine, and not too long. Don't cram gratitude into anyone. Keep the practices and your modeling of gratitude authentic. Kids will immediately catch fake expressions of gratitude. Keep the practices varied and interesting. Mix in art, demonstrations, role-playing, questions, interviews, stories, and celebrations.

Teach and practice benefit appraisal. A 2014 study with children ages 8 to 11 (Froh et al., 2014) showed that young people could be trained to think gratefully. Classes were randomly assigned to weekly activities in what was called "the benefit-appraisal curriculum" group or to a control group wherein classes did social activities not related to gratitude. In the benefit-appraisal curriculum, students participated in daily sessions for one week. This included discussions, role-playing activities, and writing assignments designed to teach students to appraise (examine and evaluate) grateful thoughts and actions. Within just a few days, researchers saw increases in benefit appraisals, grateful mood, and behavioral evidence of gratitude (as compared to the control group). A follow-up study of weekly sessions over five weeks also showed an increase in students' appraisals of the benefits of grateful thinking. In addition, researchers found increases in a positive mood, students' positive affect (well-being), general life satisfaction, and the number of outward expressions of gratitude. Furthermore, these benefits were still in effect five months after the experiment.

> *Gratitude connects humans to the best in themselves and in others.*
>
> –Giacomo Bono and Jason Sendder, Gratitude Researchers

The idea behind benefit appraisal is that teaching students to analyze the benefits of grateful thinking and actions deepens and expands gratitude. What a great set of skills for all ages—to think in terms of the broader picture of gratitude! It goes beyond the habit of saying a quick "thank you" for something you've been given.

In your plans for gratitude work, consider ways to include this skill. You can read the "Nice Thinking!" study (Froh, Bono, Fan, et al., 2014) for a more complete look at how it was carried out. To begin a simple approach, make a plan for some sessions that include assessing the following components of a beneficial act. Use hypothetical vignettes or situations and discuss them by addressing the following factors:

> **Intent:** a benefactor's intentions behind doing a beneficial act: *To what extent did the other person do this on purpose?*
>
> **Cost:** the cost that the benefactor incurs when giving a benefit: *What did the other person give up to do this?*
>
> **Benefit:** the benefits to the receiver when given something or helped with something: *How helpful or important was this for you (or what was the benefit to you)?*
>
> **Effects:** the receiver's response: *How did you feel in response to the action? What did you do, say, or think?*

This benefit appraisal can be done with any age group. Keep to appropriate topics and those that are not too emotionally charged. Invite students to suggest situations or create stories. Do be sure to practice this with colleagues.

Conclusion

The First Pillar

It's a funny thing about life, once you begin to take note of the things you are grateful for, you begin to lose sight of the things that you lack.

—Germany Kent, American Journalist and TV
Producer, Author of *The Hope Handbook*

I hope that the benefits and examples of gratitude practices I've described inspire you to dive into gratitude work in your school. However, you may have read Chapters 1-4 with an open mind but, because of circumstances in your school, are hesitant to fully embrace gratitude as a foundational element. (These might be such factors, perhaps, as uncertain or unpredictable school leadership, low academic performance, a history of apathy or disinterest in new school initiatives, inconsistent cooperation among staff members, or widely varying priorities). If so, I invite you to consider this: In environments with low morale and diminished trust, gratitude is just the point on the compass that can guide our response to distrust or pessimism. This does not mean that we simply replace resentment with gratitude; that's but an attempt to paint a positive veneer over negative situations crying out for our attention.

Expressions of gratitude unite us with others. They nudge us to recognize and acknowledge the contributions of others. Where resentment leads us to reject, divide, ignore, lament, blame, backbite, and criticize—even minor, awkward, hesitant experiences of realizing or expressing gratitude automatically take us in opposite directions. Our school communities cannot afford to dwell in the divisive, judgmental, "No-Brain" cultures. We must work overtime to create and sustain communities where gratitude is a centerpiece. This can be just the catalyst needed to turn from debilitating discouragement to energetic hope.

Gratitude generates connections and enlivens relationships. Relationships spark situations for gratitude. Gratitude, in turn, ignites and strengthens relationships. The Second Pillar focuses on the "R" factor in the description of G.R.E.A.T. leadership for a brilliant school. As you explore the critical elements of **relationships**, you'll see more clearly how gratitude is essential to healthy, substantial relationships in any school community.

> *To speak gratitude is courteous and pleasant. To enact gratitude is generous and noble, but to live gratitude is to touch heaven.*
>
> –Johannes Gaertner,
> Educational Theorist

The Second Pillar of a Brilliant School

Relationships

Through others we become ourselves.

—Lev S. Vygotsky, Educational Theorist

*C*hristina was in ninth grade when I first met her. I was the new assistant principal at a large high school where two of my main roles were handling disciplinary infractions and helping students with attendance issues.

She was a kind, brilliant, outspoken young woman who stood about five feet tall. Christina was a "frequent flyer" in my office—mostly for getting to school late and for not attending Saturday detention. At any rate, doling out her consequences was always a positive experience because of her sweet, happy demeanor.

All of Christina's siblings also struggled with getting to school on time. Her mother suffered from several health ailments and never came to the school, but I talked to her each time Christina had to serve an in-school suspension for missing Saturday detention, excessive tarries, or the occasional episode where she forgot that she was talking to her teacher and not her friend.

One Monday morning as I was processing Saturday detention skips, Christina appeared in my doorway, saying, "I'm next. I had to skip Saturday detention this week, but I promise I have a good reason."

Now, for those of you who deal with teens frequently, you know that most of them do think they have good reasons for doing what they want at the moment. Christina was usually no different; however, this time she did have a good reason. "My mom is in the hospital. She had to have surgery, and I had to watch my little brother and sister."

I asked her about her mom, and she said that the surgery went well but that she had some other health issues that were complicating her recovery. We talked a little more; I gave her grace until the next Saturday's detention, and she was on her way.

A few days later, just after lunch, a woman came into the attendance office and told my secretary that she was there to pick up Christina but that she wasn't on Christina's checkout card as an authorized adult to pick her up. Meeting immediate resistance from Ms. Hamilton, our attendance clerk, the lady said, "Listen, her sister sent me to pick her up because her mother has died, but she doesn't want Christina to know until she gets to the hospital."

Ms. Hamilton came into my office, closed my door, and apprised me of the situation. I sat at my desk thinking how this girl who struggled already to get to school and to do the things she needed to do was about to learn that another obstacle had been added to her life. I compartmentalized my emotions and called for Christina to come to my office.

She arrived, nervous and with questions. I explained that her sister had sent the lady in the lobby to pick her up because her mom wanted to see her. She fidgeted in the chair as she faced me. Staring directly into my eyes, she said, "Something has happened; I know my mom has died. I don't know that lady, Mr. Parker. I can't go with her. I have to go with someone I know." Tears began to fall from her eyes, and she repeated, "I need someone to go with me who knows me. I need you to take me, Mr. Parker."

I fell completely apart inside; but on the outside, I said, "OK, sweetie. I'll take you."

Ms. Hamilton, a stern rule enforcer herself, gave me a glance of empathy and said, "I'll let Mr. Vaughn know you'll be off campus for a bit."

Christina and I got into my car and began the 10-minute ride to the hospital—one of the longest, most difficult rides of my life. As we passed over the giant bridge that led into the neighboring town, she said, "Mr. Parker, you can go ahead and tell me that my mom has died. I know she has. I can hear that from you."

Because the woman in the office said that her sister wanted to tell her, I lied to her and said, "Honey, we don't know that. Let's just get to the hospital and find out what's going on. I will go with you. I'm here for you."

She was quiet the remainder of our ride. I pulled up into a parking spot, got out of the car with her, and walked toward the hospital doors. Her sister was waiting, and when she appeared from the mirrored doors, Christina fell to her knees on the concrete sidewalk and sobbed. I knelt beside her, mustering every muscle in my face and body so that I, too, would not fall apart and cry. (Today, I would have just cried with her; but at that time in my life, I thought that being strong was keeping a stiff upper lip and being there as emotionless as possible as a caregiver.) I hugged her tightly, and with one hand on her sister and the other on her, I passed her to her sister, and I turned and went back to my car.

During the entire ride back to the school, I thought about what would happen to Christina and her brothers and sisters now that their mom was gone. I was still fighting back tears in the privacy of my car. I turned into the school parking lot; school had just been *dismissed, and the campus was mostly clear of students. I got out of my car and began walking to the front of the school. One of the doors opened, and Ms. Hamilton, my attendance clerk who had clocked out earlier at her designated time, was there waiting for me. I don't remember my feet touching the covered sidewalk as I rushed to her open arms, where she held me in the doorway of the school as I released all of my be-a-man bullshit and sobbed for Christina and her family and Ms. Hamilton and myself.*

About a week later, Christina returned to school. We caught a glimpse of each other across the school's courtyard during the student break time. Like magnets, we began walking to each other. She dropped her book bag and hugged me tightly, and with her signature smile, she said, "Thank you for taking me to the hospital. I could not have survived that time without you, Mr. Parker. I know that had to have been really hard for you to do. Thank you. I love you."

I gave her a tight hug and said, "I love you, too, kiddo, and I'm here for you."

Thank you, Christina, for teaching me that it's okay to break my shield of invulnerability with my students and staff. You helped me learn that vulnerability is the place where trust is formed or strengthened; it is where relationships are born and cultivated.

Chapter 5

What Are Relationships?

*The greatest compliment that was ever paid me
was when someone asked me what I thought,
and attended to my answer.*

—Henry David Thoreau, American Philosopher and Poet

A school community is a dynamic beehive of relationships. Hundreds of relationships are at work at any moment and any location—to name a few: student-to-student, teacher-to-student, teacher-to-teacher, support staff member-to-support staff member, teacher-to-support staff member, administrator-to-staff member, administrator-to-student, bus driver (or any other member of the school support staff-to-student), student-to-coach, parent-to-teacher, parent-to-administrator, parent-to-support staff, parent-to-parent.

Relationship: A Working Definition

A basic definition of a relationship is generally something like this: *how two or more people or groups regard (perceive and value) each other and behave toward each other.* From life experience, I'd add that any relationship *involves connections that develop through interactions and emotional ties.* Also, even a basic denotation of the word includes the implicit understanding that not all relationships are interconnections between **two or more** people or groups. One key, foundational relationship for every human being is the relationship she or he has **with herself or himself**.

Of those hundreds of relationships within our school communities, some are types that diminish or threaten the well-being of the parties involved. It's important to acknowledge all the various forms of relationships that affect members of the school community. But most critically, we must define the **kinds of** relationships we **want** to find, nourish, inspire, and build in our schools—the kinds that we know **will** further well-being.

So, when you see the word relationship in this book, know that I have this definition in mind for what forms a pillar of a brilliant school:

Relationship: *a connection with oneself or with another person or group of persons that is based on positive bonds—a relationship that is respectful, caring, and trusting. In addition to being trusting, it is trustworthy—something one can count on.*

Here's more about what the *relationships* we want in our schools look like: All members of the school community should be able to walk into school on any given day and feel valued, respected, and connected. In the encounters and connections among and between students, teachers, administrators, other staff members, and parents, each individual should enjoy a setting where

- Collaboration is the norm.
- Kindness, not criticism, is the norm.
- Discrimination is not the norm.
- Respect can be counted on.
- Appreciation and acceptance of individual and cultural differences are the norms.
- Members are truthful and trustworthy.
- Everyone can feel safe—physically and emotionally.
- Students and adults advocate for themselves and each other.

- Everyone's voice is invited and valued.
- All members can feel that they belong.
- Expectations and consequences are clear and consistently followed.
- Everyone is seen and treated as an equal participant.
- Students can count on adults to have their backs.
- Adults can count on each other to have their backs.
- Everyone can feel free from exclusion, derision, stereotyping, or bullying.
- Everyone keeps learning and growing.
- Expressions of gratitude are ubiquitous.
- Everyone matters and knows it.

The next chapter of this relationship pillar (Chapter 6) gets more specific about how those "caring, trusting, healthy" relationships take shape for particular types of connections. It explores the research findings on many kinds of relationships within schools: the educator's relationship with self, teacher-to-student relationships, student relationships with other adults in the school community, student-to-student relationships, and relationships among the adults in the school community. The chapter will also identify many benefits of the hard, satisfying work of building positive relationships that make a difference in everyone's well-being—that contribute to the culture we want in our schools. Chapter 7 offers suggestions about how to initiate and sustain strong, positive relationships to get the many resulting benefits of such work.

And here's some good news as you learn more about relationships in schools: With your base of gratitude practices learned and strengthened (in the First Pillar), you already have a wonderful foundation for the relationships you'll want for yourself, your colleagues, and your students and their families. Gratitude strengthens positive social bonds and relationships; it helps friendships grow. It increases satisfaction with school life (for students and educators) and inspires prosocial (generous, kind) behavior.

According to Kerry Howells (2013), a gratitude researcher, in a relationship, gratitude "calls upon us to give back **to** another. It also strengthens a relationship by recognizing what we **receive** from another person,"—thereby contributing to flourishing relationships (para. 10).

Chapter 6

Why Relationships?

No road is long with good company.
—Turkish Proverb

What do relationships have to do with building brilliant schools? Relationships are absolutely one of the most influential factors in the success of a brilliant school culture (or in the failure to achieve a brilliant school culture). Here's why: Nothing happens in a school outside of one or more relationships—not teaching, learning, or any of the other features of "doing" school. The kinds of relationships students encounter (and participate in) **make all the difference** in whether they flounder or thrive. As well, the forms and nuances of adult relationships in the school (with students or with other adults) make all the difference in whether **the adults** flounder or thrive! Without safe, caring, and supportive relationships, all the other good work we do in schools (i.e., great organization, strong academics, sound management and behavior policies, high expectations, engaging activities) is diminished.

Among policy elites and pundits in education, the urgency to improve academic achievement has stoked a raging debate. On one side are those who prioritize rigorous cognitive and academic development; on the other, those who care most about students' noncognitive skills and the physical, social, and emotional needs of the whole child. To many teachers, the debate seems ridiculous—because they have long known the answer is "both." Now, science is on their side.

Teachers, like parents, have always understood that children's learning and growth do not occur in a vacuum, but instead at the messy intersection of academic, social, and emotional development. And they know that students' learning is helped (or hindered) by the quality of students' relationships and the contexts in which they live and learn. (Shelton, 2018, para. 1 and 2).

These comments (above) are from Jim Shelton, president for education at the Chan Zuckerberg Initiative. (The Chan Zuckerberg Initiative is a philanthropic venture using technology to help solve some tough challenges—from preventing and eradicating disease, to improving learning experiences for kids, to reforming the criminal justice system.) In an article for *Education Week* titled, "The Brain Science Is In: Students' Emotional Needs Matter," Shelton (2018) shared the above empirical view, taken from a close look at meta-analyses bringing together research on learning and development from neuro, cognitive, and behavioral science. He asserts what so many of us practicing education in schools have known from experience—**it is not a choice between student achievement or relationships**. We do not sacrifice one for the other. Instead, we recognize the social nature of the human beings in our care and create opportunities to develop and sustain relationships to support their academic, social, and emotional well-being.

> *Without safe, caring, and supportive relationships, all the other good work we do in schools is diminished.*

The academic, social, and emotional well-being of students hinges on school communities providing consistent opportunities for connection and socialization. Classrooms are not going to serve kids well if the primary purpose is to sit in siloed desks doing independent work for six hours each day. By providing opportunities for collaboration—in and out of the classroom—we are responding to the brain's need to form connections. By recognizing that kids are social creatures, our spaces and learning opportunities can reflect what we know from science: that human beings are social beings from birth.

In recent decades, educators have become increasingly attuned to the importance of relationships in the classroom and school. The most voluminous relationship research has focused on the effects of teacher-student relationships on achievement, student behavior, and other facets of school life. But other relationships within the school setting are also the subjects of serious research. No longer is this topic sidelined to academics. It is widely understood that relationships, and other aspects of social development, are partners with academic learning.

Benefits of Your Own Self-Awareness

It's easy to bypass one key ingredient necessary to becoming a brilliant school: your brilliant self! As I see it, educators' relationships with themselves are the relationships that receive the least attention. We educators diligently work to support healthy relationships with our students and among our students. We put planning and effort into meaningful, positive connections with parents and colleagues. But attention to ourselves—our social, personal, and learning needs, attitudes, and behaviors—falls to the bottom of the priority list. This is a mistake! We won't have nearly the success we want with all the other relationships in our schools without first attending to relationships with ourselves. That's why I'm beginning this section with a focus on **the relationships that leaders, teachers, and other staff members have with themselves** and how that impacts their work in schools.

People with high self-awareness are honest with themselves about themselves.

At the beginning of the book, I told my story of a personal loss that compelled me to a major life reexamination. As I expressed in the chapters on gratitude, the growth process thrust upon me by Hurricane Katrina was able to flourish only within a mindset of self-awareness. Thankfully (and unexpectedly), I was given many hours standing in that Kmart parking lot to reflect. I became more self-aware—more in tune with my perceptions, feelings, values, and motives—and how these affected my behaviors.

Daniel Goleman (2012), author of *On Self-Awareness,* describes self-awareness as "the ability to recognize and understand personal moods and emotions and drives, as well as their effect on others" (para. 4). "This means having a deep understanding of one's strengths, limitations, values, feelings, and motives. People with high self-awareness are honest with themselves about themselves. They are realistic, neither overly self-critical nor excessively optimistic" (Goleman, cited in Kamath, 2019, para. 2-3). In his book *Emotional Intelligence* (2006), Goleman also notes that self-awareness is a core component of emotional intelligence—the necessary block upon which the other components (self-regulation, social skills, empathy, and motivation) are built.

Research has found that the intentional practice of self-awareness increases positive self-development and self-acceptance, boosts self-control and self-esteem, and leads to better decision-making. It allows people to see things from the perspective of others (Ridley et al., 1992; Silvia & O'Brien, 2004; Sutton, 2016). In work settings, self-awareness contributes to better communication and greater self-confidence, productivity, and job satisfaction (Silvia & O'Brien, 2004; Sutton et al., 2015).

For a long time, teacher training in content knowledge overshadowed the development of skills of self-awareness. In time, we have become savvier about the benefits of social-emotional learning for our students, including the critical nature of self-awareness in their learning and relationships. Now researchers are discovering that self-awareness is just as powerful a tool as content expertise for the success of teachers (and other educators). Just as we'll focus on how you must

62

know your students, we'll emphasize that you must know yourself. By examining our beliefs and biases, identifying your strengths, and identifying areas of needed growth, we leaders and teachers can co-create learning plans for our schools and classrooms alongside our students. Research has found that self-aware teachers (in comparison with those who indicate less self-awareness)

- Are more attuned to their strengths and weaknesses.
- Are better able to (and more likely to) help students with self-esteem and self-awareness.
- Have higher levels of self-efficacy (belief in their abilities to deal with situations).
- Have a more accurate understanding of their emotional responses to students.
- Have a better understanding of how their behaviors affect students.
- Are better able to help students understand themselves.
- Are more aware of students' emotional triggers and behavior choices.
- Positively affect student academic success.
- Have more success with positive classroom management.
- Give positive feedback to students more often.
- Experience fewer behavioral disturbances in their classrooms.
- Are better able to deal with student misbehavior.
- Are less likely to take student misbehavior personally.
- Can minimize the likelihood of power struggles with students.
- Can remain calm in tense situations with students.
- Have stronger personal relationships and better communication with colleagues.
  (Caprara et al., 2003; Kaufman & Wong, 1991; Richardson & Shupe, 2003; Ryan & Deci, 2000; Zee & Koomen, 2016).

Enhanced self-awareness skills increase self-efficacy—the belief or confidence that one can handle a situation well or do a job well

(Bandura, 1997). Teachers who perceive themselves as having the ability to affect student performance are more likely to perceive their students as teachable and worthy of their attention and effort. And higher levels of teacher self-efficacy positively affect student achievement. In addition, teachers' job satisfaction increases when they have confidence in their abilities as teachers (Caprara et al., 2006; Kaufman & Wong, 1991). **By the way, all of these characteristics above are not only true for teachers but hold for school leaders and others in non-teaching roles as well.**

Benefits of High-Quality Teacher-Student Relationships

Many researchers and educators believe this to be the most critical relationship of all in any school. We all remember THAT teacher who had a profound impact on us. We remember the name, can visualize the face, and can even hear the cadence of the speech (or certain frequent phrases of advice or encouragement). We can pinpoint the impact of these teachers because they created a safe, caring environment for the teacher-student relationship to bloom and for learning to take place. For some of us, our teachers and school staff were what "made" our school experience and influenced us to become teachers. The reach of the adults in a school building extends well beyond the school year or school setting. Many anecdotes of influential teachers give testimony to research findings that the effects of teacher-student relationships are long-lasting. Relational experiences accumulate with each student, influencing what they become and how they view the world (Giles, 2011).

Teachers and students are always in a state of relationship. Whether or not either party realizes it at every moment, these relationships matter—always. And when teachers and students are comfortable with and value the relationship, learning is enhanced for both. On the other hand, when teachers are indifferent to the relationship or the student perceives that her or his relationship with the teacher is not important to the teacher (or is adversarial), learning for both is diminished (Giles, 2011).

In an interview with *Education Week,* James Ford, North Carolina State Teacher of the Year 2019 and program director for the Public School Forum of North Carolina, said,

> The relational part of teaching may very well be its most underrated aspect. When teachers are good at building relationships with students, the skill is seen more as cover for a lack of content knowledge or wherewithal to instruct with rigor. On the contrary, our first job as teachers is to make sure that we "learn" our students, that we connect with them on a real level, showing respect for their culture and affirming their worthiness to receive the best education possible. (Cited in Sparks, 2019, para. 6).

Benefits for Students

Extensive research has focused on the effects of teacher-student relationships. Researchers Bridget Hamre and Robert Pianta (2001) found that the bonds of a positive teacher-student relationship give students a secure base for social and academic development over a long period of years. One systematic review and analysis of 46 published studies on the topic (Quin, 2016) affirmed what many other investigations found: Strong, healthy teacher-student relationships are associated with improvements on practically every measure important

Strong, healthy teacher-student relationships are associated with improvements on practically every measure important to schools.

to schools (attendance, grades, behavior, dropout rates, achievement, and school satisfaction). Over and over, we learn that trusting, caring teacher-student relationships contribute to such results for students as

- Increased academic performance and academic resilience.
- Scaffolding for important social and academic skills.
- Higher levels of motivation and engagement.
- Greater feelings of safety and security for students.
- Increased prosocial skills and behavior.
- Higher levels of students' sense of school belonging.
- Fewer behavioral disruptions in the classroom.
- Enhanced autonomy, self-direction, self-confidence, and self-esteem.
- Increased academic self-esteem.
- Increased academic tenacity.
- Reduced stress, isolation, and depression.
- Increase in overall school adjustment, satisfaction, and connection.
- More satisfying, trusting relationships between peers.
- Higher attendance and lower dropout rates.
  (Alexander et al., 1997; Baker, 2006; Baker et al., 2008; Birch & Ladd, 1998; Bryk & Schneider, 2003; Chiu et al., 2016; Deci & Ryan, 2014; Decker et al., 2007; Hamre & Pianta, 2001; Kemple & Hartle, 1997; Konishi et al., 2010; Konishi & Wong, 2018; Ladd, 1999; Ladd et al, 1999; Leadbeater, 2008; Martin & Collie, 2016; Marzano et al., 2003; O'Conner et al., 2011; Pianta & Stuhlman, 2004. Rimm-Kaufman & Sandilos, 2011; Ryan et al., 1994; Silver et al., 2005).

High-quality teacher-student relationships have also been found to
- Help to diminish negative behaviors toward others in the present and future.
- Enable students to develop protections against long-term internalization of negative internal behaviors (behaviors directed at themselves).
- Contribute a positive impact on long-term success in school and employment.

- Diminish chances of anxiety or withdrawal.
- Offer a buffering effect in the presence of bullying and distress in students' lives.
- Strongly protect students against the consequences of even the worst psychological trauma.
  (Hamre & Pianta, 2001; Headden & McKay, 2015; Konishi et al., 2010; Konishi & Wong, 2018; Leadbeater, 2008; O'Connor et al., 2011; Rudasill et al., 2010; Deci & Ryan, 2014).

Those of us who have taught and served in historically disenfranchised communities understand the wide-reaching effects that poverty can have on our students, and many of us have seen in our daily school lives how critical adult relationships are for these students. Researchers Christopher Murray and Kimber Malmgren (2005) affirm that, because of the risks associated with poverty, **students in high-poverty urban schools may benefit from positive teacher-student relationships even more than students in higher-income schools**. Risk outcomes associated with poverty include low academic self-esteem and low confidence in their academic futures, high rates of high school dropouts, lower rates of college applications, low self-efficacy, and low self-confidence. A positive and supportive relationship with an adult, most often a teacher, is one of the most powerful protective factors against the negative outcomes often associated with the schooling of low-income children. Low-income students who have strong teacher-student relationships have higher academic achievement and more positive social-emotional adjustment than their peers who do not have

> *Children learn best when they like their teacher and they think their teacher likes them.*
>
> –Dr. Gordon Neufeld, Child Development Specialist, Author

a positive relationship with a teacher (Leadbeater, 2008; Murray & Malmgren, 2005).

Probably most teachers find that some students are easier to get to know and relate to than others. As a teacher, don't give up on working to develop positive relationships with difficult students. As a school leader, don't give up on doing the same and supporting your teachers to learn ways to reach these students. Such students benefit from strong teacher-student relationships as much as, or even more than, their peers (Baker, 2006; Birch & Ladd, 1998).

Benefits for Teachers

It is not only the students who gain from a high-quality relationship. **The teacher benefits too.** A study exploring teacher emotions in connection with student behavior and teacher-student relationships found this: A teacher's relationship with students was the best predictor of the amount of joy the teacher experienced in the classroom. Teachers who developed high-quality relationships with students reported more joy, less anger and anxiety, and greater job satisfaction (Hagenauer et al., 2015).

Researchers who study teacher resilience have found that warm, connected relationships with students contribute to teachers' abilities to successfully cope with job responsibilities. As teachers work to enhance relationships with students, they improve their interpersonal and communication skills; they do better at managing stress and appropriately expressing frustration (Day & Gu, 2014). Stronger interpersonal skills contribute to better relationships with co-workers and parents, as well.

Signs of Good Teacher-Student Relationships

The teacher-student relationship is continually in play. This means that hundreds of small, everyday interactions are opportunities to seize (or miss) building the kinds of trusting relationships that impact student outcomes in desired ways. So, let's not miss even one such opportunity! Let's show students that relationships with them matter to us.

How do these high-quality teacher-student relationships look in action? There are dozens of attitudes to cultivate and behaviors to practice to develop the relationships that help students thrive. Start with the Chapter 5 list of features that apply to **all** the relationships in a school. (See the bulleted list under the working definition of a relationship.) Then move on to this group of suggestions specifically for teachers. Here are some signs that such relationships are present:

> *A teacher's relationship with students was the best predictor of the amount of joy the teacher experienced in the classroom.*

The students
- Appear to be comfortable with the teacher.
- Believe that the teacher likes them.
- Feel noticed (they don't look alienated).
- Feel safe (they don't look scared or wary).
- Each have a voice and use it comfortably.
- Are free to ask questions.
- Show signs of engagement with the teacher and the class.
- Exhibit high motivation to perform well academically.
- Feel respected by the teacher.
- Show respect to other students.
- Acknowledge the teacher (including out of the classroom).
- Laugh, smile, show signs of enjoyment.

The teacher
- Is warm and welcoming to all students.
- Is agreeable, patient, and empathetic.
- Shows that she/he likes the students, wants to be with them, wants to teach them.
- Shows a passion for the subject matter.

- Encourages and plans for autonomy for students (in contrast to control and contingent regard).
- Is positive and affirming in explicit and implicit messages, and in body language as well.
- Shows an understanding of the needs, characteristics, and interests of the age group.
- Puts serious effort (visibly) into getting to know students.
- Learns about students' interests, backgrounds, activities.
- Shows genuine interest in students' overall (not just academic) wellbeing.
- Accepts and respects every student's culture and individuality.
- Believes that each student can succeed and shows it.
- Notices, appreciates, and affirms everybody's talents.
- Helps students meet their academic and social goals.
- Affirms students' accomplishments.
- Asks for and listens to all students' opinions, ideas, and perspectives.
- Sets high (attainable) expectations for each student, holds to them, and helps students reach them.
- Invites student participation in decisions that affect them.
- Does what she/he says; follows through.
- Deals with student issues privately; never embarrasses a student in front of others.
- Makes contact with every student every day.
- Honors others' privacy and confidentiality.
- Is honest, authentic (not phony), and direct—does not play games or give mixed messages.
- Does not threaten, yell, shame, label, judge, or belittle students.
- Shows absolutely no favoritism, bias, or predetermined judgments.
- Enjoys humor and uses it appropriately; laughs and smiles a lot.

Benefits of Other High-Quality Adult-Student Relationships

The classroom teacher is not the only important adult in a student's school life. While the role of the teacher cannot be overstated, students interact with numerous teachers other than their own and with a variety of other adults. All adult contacts make an impression on a student. From our custodians Mr. Delfred and Ms. Kathy who hug, greet, and counsel students during morning entry to Ms. Lisa and the other lunch workers who provide smiles while serving lunch on the line to the coaches, bus drivers, librarians, student teachers, after-school staff, and all others who have touchpoints with kids—those relationships are critical to a student's social, emotional, and academic well-being as supports to the classroom teacher-student relationship. Indeed, sometimes it is one of these folks who makes the most difference in a student's life. The quality relationships with the student's teacher or teachers can be multiplied many times by contacts with supportive staff members throughout the school, on the bus, in the gym or hallways, and on the playground or sports field. The characteristics of good teacher-student relationships apply to all those connections. So do the benefits!

> *There is something in that bond, in that connection to school, that changes a life trajectory.*
>
> –Robert Blum, Professor, Johns Hopkins Bloomberg School of Public Health

Robert Blum (2005), Professor at the Johns Hopkins Bloomberg School of Public Health, defined school connectedness as referring to "an academic environment in which students believe that all adults in the school care about their learning and about them as individuals" (para. 1). He summarized the research about the importance of this experience of connectedness for students:

> Students who feel connected to school (independent of how these students are faring academically) are less likely to use

substances, exhibit emotional distress, demonstrate violent or deviant behavior, experience suicidal thoughts or attempt suicide, and become pregnant. In addition, when young people feel connected to school, they are less likely to skip school or be involved in fighting, bullying, and vandalism. These students are more likely to succeed academically and graduate.

From our research, we have found that kids who felt connected to school . . . smoked less, drank alcohol less, had a later age of sexual debut, and attempted suicide less. On top of this, from the educational literature, they do better across every academic measure we have.

As our research expanded, [we learned that] this is not just an association—kids who smoke less also felt more connected to school. It is a causal relationship. There is something in that bond, in that connection to school that changes the life trajectory—at least the health and academic behavior. It is very powerful—second only to parents in power. In some contexts, it's more powerful than parents. (Blum, 2005, para. 7).

This is powerful, striking evidence of the absolute necessity for our students to experience strong, caring relationships with all the adults in the school! And those relationships have a foundation in our (administrators, teachers, support staff) relationships with each other. Furthermore, the best scenario is that the families of all students pick up the same caring from school personnel.

Recently I watched an online video that, as I understand, went viral shortly after its release. As I viewed (and read) the story of a Texas school bus driver, I couldn't help but feel the power of "wraparound" relationships that spread across a school setting (Hartman, 2019). Well before students enter the building and well after the final bell has rung, students feel cared for and connected. Curtis Jenkins, a Lake Highlands Elementary School (in Dallas, Texas) bus driver in his seventh year of service, told a local TV reporter that he wants kids to know they are appreciated. He spreads care, respect, and important life lessons, along with special personalized gifts to students. He helps anyone in need, spending thousands of dollars out of his own pocket. But the interviews with students show that it is the motivation, inspiration, and love from Curtis—not the gifts—that are what the students need and remember. Can you imagine how such a relationship—one that begins before the school day, impacts a student's learning, confidence, and approach to school?

Curtis Jenkins' bus is a microcosm of what all brilliant schools strive for. This "mini-community" cultivates teacher-student and peer-to-peer relationships which bloom in earnest across various school settings. These relationships can't help but flourish when given the kind of consistent attention that he gives. From the bus to morning breakfast, into classrooms, and through our afternoon routine, students work with social systems in the school building. Just think about how the caring culture of that bus affects the entire school day!

Jenkins' story serves to remind us of the power that an individual could use to affect a whole system; in this case, the system is the school. Jenkins tells the reporter, "Every morning we say, 'Listen, love, and understand each other'" (Kuruvilla, 2018, para. 12).

Benefits of High-Quality Student-Student Relationships

A host of peer encounters play powerful roles every day for every student. These student-to-student connections and contacts are a major factor in the success and comfort (or failure and discomfort) of the entire school experience for any given student. This is true for all grade levels and in all kinds and sizes of schools. And the impact of peer relationships increases as students proceed to higher-grade levels (Steinberg & Monahan, 2007; Yibing et al., 2017).

School can be a rough place for many children. Peer rejection, exclusion, and interpersonal conflicts are normal parts of school for many students. Unfortunately, a surprising number of students each day are reluctant or outright afraid to go to school. They fear that they will be bullied or otherwise mistreated. Not only can being rejected by a school peer group or feeling unsafe at school make a school experience miserable, but it can also have long-term, negative effects—social, academic, and personal—as well (Buhs et al., 2010; Ladd, 2005). On the other hand, the successful development of healthy peer relationships leads to short-term school comfort and success and long-lasting positive effects. It is a critical part of building a brilliant school.

Student-to-student contacts are a major factor in the success and comfort (or failure and discomfort) of the entire school experience for any given student.

Early developmental theorists proclaimed that quality peer relationships are critical for developing a sense of self, social competence, and sense of justice (Piaget, 1997; Sullivan, 1953). For decades, researchers have studied multiple aspects of peer relationships, in and out of the school setting. It's been shown that the peer group plays an important role in social and personal development. Peers also have a huge impact on the learning environment—affecting academic experiences for every student.

As all educators know, students are highly affected by their social groups. Peers help shape outlooks, ideas, biases, and behaviors for one another. **Peer contacts and influences can serve as powerful, positive forces.** Research has found that, in the presence of relationships characterized by safety, support, and trust, peers (individually or in groups) can provide to each other

- A sense of belonging separate from families.
- Emotional and social support.
- Emotional and social connections to school.
- Help to shape prosocial behavior.

74

- Opportunities to learn appropriate social interactions.
- Models and motivation for self-management.
- Help for crossing barriers and adjusting to school.
- Protection against stress.
- Models of willingness to help.
- Situations for learning and honing such skills and behaviors as caring, empathy, communication, cooperation, compromise, social responsibility, negotiation, conflict resolution, and problem-solving.
- Enhanced learning that comes from social interaction (as brain-compatible learning research that tells us brains learn and remember better when working with other brains).

And peers can enhance for each other

- Self-confidence and self-belief.
- Self-awareness.
- Self-direction and independence.
- Awareness of others' needs, values, and perspectives.
- Engagement and success in learning activities.
- Favorable views of school.
- Academic challenge and academic risk taking.
- Overall school satisfaction and well-being.
  (Bryk & Schneider, 2003; Chiu et al., 2016; Furrer & Skinner, 2003; Ladd, 1999; Ladd, 2005; Ladd et al., 1999; Ming-tak, 2008; Roffey, 2011; Rhorbeck, 2003; Rohrbeck & Gray, 2014; Rubin et al., 2005; Ryan et al., 1994; Wentzel & Caldwell, 1997).

Furthermore, the more students get to know each other, set and accomplish goals together, and listen to each other, the greater are the benefits listed above (Headden & McCay, 2015). Cooperative learning has a powerful effect on student relationships. Students come to value and care about one another as they have more experiences working, communicating, problem-solving, and decision-making together.

Shelly Berman (1997), a cooperative learning researcher, found that the kind of group learning that involves *interdependence*—that is, where each individual is needed to reach a group goal, giving each student a valuable place in the group—leads to significant bonding among group members. Students contribute more to the well-being of others, and prosocial behavior increases. Further research into the outcomes of the *positive interdependence* that is central to true collaborative learning found that it is this kind of student interaction that breaks down biases among students, causing them to rethink their previous conclusions about the social desirability of someone else and increasing empathy for and reduced prejudice toward people they previously avoided or rejected (Bierman, 2004; Pettigrew, 2008; Pettigrew & Tropp (2008).

In contrast, negative peer encounters can have devastating and long-term effects. Among such social contacts are rejection, victimization, teasing, exclusion, demeaning—and any other of the many forms of bullying. In effect, negative experiences with peers diminish or erase many of the above benefits of caring connections. Relationships that are hurtful, frightening, or dismissive, can lead to

- Battered self-esteem
- Loss of confidence
- Educational difficulties
- Waning motivation and academic connection
- Withdrawal
- Antisocial behavior
- Negative behaviors turned inward
- Disengagement from school
- Insecurity
- Depression

  (Furrer & Skinner, 2003; Hughes et al., 2001; Ladd, 1999; Ladd, 2005; Ming-tak, 2008; Rohrbeck & Gray, 2014; Rubin et al., 2005; Rubin et al., 2009; Wentzel & Caldwell, 1997; Yibing et al., 2011).

Just think of the number of peer interactions each student encounters on the way to school, in the hallways, in classes, between classes, and after school—every single day! Schools can't ride a middle ground when it comes to student-to-student relationships; we must choose between engagement and disengagement, inclusion and exclusion, joyful participation and withdrawal, success and failure, security and dread. We must work tirelessly toward the outcomes that will result from serious efforts to model, develop, spread, and sustain satisfying, safe relationships among students.

There is no doubt that consistently positive peer-to-peer relationships are critical to building a brilliant school. Kenneth H. Rubin, Professor of Human Development, has spent a career studying peer relationships in children and adolescents. In the publication, *Peer Relationships in Childhood,* Rubin and his colleagues (2005) asserted: "'No child left behind' movements in public schools should incorporate children's social skills and relationships into the academic curriculum" (p. 68).

Benefits of High-Quality Adult-Adult Relationships in the School

We're all eager for students to behave appropriately and to treat each other with respect. We recognize the monumental importance of teacher-student relationships, and we have grown to understand that time spent on this is as important as time spent on academic matters. But it is the adults in the school who are the models for trusting, respectful relationships. And the school leaders, in particular, are the models for the teachers and the rest of the staff, as well as for the students. The "relationship climate" starts at the top. The climate of relationships in a school is heavily influenced by the ways adults treat each other. Nobody is happy in their jobs as students, teachers, staff members, or administrators without experiencing value, trust, kindness, gratitude, and respect for their competence from those around them.

High-quality relationships among adults in the school, and in particular the relationships the administrator forms and maintains, are key factors in high-performing schools. These are critical for student achievement and a healthy school culture to prosper (Barth, 2006; Louis, 2007; Louis et al., 2010; Knapp et al., 2010). And here's the thing: **The characteristics of high-quality relationships and the benefits of good relationships already mentioned in Chapter 5 and earlier in this chapter— all of them—apply to adults as well as to students.** They apply to every relationship within the school community, no matter who the parties are. Each adult should learn the behaviors and benefits well.

> *The nature of relationships among the adults within a school has a greater influence on the character and quality of that school and on student accomplishment than anything else.*
>
> —Roland Barth, Director, Principals' Center, Harvard University

We can certainly think of the "trickle-down" theory (from adults to students) when we consider relationships. But it's not just a one-way matter. **Relationships in the school flow in all directions, and everyone is affected by the relationship behavior of everyone else.** We certainly know that our students, at any given moment in school, are noticing everything. They may not appear to be paying attention to adults (especially at the middle- and high-school levels), but you can be sure they catch every adult-to-adult, leader-to-teacher, teacher-to-student, staff member-to-student, administrator-to-cafeteria worker, teacher-to-parent, parent-to-parent encounter within their hearing. All students and adults can feel treasured, secure, capable, and uplifted in the presence of healthy relationships. All students can feel insecure, worried, marginalized, or untrusting in the presence of antagonistic or toxic relationships.

The Power of Leadership in School Relationships ───

School leaders are critical "movers" in the relationship status of any school. Relationships are at the foundation of educational leadership. According to Peter Northouse (2015), author of several books on leadership theory and practice, any school leader position is a job of a relational nature. That is, relationships are a part of virtually every decision and situation in which an educational leader finds herself or himself (Lasater, 2016). The 2015 National Policy Board for Educational Administration's *Professional Standards for Educational Leaders* (2015) addresses the importance of relationships in the role of a school leader. They call leaders to "empower and entrust teachers, establish "trust and open communication, and develop and support open, caring, and trusting working relationships among leaders, faculty, and staff" (p. 15).

> *Relationships are a part of virtually every decision and situation in which an educational leader finds herself or himself.*

Relationships among leaders and the teachers affect all other relationships in the school and have major impacts on students and their learning and overall school effectiveness (Goleman et al., 2013; Price, 2012; Weber & Scott, 2013). Furthermore, say researchers Weber & Scott (2013), leadership is **the** major determinant of levels of academic achievement and overall success for students. One of the major reasons that teachers leave the profession is a lack of professional support. But when leaders set the establishment and nurture of relationships as priorities, teacher retention increases (Brownell & Skrtic, 2002).

If relationships in a school are toxic, strained, or destructive, a school cannot have a healthy culture. But when relationships between administrators and teachers are kind, cooperative, and trusting—the relationships between teachers and students and parents will be the same (Barth, 2006). Successful schools are marked by a culture of value, respect, trust, and cooperation among all stakeholders.

Here are some of the benefits evident in schools where leaders are transparent, compassionate, trustworthy, and open—and where teachers, support staff, parents, and students see and feel that they are included, trusted, and valued:

- Teacher trust in school leadership is enhanced when they feel valued by the administration.
- Teachers and other staff members feel more connected to the school and more concerned with its welfare.
- Staff members, parents, and students reciprocate by trusting their leaders.
- Teachers collaborate more willingly with colleagues on effective teaching practices.
- Teachers and staff are more open to the practices, programs, and input of administrators.
- Teachers, staff, and leaders all have higher job satisfaction.
- Students feel safe and more connected to their schools.
- Students feel that their teachers and others are invested in their success.
- Students have higher levels of achievement.
- Families feel more connected to the school.
- Parents are more likely to work in support of the school staff and school ventures.
- School improvement efforts have higher rates of success. (Barth, 2006; Bryk & Schneider, 2003; Price, 2012; Weber & Scott, 2013).

Chapter 7

How Do G.R.E.A.T. Leaders Get Results with Relationships?

Three things in human life are important:
the first is to be kind; the second is to be
kind; and the third is to be kind.

—Henry James, American writer

Everyone in the school community benefits when we establish deep, meaningful connections. To interact and regard one another in ways that support and improve outcomes for our students serves us all.

How do we work to develop relationships in ways that bring the kinds of benefits named in chapters 5 and 6? How do we make this long-lasting? What can leaders do? What can teachers and other staff members do?

The research, born out by the experiences of many educators, gives us clues to answer these questions. Based on those clues, here are some suggestions and advice for administrators and other leaders. These attitudes and practices get proven results! There are small, powerful ways to forge these connections so that they ripple and multiply. I hope you'll understand that these ideas can be adapted to fit your purposes. I invite you to think about ways to implement these experiences with your teams, parents, students, and staff.

Brilliant schools use such relationship-building strategies to jumpstart the year and develop them into powerful habits throughout the year. Often, our best relationship-building strategies stem from well-intentioned mistakes we've made or witnessed. The goal in offering the kinds of ideas that follow is to allow you to make deposits in what I call "the Student's Bank of Trust, Care, and Safety" **before** a challenging situation presents itself. We must be proactive, not reactive, with the steps we take. All in all, the strategies are opportunities to connect in meaningful ways so that you can build and sustain a brilliant school.

Keep These Discoveries in Mind

- Humans need to feel valued, respected, known, wanted, capable, and useful—in whatever social setting they must operate.
- The intentional practice of high-quality relationships between and among all members of a school community yields a multitude of benefits.
- When students experience connectedness to school and the people in it, they do better—socially, academically, and emotionally.
- Negative peer relationships or encounters harm academic performance and a host of personal and school factors for those who are victimized as well as those who do the bullying.
- School staff members who experience satisfactory, supportive relationships have higher job satisfaction. (This includes leaders—who otherwise are often the most isolated members of the school staff.)
- Teachers and other adults in the school have powerful influences on the relationships among peers; students who have positive relationships with teachers fare better in their relationships with their peers.

- The model for quality relationships begins with the school leaders and spreads up and down and back and forth to all staff, students, and school families.
- With joint effort, commitment, and practice, all of us in schools can learn to build and continue caring, nurturing relationships.
- The regular practice of gratitude leads to deeper, more meaningful relationships.

Start with These Steps

Define and describe relationships. Do this together! What kinds of relationships do you want in your school? With the whole staff, reflect and discuss this thoroughly. Don't leave students or parents out of that process. Listen to (and incorporate) students' definitions and descriptions. Discuss, demonstrate, draw, and describe what quality relationships look like. As you move forward, your plans can be built on your own group's understanding and statement of what everyone means by the relationships that are best for everyone. (Reflect on that list of relationship characteristics that followed the definition of *relationships* in Chapter 5.)

Revisit understandings about relationships. Continually revisit, revise, and expand the descriptions and criteria. Talk with students about the markers of healthy and unhealthy relationships. Be sure that students and adults know that as they practice healthy, quality relationships and watch them in action, they will learn new things about what good relationships are.

Believe in relationships. Expose members of your

> *Our first job as teachers is to make sure we "learn" our students, that we connect with them on a real level.*
>
> –James E. Ford, 2014-2015 North Carolina Teacher of the Year, Consultant, Writer, Speaker

school community to as much information as you can about what good relationships are and how they benefit everyone. Share the research. Encourage staff members to read and explore further. Even share research findings with students (explained appropriately for their ages) and with their parents. Adults who work on relationships will do better if they wholeheartedly embrace the idea that time spent building relationships is worthwhile. And if they are clear about what the benefits of good relationships are (as well as the consequences of the lack thereof), they'll be highly motivated to keep up the efforts. Do your best to garner everyone's commitment to being an eager part of the relationship work. If some aren't ready to be "all in," ask them to participate in relationship-improving practices enthusiastically anyway for several weeks. (They will likely become converts!)

Plan together. As you make plans to build quality relationships, draw input from all parties about what to do. Do come armed with information about what has worked in other places, what is learned from research, and such. But hear all the suggestions from all the voices (including students). Decide together what to try. When you're ready to kick off any new or expanded effort, enlist a wide range of stakeholders to join in.

Make staff dialogue part of the plan. From the very beginning, provide time and settings for staff members to learn, grow, share, and evaluate together. Teams or grade-level groups (or the whole staff) can share ideas about and experiences and support one another in the journey of relationship building and maintenance. They can try out new strategies and share with colleagues their successes or challenges in doing the work with their students.

Make sure you, the leader, are completely on board. Take the lead. Whatever descriptions of relationships, decisions about approaches, or commitments are set in motion—you, the leader, must visibly, consistently embody these in your actions. Period.

Include These Attitudes and
Actions Throughout the Year ───────────

Teach and practice self-awareness. We opened the chapter on relationship research (Chapter 6) with a focus on the relationship with self. That chapter outlined many benefits of increased self-awareness within the school community. Here are some steps to increase self-awareness. Leaders, practice these yourself. Then, share them with your staff:

1. Ask yourself such questions as:
   - *Do I know my emotional triggers?*
   - *Am I learning to defuse them?*
   - *Do I pay attention to my mental health?*
   - *Do I intentionally do practices to manage my stress?*
   - *Do I have help and support?*
   - *Do I have a sense of humor?*
   - *How do I feel about myself?*
   - *What words come to mind when I think about yourself? Are they positive or negative? A mix of both? What are those words? (Write them down.) Use the margin to write them down.*
   - *Do I love myself?*
   - *What are pieces of evidence from my words or behavior that prove my self-love?*
   - *Do I want to spend time with myself? Why or why not?*

If we're honest with ourselves, many of us might see that we have some work to do on knowing and loving ourselves. Asking these questions helps each person notice and ponder feelings about herself or himself.

2. Notice how you talk about yourself (or to yourself).
   Ask yourself:

- Do I denigrate myself?

- Does my talk show self-doubt?

- Do I compliment myself (to myself)?

- Do I "beat up" myself when I talk to myself?

- Do I brag? Do I sound arrogant?

- Do I overcompensate for self-doubts or feelings of powerlessness by talking about myself in grandiose terms?

Being aware of how you talk about yourself and to yourself is an important early step in self-awareness.

3. Check-in with yourself.

Just as you might monitor your students or staff, you have to monitor the thoughts and words that drip into your mind. How you see yourself is often the way you will see others—and nothing can kill a brilliant school more than trading in a group of grateful, Yes-oriented minds and hearts for a bunch of negative thinkers/reactors running around any day! We've all worked in toxic situations and can identify the culture killers in a second. Don't jump on board that train, even when tempted. Stay the course and mine the data; successful relationships with others begin by examining the one we have with ourselves. The way you see and treat yourself will affect or become the way you see and treat others.

> *The curious paradox is that when I accept myself just as I am, then I can change.*
>
> –Carl R. Rogers, Psychologist, Author

4. Know the skills of self-awareness.
   - Identify and notice your emotions and how you handle them.
   - Identify what triggers particular emotions.
   - Analyze how your emotions affect your behavior.

- Analyze how your emotions affect others.
- Work toward an accurate perception of yourself.
- Notice how others see you.
- Identify your strengths and build on them. (Make a written list.)
- Identify where you need growth and work on those areas. (Make a written list.)
- Accept yourself. Like yourself.
- Have patience with yourself and compassion for yourself.

5. Work at developing self-awareness skills.

   Here are some ways to do that:
   - Practice mindfulness. Pay attention to your inner state as it arises.
   - Process your thoughts; keep a journal; take notes.
   - Practice listening to others, to yourself.
   - Observe other people's body language and emotions.
   - Observe how people respond to you.
   - Don't jump to judge yourself or others.
   - Ask trusted friends or colleagues to give feedback about your strengths and needs. Ask people how they see you.
   - Practice perspective-taking (actively imagining how the other person might perceive or be affected by a situation).
   - Listen—really listen—to other perspectives.
   - Practice self-awareness skills with each other!
   - Discuss self-awareness—with colleagues, friends, students.
   - Have ways and places to talk with colleagues as an effective coping tool.
   - Acknowledge to yourself and each other the significant differences you are making.
   - Look for and engage in appropriate, light-hearted humor. Work at developing your sense of humor.

- Don't ignore signs of burnout, loss of interest, or being overwhelmed. Ask for help.
- Develop a growth mindset.
- Practice optimism. (I'll recommend a great book, *Deliberate Optimism*, by Debbie Silver, Jack Berckemeyer, and Judith Baenen, 2014.)

Model and Promote Quality Relationships. Yes, leadership matters! If you've been in the education game for a while, you've likely been led by different types of school leaders. Even if you've called one school home for the majority of your career, you've likely witnessed leaders sticking to the tried and true, trying on various leadership styles, or implementing new approaches or systems like a new wardrobe. The vision-setting, the questioning, the daily decisions—these all play a role in what makes a brilliant school. It is only together that any school community (administrators, teachers, support staff, students, families) can achieve and sustain what is needed for an effective school. We all must work collaboratively. But it is the leader that models this belief—demonstrating it in action.

> *In high-performing schools, a large percentage of teachers report strong relationships with fellow teachers and principals.*
>
> –Anthony Bryk and Barbara Schneider, Authors of *Trust in Schools*

The primary leadership behaviors associated with strengthening relationships are compassion, openness, authenticity, consistency, and involving all parties in decisions (Goleman et al., 2002). Start by embracing and practicing these yourself. Then work to help everyone realize the interdependency of the school community. One individual cannot succeed without the other. The needs of one or one group cannot be met without the help of the others.

Here are some active ways that the leader can show and encourage quality relationships. Use this as a checklist for monitoring yourself periodically throughout each school year:

- Express care and connection by extending a high level of personal regard to staff, students, and parents.
- In all your actions, show value to all members of the school community.
- Regularly, visibly, practice gratitude.
- Work to inspire and spread trust throughout the members of the school community.
- Operate transparently yourself; foster a transparent environment.
- Promote school-wide practices that support and encourage students and that attribute worth and equity to all.
- Practice the kinds of relationships you know are good for your school and yourself. Your staff, students, and students' families see how you interact with others. When you're in view, you're going to be noticed. Members of the school community observe you in normal, fun, crisis, or high-frustration situations. They see how you handle your feelings, students' behaviors, and visitors.
- Gauge how your feelings and actions affect others; make changes when your behaviors impact negatively.
- Control your emotions and the behaviors that follow. Disturbing behavior, erratic decisions, or toxic moods in a leader can wreak havoc on relationships and morale.
- Make every effort never to become the enemy—the one staff members, parents, or students refer to as the "they."
- If you're ever tempted to say, "No way!" quickly change it to "Yes . . . here's a way!" Keep that Yes Brain tuned up!

- Develop positive relationships with all students and their families. In particular, work at caring, supportive relationships with students who have challenges or difficult behavior.
- Be trustworthy. Do all that you can to spread trust schoolwide.
- Be respectful, trusting, and supportive with your staff. Make sure that teachers and other staff members feel treated like the professionals that they are.
- Treat all staff members with equity. Each one deserves to have the same level of regard, value, dignity, and trust afforded to them.
- Do the same (as above) with students' parents and family members.
- Be present and available. Greet staff, students, and visitors. Offer help, show up in hallways, in the lunchroom, and on the playground. Go to extra events. Take part in professional development—as an equal participant. Keep your office door open. Eat lunch in the faculty room or cafeteria.
- Tell the truth. Be straightforward and transparent about your actions and decisions. Give clear reasons for these. Honest information (even when unpleasant) stated clearly to all parties helps to circumvent rumors and avoid confusion. State expectations clearly.
- Seek teachers' professional perspectives and input; honor their knowledge, experience, expertise.
- Do the same with other staff members, parents, and students. Honor what they have to teach you. Enlist their help.
- CELEBRATE and affirm your staff members. Make a big deal out of things that are going right. Congratulate, affirm, and build on accomplishments.
- Act with integrity; be reliable and be adaptable.
- Stay alert to sense the emotions of others and show gratitude and caring.

- Problem-solve and manage conflict with enthusiasm, kindness, and humor.
- Share the power. Ask for teachers' input and honor it. Honor veteran teachers (many of them have been there before you and will be there after you!) Get input from non-teaching staff members, students, and parents on matters that involve them. Take the input seriously. Let others know what you learned from them and what you will do about it. Then let them see you DOING it.
- Don't be arrogant. Just because you are a leader, does not mean you need to be bossy.
- Keep people informed. No mandate should come out without people knowing about it. Work together.
- When things are tough or when people seem confused, upset, or disappointed, acknowledge the difficulty or solemnity. But also respond with gratitude and optimism.
- Show enthusiasm! Be realistic, hopeful, and positive. Without being haughty, show confidence that you all can make a change, grow and develop, or get through something hard—together.

Enlist staff in a commitment to non-stop modeling of caring relationships. The training is essential. But it has to be put into practice. Students learn from watching the adults. Parents notice how each member of the school staff relates to colleagues, students, and students' families.

Make relationship-building a regular, intentional part of teacher and staff training. Don't assume that educators automatically know how to relate well to others or how to teach students to get along with each other. See that "relationships" remain a consistent topic of your professional development program. Teachers (and other staff members, including leaders) need explicit training in many facets of relationship building for the work they do with each other and with students and their families.

- Plan specific PD sessions, getting the best help you can. Include aspects of relationship work as regular, short features faculty-staff meetings. This is good work for all adults in the school. Teachers can apply some of it for student work as well.
- Give training in relationship-related topics such as identifying and counteracting biases, bridging cultural gaps, restorative management, trust, communication, interventions with difficult student behavior, managing conflict with colleagues, helping students feel a sense of belonging, etc.
- State, clearly, your expectations about relationships. Let staff members know that you expect them to value one another, show it, and work together. Remember: people tend to rise to high expectations!

Make relationship-building a regular, intentional part of teaching plans. In outlining characteristics and evidence of quality teacher-student relationships, Chapter 6 described many actions for developing caring, supportive relationships. Here are a few other tips to share with your staff:

- One of the most effective tactics teachers can use to give value, support, and validation to students is to help them succeed academically. Teach well. See that each student learns. Adapt and scaffold to present material in ways that help each student succeed. When they achieve goals, master concepts, and skills, and participate meaningfully—students' beliefs in themselves as learners soar. So does their satisfaction in the relationship with the teacher who helped them succeed.
- Model quality relationships. Yes, this has been said before. But it is a key way that students learn about relationships, so I'll put it on this list too. Whether they show it or not, whether you notice or not—students notice all your interactions with other

students, with your colleagues, and with visitors to the school—including their parents and other parents. Let them see you interacting with respect, gratitude, humility, and care in every situation. Be sure to model, not only with kindness and regard for others, but with full control of your emotions and behavior, and with full self-awareness of how you are perceived.

- Invite students to give you feedback about your lessons, communication skills, engagement with students, and teaching techniques. Let them tell you what works for them. This shows that you trust their thinking and evaluating abilities.
- Don't be afraid of the "difficult" students—those who seem defiant, resistant, or withdrawn. Work hard to develop positive relationships with these kids. They need it! They (and you) will feel better and learn better when they see that you care enough to be persistent in reaching them. Note the students with whom you realize you don't have much of a relationship. Get to work—hard—at building connections with those students.
- Spend time individually with each student. Connect with each student—as often as possible. Show each that you know some things about him or her. Show interest in learning more.
- Show all your students that you enjoy them! Have a sense of humor! Show that you like being with students and that you like your job.
- Be absolutely unbiased. Watch yourself carefully to be sure that you demonstrate (by words, nonverbal cues, actions) that you value, respect, and believe in all students equally. If a student picks up clues that the teacher has a stereotypical attitude, a fear, a doubt related to the gender, siblings, family situations, sexual orientation, ethnicity, appearance/physical attributes, religion, or to any other personal attribute—this is a relationship killer!

- Get as much equity training as you can to learn about sneaky biases, how they evidence themselves, and what to do about them.
- When a sticky discipline situation arises, particularly in cases where a problem is persistent, look closely at the root causes. Sometimes the root cause of the behavior is related to implicit biases that unconsciously affect teachers or other students in relationship to the particular student.
- Polish and practice perspective taking. This means actively imagining how a student might perceive or be affected by a situation. This can help reduce bias, help teachers get to know students better, and deepen positive student-teacher relationships (Niskioka, 2019).
- Talk about relationships! Becoming more comfortable with others is not a taboo subject. Students of all ages can, and usually are willing to, talk about relationships—what works, what doesn't, what helps, what doesn't. Invite students to talk about what they need, what they can do, what the group can do—to improve relationships with the teacher and each other.

Don't sweep bullying—in any form—under the carpet. U.S. Department of Education (2016) statistics report that over 20% of students ages 12 through 18 are regularly bullied at school. In addition, most bullying incidents are not reported. And peers intervene only about 10% of the time. And more alarming, *The Eyes on Bullying Toolkit* (Storey et al., 2013), developed by the Education Development Center found that "adults intervened in only 4% of the bullying incidents they witnessed on the playground" (p. 24). Recognize it in all its forms. Name it. Make sure staff members and students know that bullying, too, may be verbal, social or emotional, sexual, ethnic, digital (cyber, Internet). It has a wide reach and the ramifications can be brutal. Hold lots of conversations about bullying. Talk about how private and subtle it can be. Tackle the very real problem of bystanders to bullying—roles they play in making it worse and roles they can play in diminishing it. Promote the power of students standing up as a group to bullying. See that intervention is immediate and follows all the school's stated processes.

Give a high priority to relationships with parents. Across the school culture, do whatever you can to build trust and build strong family relationships by including parents, building them up, showing that they are respected, important players in their child's education. This is a regular task for classroom teachers. But responsibility for this extends to administrators and all members of the school community.

> *In the end, we will remember not the words of our enemies, but the silence of our friends.*
>
> –Rev. Martin Luther King, Jr.

Parents are an integral part of everything that has to do with their children. Never let them be far from your mind, no matter what your role at the school. In addition to many other benefits, good relationships with parents improve students' academic achievement.

- Communicate often with parents. Make most of the communications positive. Celebrate the things their children are doing, accomplishing, mastering. Keep them informed about what is going on in your classroom. Find ways to invite them to participate in projects, assignments, and celebrations.

- Help parents belong. All the research tells us that students do better when parents are involved with the school (Comer et al., 1996). Realize that, just as students need a sense of belonging in their classrooms and schools, so do parents. Any time and effort you put toward bonding positively with parents will multiply in rewards to students' success and wellbeing. And when students notice that their parents are valued and treated, respected, and helped equally to others, they can better trust their school and the people in it.

- Plan for parent connections. For each week or unit you plan, add a spot for a "parent" idea. Think of a way to inform the parent, get ideas from the parents, share something with families, or include the families in a fun assignment. The basis of good family-home

> *A huge part of the message schools impart to students about relationships is not spoken or written. It is demonstrated in the ways we treat their families.*

connections lies in the teacher's belief that parents know and care about their children (more than the teacher), are competent adults, and have gifts and insights to offer. So many teachers dread seeing a parent show up at school or getting a text from a parent. If we teachers are gifting parents with our trust in them and need for them as partners, those incidents will be joyful, not fearful! And all the students will be in a better place.

- SHOW! Don't just tell. A huge, huge part of the message teachers, administrators, and all school personnel impart to its students and parents about relationships is not spoken in words. Nor is it written in the student handbook. It is demonstrated in the ways we treat their families. Likewise, a huge part of the message we at the school communicate with parents about anything related to the school is conveyed by the way we treat their children—by the relationships we develop with their children.

Help students build high-quality relationships with each other. Peer relationships (or lack of relationships) are at the heart of each student's school experience. The human need to connect is a powerful factor in learning and achievement. Teachers can support and sustain peer relationships with numerous intentional actions and attitudes every day. Here are some ways that administrators and teachers can help students develop positive relationships with one another, so that each student feels the sense of belonging that is so important, and so that each student is comfortable and valued at school.

> *The positive interdependence that is part of true collaborative peer learning can motivate kids to reevaluate previous conclusions about others' social desirability.*
>
> –Karen L. Bierman, Author of *Peer Rejection: Developmental Processes and Intervention Strategies*

- Set school-wide programs and traditions that promote core values and focus on prosocial outcomes such as kindness, respect, and equity across the school culture. These apply to all students and staff members, in and out of classrooms, throughout the school grounds.

- Adults in the school—demonstrate civil behavior and caring relationships with each other, with parents, and with students. Let students witness adults in many situations, including tense, emergency, or other difficult circumstances, act with calm clarity and regard for other persons. Let them see good communication that solves problems and gets things done while treating others well.

- Teachers, include plenty of collaborative learning in your lesson plans. When you put students into pairs or groups, make these groups random. Throughout many collaborative learning experiences, students will thus mix with the whole class— working in groups that draw from all social groups, academic levels, and personality types! Students get to know each other when they work together—when they have to plan, discuss, think, make decisions, come to conclusions, create, and solve problems together. I'll reiterate here a lesson learned from research on peer relationships at school. This was described in Chapter 6: True collaborative learning (where students in pairs or small groups work together and depend on each other's equal participation to reach a group goal, along with individual goals) deepens peer relationships. Furthermore, this is a kind of interaction (called "positive interdependence") that leads to a breakdown of such barriers as bias, stereotype, fear, and rejection.

- Arrange classroom settings that nurture relationships. Away with the rows! Set things up so that students face each other—sitting in circles or U-shaped tables. The setting allows for lots of face-to-face contacts where students can collaborate, discuss, pair up to generate ideas, make decisions, put their heads together, move, co-create, co-design, and co-solve problems. This arrangement, along with interactive activities gets kids relating, relying on one another. They learn to know, appreciate, value, accept, admire one another—and learn from one another.

- Focus on strong student-teacher relationships. Remember from the research: Students that have satisfying, trusting relationships with teachers (no matter what their academic record) learn better, behave better, and have better relationships with their peers at school. Furthermore, the quality of a teacher-student relationship significantly affects the social preference of students and other factors such as rejection and victimization (Elledge et al., 2016).

- Teachers, be aware, at all times, of the way you interact with students. Teachers' interactions with students can affect classmates' perceptions of individual students, in turn affecting which students the classmates choose to interact with and accept or reject (Hughes et al., 2001).

- Intentionally and regularly teach social-emotional skills (e.g., conflict resolution, problem-solving; group work skills, self-awareness, self-regulation, listening, etc.). Integrate these into the academic curriculum.

- Keep up the regular habit of gratitude practices in school. You saw in the First Pillar (Chapters 1-4) how gratitude supports flourishing relationships.
- Understand that peer relationships are highly influenced by the way teachers relate to students and by the supports teachers provide for healthy, equitable peer relationships (Kemple & Hartle, 1997).
- Hold class meetings to discuss and solve problems, get feedback on classroom procedures, and learn more about each other.
- Build whole-school community-building activities into the school program.
- Develop activities that involve parents and other family members
- Find ways for students to have some relationship-building activities across classes or grade levels.
- Be aware that group-based learning activities help break down biases and prejudices among students belonging to different social groups.
- Do your best, in classrooms and across the school, to build students' self-esteem. Students with high self-esteem are more likely to have positive relationships with peers as well as with adults (Orth et al., 2012).

A final, personal note: In my last school, with relationships as a dedicated focus, strong relationships among staff, students, and leaders propelled us to achieve amazing results over five years. Our team:

- Grew student performance and achievement each year, moving from one of the poorest-performing high schools to one of the highest-performing in the state.

- Increased scholarship offerings from just under $700,000.00 to over 5 million dollars.
- Transformed graduation rate from one of the lowest in the state to one of the highest.
- Reduced the dropout rate from one of the highest to one of the lowest in the state.
- Increased the number of state championships from one in the school's history to seven.
- Decreased the number of serious disciplinary offenses like fighting and assault to under 5 for the collective five years.

Conclusion

The Second Pillar

Think of each student and the backpack of
hopes, concerns, joys, anxieties, or trauma they
carry into your school building each day.
—Dr. Andy Parker

Back at the beginning of this pillar, I used a quote from Lev Vygotsky: "Through others we become ourselves." Others have given similar thoughts to communicate this truth: we learn and grow in relationship to others. Dr. Patricia Kuhl (2018), who researches brain development and learning says, "We use a social context to learn about the world. We learn from others by watching what they're interested in, and we learn by collaborating with them and discovering their ideas" (para. 1).

If we agree that the construction of knowledge and development as humans is a social process and that it is a school's responsibility to provide the structure and means to support the process, then we must recognize that substantial relationships lie at the heart of this work. The relationship we have with ourselves impacts the relationship we have with others and vice versa. Students construct their understanding of the world in both independent and collaborative ways; relationships are a tool critical to this work.

If you concur that learning about our students is as important as teaching them the content and how interconnected relationships are with academic growth and success, then you're on the right track. Our students bring a myriad of needs rooted and influenced by endless factors outside of our control. Socioeconomic status, abuse, parental involvement, mobility issues, etc., impact our students and their relationship to school. For some of our students, their basic needs are not met when they come to us. For others, while food or shelter might not be a pressing issue, parental pressure or absence may play a role in a student's relationship to school. Think of each student and the backpack of hopes, concerns, joys, anxieties, or trauma they carry into your classrooms or buildings each day. Then, you'll be reminded why knowing your students is so critical to students' social, emotional, and academic growth and why **relationship***s* are a pivotal tool in building brilliant schools.

But it is not only the students who are working and growing and understanding the world! All the humans in a school community are, to paraphrase Vygotsky (see quote at the beginning of this pillar, before Chapter 4), **becoming themselves through others**. This means that every relationship in the school setting, including the relationships we have with ourselves, contributes to the persons we become. And there are hundreds of these at work for each student, staff member, or parent every day.

In the Third Pillar, I will discuss **expectations**—a structure that G.R.E.A.T. leaders use to build brilliant schools. As the pillar, Gratitude intertwined with high-quality relationships, you will see how this pillar, Relationships, is a partner with efforts to set, meet, and exceed expectations in a school community.

The Third Pillar of a
Brilliant School

Expectations

Nobody rises to low expectations.

—Steve Maraboli, Behavioral Scientist,
Author, Decorated Military Veteran

*W*hen I was about five or six, a set of twin girls lived down the road from me. They couldn't **not** be twins. I remember their birthday cake complete with a pair of paper tiaras, and I concluded that they were identical twins. The blonde-haired, blue-eyed sisters always dressed in the same outfits, even down to the socks. From their haircuts to the shade of aquamarine in their eyes to the cadence of their speech—they appeared identical. I could never tell them apart. Strangers expected them to be twins. The information "fit" with what I knew to be true about being a twin: They looked alike + dressed alike + looked to be the same age = twins. Check! ✓

Wrong! What a mistake I made! The set of "twin" neighbor girls weren't twins at all. They were sisters— close in age, but not twins. Their mama had a station wagon full of other kids and chose to dress the girls alike because it was just easier. She was able to forgo potential fussing and fighting at the store over who-gets-this-or-that and decided to cut the nonsense and buy them the same outfits and toys. The duo continually confirmed what I knew about twins—similar features, outfits, birthdays, gestures, sound of voice, and so on.

Years later, in my first role as a middle school principal, I sat one morning at my desk, perusing the latest issue of Educational Leadership. I flipped through, finding an article that I thought was most *appropriate for my staff to read and discuss in an upcoming faculty meeting. I left my desk and headed into the main office lobby. As I hurried across to the copy machine, I noticed in my periphery a young, Black mother standing behind the front counter talking to my school registrar. Beside her, was a tall, young Black male wearing a cap. I began to copy the article, and as I waited, subconscious responses washed through my brain: "Gosh, not another student with disabilities; how will I ever hit my school performance target if I keep getting these SPED kids? I bet he has a discipline sheet a mile long. He's probably a gang banger who will keep my disciplinarians busy."*

I was on autopilot. These thoughts were instinctive. I didn't even realize at the time quite where they were coming from. The copier stopped. I grabbed my papers from the tray and turned toward the front counter on my way back to my office. On my second step, the young woman said, in an astonished voice, "Mr. Parker?"

Drawn back to reality, I looked up from my papers, stared at the woman, and—awed—responded, "Nikki?"
"Oh, my God! It is so good to see you," Nikki said. "This is Deshaun. You remember him, right? He was much smaller then. He is gifted, and I expect him to make straight A's, and he'd better not misbehave in any way, or you have my permission to do what you need to do to get him in line. He is so talented, and he's going to make something of his life."

It had been almost fifteen years since Nikki, who I realized was now the mother of Deshaun, sat in my Speech and Debate class as a senior. I remember her and her son vividly, because Nikki did her demonstration speech on how to change a baby's diaper, and Deshaun was her model in the speech.

"I do remember him. He's gotten much taller! And yes, I, too, expect Deshaun to make A's in every class he takes. I'm sure we won't have any problems with his behavior, or I'll tell everyone that I changed his diaper when he was a baby!"

They both laughed, we hugged, and I went back to my office to resume the planning of my professional development discussion on the article's topic: how racial bias impacts our decisions in schools. As I read the article title, my mind did a complete rewind back to the copy machine and my own racially biased thinking—even as I was copying such an article! Immediately, I was taken aback. "What would have happened to Deshaun if Nikki had not recognized me and said hello?" I said to myself. "How have my biases, even if unintentional or unconscious, impacted other students like Deshaun?" My mind and heart were heavy, but I knew I had to own these thoughts. I knew I must explore and understand the sources from which they were born and find ways to reprogram my brain to erase or stop these thoughts when I become aware of them.

Chapter 8

What Are Expectations?

*You are one of the rare people who can separate
your observation from your preconception. You see
what is, where most people see what they expect.*
—John Steinbeck, Author, in *East of Eden*

Most often, when we educators speak of "expectations," we have in mind what teachers and school leaders expect academically of a student or group of students. A main focus of this pillar is just that—teachers' expectations of students. But the concept goes further because, at all times, every school community is alive with expectations. In the process of the many interactions among community members, people have myriad expectations of one another and themselves. Like relationships, expectations flow back and forth among students and adults in a school.

In this chapter, you'll find some denotations—that is, "official" definitions of *expect, expectation,* and *teacher expectations.* But as we come to put our expectations into practice for brilliant schools, I'll reshape this definition somewhat. I'll add some comments on other factors that must be encompassed into our understanding of expectations, of what they are. And of where they originate (what shapes them).

Expectations: A Working Definition ━━━━━━━━━━

These are representative definitions of *expect, expectation,* and *teacher expectations:*

> Expect: *to consider probable, reasonable, or certain* (Merriam-Webster, 2021).
> Expectation: *a strong belief that something will happen or be the case in the future; a belief that someone will or should achieve something* (Lexico, 2021).
> Teacher expectations: *ideas that teachers hold about the potential achievement of students* (Rubie-Davies, 2015).

For this book, the discussions and research presented here, and our work together as educators, I'll use this definition that combines the above:

Expectations: *beliefs about and in persons, about the potential they have to achieve, and about their probable behaviors or characteristics now or in the future.*

At the beginning of this pillar on Expectations, I wrote about two experiences. In the first example, I thought two neighborhood sisters were twins; the pair confirmed what I believed to be true about twins. I had seen twins who looked alike and dressed alike. So, I assumed that pairs who looked and dressed alike were twins. I expected it to be true. It was a constant loop in my mind—what I inspected, I expected. I'll repeat that: **what I inspected, I expected.** Once I thought it was true, I kept looking for signs to affirm that I was right—noticing hairstyles, eye color, speech patterns, and such. This is a form of *confirmation bias*—an active seeking of information that confirms our existing beliefs (Facing History and Ourselves, 2021, para. 8).

In my second story, the expectations I had about Deshaun were rooted in my experiences and biases and shaped by my personal history.

Although sometimes the roots of our expectations can lead to positive outcomes, in this case, the outcomes were negative both for me (the person setting the expectations) and Deshaun (the one receiving the expectations). Since I did not outwardly express my thoughts in that situation, he didn't know what had been running through my mind. Maybe. Then again, he might have noticed the look in my eyes or my body language before I learned who he was. Whether or not he picked up on my biases—my judgmental spirit was not good for me and was disrespectful to him and his mother (if only silently).

Moment by moment, our minds gather, sort, and label information. Our personal story, consisting of our historical data—interactions, experiences, nuanced or "judgy" language, and sets of beliefs—mold the feelings and viewpoints. Throughout each day, we unknowingly archive, access, and reference these "file folders" in our minds. We then use the stored data to inform our behavior and decisions. Sometimes our brains digest these unconscious associations as facts. In actuality, some may be more fiction than fact. We create stories from the associations. These stories can take on a life of their own and become helpful or hurtful. And, fact or fiction, the judgments that result from this data have powerful consequences for ourselves, our expectations of others, and our relationships—particularly when the judgments go unquestioned.

Embracing Cajun country as I have, I love a good mirepoix! (A *mirepoix* is a mixture of chopped vegetables, sauteed to use as the base of a sauce—and always including onions!) I often say that a person is like an onion you find at the bottom of the pot—layered with concentric circles, each one contributing to the whole of the wonderful flavor. As discussed in the Second Pillar (Relationships), our understandings (or lack thereof) about our own complexities and inner worlds affect the ways we perceive others. If we lack self-awareness about the sources of our beliefs and biases, we likely have poor awareness of who other people really are. We can fail to notice some of the layers in individuals. When we allow our assumptions (not all of which may be rooted in objectivity) to dictate our expectations of people, we often underestimate someone's potential. In doing so, we damage the trust and value that we know are so critical to nurturing relationships.

Folks in brilliant schools understand that the quality of relationships is greatly influenced by our expectations. Our work as educators requires us to appreciate the layered, nuanced nature of people and to create opportunities for all of us to set and receive high expectations from one another.

Because bias is an automatic part of being human, and because biases are tightly connected to expectations, we must define and explore *bias* along with the definitions and examination of *expectations*. And since many of our biases are those of which we are unaware—a definition of *implicit* (or *unintentional) bias* is also important.

Bias and Implicit Bias: Working Definitions

For this book and our work together, let's think of *bias* and *implicit bias* in these terms:

Bias: *a tendency to believe that some people, ideas, etc. are better than others, which often results in treating some people unfairly* (Facing History and Ourselves, 2021, para. 5); *a natural inclination for or against an idea, object, group, or individual. It is often learned and is highly dependent on variables like a person's socioeconomic status, race, ethnicity, education, background, etc.* (Psychology Today, 2021, para. 1).

Implicit (unintentional) bias: *a judgment or behavior that results from subtle cognitive processes—attitudes or stereotypes—that often operate at a level below conscious awareness and without intentional control* (Facing History and Ourselves, 2021, para. 7).

If you have worked in a school for any length of time, you have heard other people's stories about students, co-workers, administrators, and even the families we serve. I'd bet that an image, perhaps a bit out of focus, began to emerge of that individual or family. The stories, birthed from our personal histories, experiences, and cultural, racial (or other) stereotypes, affect our expectations.

I'll reluctantly admit: I have participated in some storytelling and sharing that I am not proud to report. The teacher's lounge can be a factory where stories are retold or manufactured and passed on for others to consume. These stories might begin well before we ever meet a new student or colleague—perhaps in anticipation of the coming school year. In my case, I generally practiced a cautiously optimistic mindset, listening and perhaps filing away a suggestion for future reference upon meeting the individual. Other times, the story was a list of grievances handed to me with the expectation that I'd either sink or swim with the said student in my class. Truth be told, my cautious optimism waned while I listened to these types of stories. How could I not be influenced by the less hopeful, detailed accumulations of negative perceptions retold?

Yet, although some stories are woven into the fabric of a school like family lore handed down from generation to generation, I had to try to remain unbiased. I remember one such instance (when I was a new teacher) that challenged my commitment to high expectations. As our school clerk handed me the print-out of my class list, her face said it all. With her reaction to my class list on my mind, I approached an administrator with great trepidation. His response was not at all what I wanted. But it was what I needed. He said to me, "Andy, what we perceive we receive."

Certainly, that nugget of wisdom wasn't what I expected. I expected him to commiserate with me or coach me into solving this potential crisis. But he knew better. I replayed that phrase as the chorus of voices in the teachers' lounge shared such "information" as this about kids on my class list: *I saw your class roster; it looks like you ended up with Tony this semester. He's a great kid--super smart and super easy. He might just give you a run for your money! By the way, did you see the file on that transfer student? It's as long as my arm! Buckle up.*

111

The stories or lists of information about a student, colleague, or family are often tethered to assumptions or old narratives, riddled with gaping holes that our minds fill in—however inaccurately. Reminding myself of this, I held in my mind the refrain: *What we perceive we receive. What we perceive we receive.*

As we explore the topic of expectations, we must be aware of its constant companion—bias. Given all the biases (many of them unconscious) each individual holds, it should not be hard to understand the broad impact of our expectations for students, families, and colleagues.

It's fitting that the Expectations Pillar follows the Relationships Pillar. When various studies describe elements of successful schools, the element of relationships is always on the list. High levels of trust and cooperation among leaders, staff, students, and parents play a significant role in a school's success. The safe and trusting relationships we establish with people support our work as we investigate the beliefs that shape our expectations. I remind you, in particular, of the research on collaboration and positive interdependence that was cited in Chapter 6 (in the Second Pillar). It's been found that when people get to know each other, set and accomplish goals together, listen to each other, see each other as equally valuable to the group, and depend on each other to meet the group and individual goals—biases are broken down. People rethink previous conclusions about ability or desirability of other individuals or groups. Empathy is increased and prejudices are decreased toward people who were previously avoided, rejected, or judged (Berman, 1997; Bierman, 2004; Pettigrew and Tropp, 2008).

Let me summarize the above succinctly: doing the work for caring, trusting relationships (touted in the Second Pillar) goes miles toward eliminating biases that sabotage accurate expectations of who someone is and what that person can do.

And I cannot move on without bringing us all back to the First Pillar of a brilliant school, Gratitude. If we stay with the work of practicing gratitude, that practice leads us to look at people realistically. When we are grateful for the actions, gifts, knowledge, and contributions of others, we **see** them for who they really are and with the capabilities and possibilities they truly have. This, too, helps to melt bias.

Please take a minute to reread the John Steinbeck quote at the beginning of this chapter. Then make your commitment to be one of those "rare people" he describes.

Chapter 9

Why Expectations?

*Persons appear to us according to the light
we throw upon them from our own minds.*

—Laura Ingalls Wilder, Author

What do expectations have to do with building a brilliant school? The expectations that teachers hold for their students wield tremendous power in the performance and future success of those students. Beyond teacher expectations for students, all persons in the school community affect and are affected by the expectations we have of one another. These expectations, some of them explicit (outwardly stated) and some of them implicit (unconscious, hidden, or unintentional) fan out to include teachers, all other staff members, school and district leaders, parents and families, and the wider community.

It would be hard to find an educator today who is unaware of *Pygmalion in the Classroom,* the 1968 Rosenthal and Jacobson seminal work on teacher expectations. In their study, the researchers told teachers that an IQ test had identified students in their classes who were likely to make substantial academic gains that year. Twenty percent of the total number of students in each class was randomly identified to the teachers. When those students were retested later in the year, the students in the experimental group showed significantly greater gains in their IQ scores when compared to the control group. The researchers concluded that the teachers treated those students differently because of the expectation that these students would flourish.

Effects of teacher expectations accumulate over time, and the influence grows significantly stronger as students progress through school.

Later studies followed up on this idea. Many confirmed the boost that follows from high expectations. Others identified the teacher behaviors that differed according to teacher expectations (Brophy, 1983; Brophy & Good, 1970; Johnston et al., 2019), student characteristics that seemed to influence teachers' expectations, or teachers' underlying beliefs that affected their expectations of individual students, groups of students, or entire classes (Johnston et al., 2019; Rubie-Davies, 2006, 2007, 2008; Rubie-Davies et al., 2015).

The Rosenthal-Jacobson study (1968) inspired a good deal of investigation into the concept of teacher expectations creating self-fulfilling prophecies. *Self-fulfilling prophecies* occur when a teacher believes (erroneously) that a student has less potential, and passes on these beliefs in interaction with the student, influencing the student to behave in ways to confirm the false expectation—making the teacher's belief true.

Sometimes the term *Golem effect* is applied to this situation. It names a process where teachers (or others in authority) believe that someone will give a low performance, thus causing the behavior that they predict. This happens when the person, realizing that the teacher or boss has low expectations for her or him, loses belief in herself or himself to do well. Just as evidence gathered over the years has shown the positive effects of high expectations, so an ample amount of evidence has accumulated to show the reality of the self-fulfilling prophecy or Golem effect (Busch, 2017).

Benefits of High Teacher
Expectations for Students

Over time, more research has supported the powerful effects of teachers' expectations for students at all levels of the educational system. It affirms what so many educators experience and observe. Let's look at this in more detail. Here are some findings of what can happen **when a student learns in the presence of a teacher with high expectations**. This means—the teacher believes that the student is capable of the work in the grade and/or subject area, **and** the teacher communicates that belief clearly to the student.

- When teachers expect that certain students **will** show greater intellectual or academic growth, the students **do** show greater intellectual or academic growth (Bamburg, 1994; Papageorge & Gershenson, 2016; Rosenthal and Jacobson, 1968; Rubie-Davies, 2015a).
- High school sophomores whose teachers expected them to graduate from college were more likely to eventually do so, even after controlling for other factors (Center for American Progress, 2014).
- Teacher belief in a student's academic capabilities is linked to the student's own beliefs about how the student will do in school, to the student's attitudes toward school, and to the student's academic achievement (Rubie-Davies et al., 2015).
- Students respond to high expectations by internalizing them, which can boost their academic expectations. (Gonder, 1991; Papageorge & Gershenson, 2016; Raffini, 1993; Rubie-Davies, 2015a).
- A teacher's high expectations of an entire class are related to students' academic gains (Brophy & Good, 1974; Rubie-Davies, 2010).
- Teachers who overestimate the ability of students get better results than teachers who underestimate the ability (Brophy & Good, 1974).

- Peer expectations can also affect student performance. And teachers' high expectations set the tone for expectations students have of other students (Brophy & Good, 1974).
- High school students whose teachers have higher expectations about their future success are far more likely to graduate from college (Boser et al., 2014).
- Teachers prefer students who perform above average and treat them differently. The higher expectations for these students often contribute to accelerated performance (Glock, 2016).
- The effects of teacher expectations have to do with attributes, attitudes, beliefs, and stereotypes held by the teachers rather than with the actual academic characteristics or potential of the students (Rubie-Davies, 2009).
- Teacher expectations are more predictive of future educational attainment than such other factors as academic effort, motivations, race, high school courses taken, parents' educational level, and parents' expectations for their children (Center for American Progress, 2014).
- Effects of teacher expectations accumulate over time and the influence grows significantly stronger as students progress through school (Jamil et al., 2018).

High Expectations Translate to Teacher Behavior. It is not simply having high expectations that makes the difference. There's another part of the picture: To help students achieve to their best abilities, teachers need not only to expect that the student CAN achieve but must also

- Articulate expectations to students.
- **Provide the necessary support** that students need to accomplish goals.
- Encourage students to have high expectations of themselves.
- Let parents know they believe the child can meet high expectations.

- Set high expectations from the beginning of a year, class, topic, or task.

(Busch, 2017, Rubie-Davies, 2015a; Rubie-Davies, 2015b).

To summarize, high expectations make a difference when accompanied by teacher behaviors that help students reach them.

A good deal of research already exists to show that teachers often behave differently with students they've already decided can succeed. It's been found that teachers' high expectations translate into specific teacher behaviors—communications and communication style, body language, assignments, resources used, and time spent with the student

> *It's amazing how far you are willing to go when someone believes in you.*
>
> –Kate Kacvinsky,
> Author of the Young
> Adult Novel, *Awaken*

(Brophy & Good, 1970; Johnston et al., 2019; Rubie-Davies, 2007; Rubie-Davies, 2015b). In general, teacher expectations influence their own behavior and the subsequent performance of students. Researchers Brophy and Good (1970) developed a four-step model to explain how this works: 1) Teacher develops expectations. 2) Teacher treats student differently, according to expectations. 3) Student reacts to teachers' treatment. 4) Student outcomes are improved or limited (pp. 365-366).

When teachers work with students for whom they have high expectations (as opposed to students for whom they have lower expectations), such behaviors as the following are observed. For those "high-expectation" students, teachers

- Put more effort into preparing lessons.
- Supply a wider variety and higher level of resources.
- Provide a framework for learning.
- Communicate expectations more clearly, verbally and non-verbally.
- Show positive bias when evaluating the students' work.

- Offer the students more response opportunities.
- Supply the students with more challenging instruction.
- Give more feedback—and more of it positive and helpful.
- Dedicate more time to answering student questions.
- Use higher-order thinking questions and activities.
- Criticize students' work, questions, or responses less often.
- Interact regularly with those students in more supportive, caring ways.
- Appear more devoted to the students and to teaching the students.
  (Brophy & Good, 1970; Hughes, Gleason & Zhang, 2005; Peterson et al., 2016; Rubie-Davies, 2007; Rubie-Davies, 2015b; Tenenbaum & Ruck, 2007).

Consequences of Low Teacher Expectations for Students

Most educators say that high expectations are important. Yet many of them have low expectations for at least some of their students. Some teachers do have unjustifiably low expectations for the achievement of a student or group of students based on factors that have nothing to do with academic potential. These are such factors as (but are not limited to) race, gender, or socioeconomic status. It is just a fact that, in many cases, teachers behave quite differently toward different students in their classrooms.

Let me say here that, though study after study shows that teachers' low expectations have a strong bearing on student performance, most researchers also conclude that, generally, low expectations are not formed or acted upon out of malice. Most often, teachers (or educators across a wider school culture) are not aware that they have developed lower expectations for some students or how different expectations have developed.

Most educators would say that high expectations are important. Yet many of them have low expectations for at least some of their students.

We'll examine the sources of expectations and bias a bit later in the chapter. For now, I'll reiterate that low expectations for some students do exist—widely, and that research identifies negatively biased teacher expectations as "a significant obstacle to academic achievement, particularly for disenfranchised learners" (Lynch, 2019, para.6).

Here are some findings about what can happen **when a student learns in the presence of low expectations**. This is a situation in which the teacher believes that the student is less capable of (or not at all capable of) high-level performance in the grade and/or subject area **and** the teacher communicates that belief, even if unintentionally or subtly, to the student.

- Teachers underestimating students' abilities impacts students' academic performance. When the teacher does not believe that students can perform at high levels, the students don't (Bamburg, 1994; Papageorge & Gershenson, 2016; Rubie-Davies, 2015, The Master Teacher, 2015).
- When a student senses that a teacher has low expectations, the student has low expectations for herself or himself. Students' achievement, beliefs in themselves, and feelings about school are negatively affected (Cherng, 2017; Rubie-Davies et al., 2015).
- Teacher doubts confirm students' worst fears about their potential (The Master Teacher, 2015).
- Students respond to low expectations by internalizing them, which decreases their academic expectations and performance (Gonder, 1991; Papageorge & Gershenson, 2016; Raffini, 1993; Rubie-Davies, 2015).

- Teachers who underestimate the ability of students get lower results than teachers who overestimate students' abilities (Brophy & Good, 1974).
- A teacher's low expectations of a student set the tone for expectations other students will have of that individual (Brophy & Good, 1974).
- High school students whose teachers have lower expectations about their future success are less likely to graduate from college (Boser et al., 2014).
- Negatively biased teacher expectations have a detrimental influence—not only on a student's current and future academic performance but also on the student's future career (de Boer et al., 2010; Jamil et al., 2018).
- Communicating low expectations has more power to limit student achievement than communicating high expectations has to raise student performance (de Boer et al., 2010).
- Teacher expectations are more predictive of future educational attainment than such other factors as academic effort, motivations, race, high school courses taken, parents' educational level, and parents' expectations for their children Center for American Progress, 2014).

Low Expectations Translate to Teacher Behavior. Often low achievement levels for a student, group of students, class, or school are seen as a result of students having low learning ability. The lower performance is (mistakenly) attributed to student characteristics and not to the school's or teacher's strategies. This affects the energy, commitment, persistence, instructional strategies, and resources that some educators employ or are willing to try to reach the students (Brophy, 1983).

The reality is that most teachers **do** try to help each student reach learning potential whether or not the student has been successful in the past. But often, our experiences and other influences still tamper with our best intentions. Beyond our awareness, low expectations or bias may sway behavior in ways we don't realize. Conscious or unconscious, expectations affect teacher behavior. A good deal of research already exists to show that teachers often behave differently with students they've already decided (or at least suspect) are not likely to succeed (Rubie-Davies, 2007). When teachers work with these students (as opposed to students for whom they have high expectations), the tendency toward such behaviors as the following are observed. For those "low-expectation" students, teachers

- Provide fewer learning opportunities or resources—less of a framework for learning.
- Demand less from students and are less likely to supply challenging instruction.
- Are less likely to start a conversation with the student.
- Call on those students less frequently.
- Offer briefer and less informative feedback.
- Spend less time with them.
- Communicate expectations less clearly, verbally or nonverbally.
- Are less likely to show positive bias when evaluating the students' work.

> *Not every teacher is equally likely to transmit Pygmalion effects to students.*
>
> –Babad, Inbar, and Rosenthal, Researchers on Teacher Expectations

- Ask them fewer questions.
- Dedicate less time to answering student questions or following up to expand meaning.
- Use fewer higher-order thinking questions and activities.
- Smile less or make less eye contact.
- Point out failure; criticize students' work, questions, or responses more often.
- Give less praise for success.
- Appear less devoted to the students and to teaching the students.

(Brophy & Good, 1970; Brophy, 1983; Cheng, 2017; de Boer et al., 2018; Hughes et al., 2005; Peterson et al., 2016; Tenenbaum & Ruck, 2007).

Long-Term Effects of Low Expectations

Though some evidence is found that the influence of a particular teacher's expectations can dissipate over further years of school, other longitudinal studies show evidence that effects of teacher expectations accumulate, or that a single teacher's expectations can have influence for many years (DeBoer et al., 2010; Jamil et al., 2018; Rubie-Davies et al., 2016; Weinstein et al., 2004). Researchers de Boer, Bosker, and van der Werff (2010) followed 11,000 students for several years to examine how elementary-level teacher expectations might affect the students in their secondary education studies. They found that teacher expectations in grades 6 and 7 predicted student achievement six years later.

In addition, some research has found that teacher expectations based on a student's socioeconomic status (SES) accumulate over years of students' education and contribute to the disparity between the academic performance of SES groups, in some cases 5 or more years after the encounter with a particular teacher (de Boer et al., 2018; Hinnant et al., 2009; Mistry et al., 2009). Others have found that the effects of teacher expectations have the strongest influence and most long-lasting effects on members of minority groups (Jamil, 2013), females, and older students (middle and high school) (Jamil, 2013).

Bias and Implicit Bias

Regardless of good intentions, role in society, circle of friends, or commitments to our jobs as educators or in other professions, we all hold biases. Even people who try to remain objective have developed biases that affect how they perceive the world. Yes, there are **explicit** biases that people hold and know it. Even these are not always overtly shared. Most often, in our professional capacities, we're likely to be aware of these and soften or withhold their expression—sometimes due to the need for "political correctness." Just as often (or perhaps more often), our biases are **implicit**. As defined in Chapter 8, *implicit bias* refers to ideas, attitudes, assumptions, stereotypes, categories, and reactions that affect our understanding, and ultimately, our behavior and decision-making—without us consciously recognizing it.

Now, many well-intentioned educators (along with many in the general public) may find it hard to accept the idea that we're biased—particularly when it comes to doing the best for our students. Yet, science helps us understand how this is so—how we can be biased and act in biased ways—without knowing it. Magnetic resonance imaging (MRI) has heightened awareness and understanding about unconscious (or implicit) bias. MRIs have been used to identify, observe, and validate it as something disassociated from conscious (or explicit) bias. "Unconscious bias is now acknowledged by psychologists and neuroscientists as real and measurable" (Luskin, 2016).

> *Implicit bias can operate like an "equal opportunity virus" that infects people's unconscious abilities and competencies, as well as the group's abilities.*
>
> –Nilanjana Dasgupta, Researcher of Implicit Attitudes and Beliefs

Pragya Agarwal (2020), behavioral scientist and author of *Sway: Unraveling Unconscious Bias,* has researched unconscious bias for many years. He explains the neural processes and zones (the amygdala, prefrontal cortex, posterior cingulate, and anterior temporal cortex) that "light up like a Christmas tree" (para. 3) when stereotypes are activated. He says that, within seconds of meeting someone, seeing a behavior, or reasoning about a situation, we evaluate that person and assign labels and stereotypes. These decisions take place quickly before we have the time to move to more conscious processing. The unconscious processes are triggered by a lifetime of personal memories, messages given to us, experiences, and influences of groups with whom we hold close associations. Instinctively, we rapidly categorize others "as 'like me' and 'not like me,' or 'in-group' or 'out-group'" or with other labels. This, here, is the root of prejudice and discrimination. And it all happened outside our conscious awareness" (para. 6).

Other kinds of testing strengthen these scientific findings. Awareness of the concept of implicit bias mushroomed when a test of unconscious bias went online in 1998. The *Implicit Association Test* (IAT) measures attitudes and beliefs that people may be unwilling or unable to report. It can show implicit attitudes that a person does not realize. Since then, over six million people have taken the *Implicit Association Test*. The test measures unconscious prejudice by gauging the speed at which a person makes associations. The purpose of the test is to develop an awareness of implicit biases to enable people to manage or eliminate such biases (Luskin, 2016).

In an article for *Psychology Today* in which data from both the MRI studies and the *Implicit Association Tests* are discussed, Dr. Bernard Luskin (2016) states:

> The point is that even self-possessed bias-free egalitarians, who think they have no bias, show bias when MRI comparisons are made.
>
> Neuroscience has now proven that people were not falsely claiming to believe in equality. Instead, neuroimaging shows that decision-making automatically triggers specific regions of the brain responsible for unconscious processing, including those measured by the Implicit Association Test. MRI imaging showing which regions of the brain are activated during biased responses allows us to see the occurrence of biased associations, increasing our ability to counter or diminish them. Again, the point is that bias is in place, whether you are aware of it or not, and it can be measured (para. 13-15).

It's important to note that biases, conscious or unconscious, do not always lead to overt behaviors. As said earlier, teachers are often careful not to express biases of which they are aware. Yet teachers do express biases subtly, unconsciously. And students do pick up on and interpret these subtle verbal or nonverbal clues—even students of a young age (Asendorpf et al., 2002). The teacher's behavior might be a sigh, a diverting of attention, a tone of voice, a smile or frown or grimace or other nonverbal motion, or a contrast between any one of these in response to one student as compared to other students. All of these small cues accumulate to enable students to perceive optimism or joy (or lack of these), belief or disbelief, and a level of confidence in a student's ability.

What is the source of these biases? For each of us, our biases—for and against things—have developed over a lifetime. As with the wider population, in teachers, these are subtle cognitive processes rooted deep below awareness. Attitudes about individuals or groups of individuals stem from varying personal histories, backgrounds, beliefs, experiences, and teachings. Our own school experiences as students, views of teaching, self-concept, ethnicity, socioeconomic status, families, education level, neighborhoods,

> *Teacher support, in the form of beliefs about students' academic abilities, is CRUCIAL.*
>
> –Hua-Yu Sebastian Cherng, NYU Sociologist, Researcher

friends, and other associations play a part. And we can't ignore the influences of systemic or culture-wide stereotypes, the wider cultural atmosphere, current events, powerful figures in our lives, political climate and views, and continual media messages—including those from social media (Dusek & Joseph, 1983). Each of us is different in the depths, effects, and manifestations of our biases (Rubie-Davies, 2007; Weinstein et al., 2004). Perhaps even more so, our attitudes and beliefs seem to take shape in the local social systems in which we are embedded—close social circles, job settings, organizations we support, and families (Dasgupta, 2013).

The good news about science's exposing evidence that we all have biases is this: Acknowledging and understanding implicit bias allows us to explore its implications and workings in our schools—how it affects our expectations and actions. And beyond that, it gives us chances to understand bias, to learn more about ourselves, and to work at training ourselves and our staffs to combat bias and prejudice. Knowing that unconscious and unintentional bias is documented and can be measured, and internalizing that knowledge—is the first step. Once we take that step, we can work together to make a priority of reducing implicit bias. This is a must if we are to promote equity, value, appropriate expectations, and success for each student and group of students. (See Chapter 10 for some suggested practices to help educators reduce bias and adopt realistic, high expectations for all students.)

Bias, Expectations, and Student Achievement ———————

There are dozens of situations every day in which our biases about students are activated. This activation is generally related to student characteristics such as ethnicity, skin color, gender, gender identity, religion, socioeconomic status (SES), social desirability, appearance, manners, conduct, sexual identity, personality, confidence, aggressive (or submissive) tendencies, organizational skills, seat the student selects, student's track or ability group, annoying behaviors, language patterns, writing patterns, physical abilities, physical disabilities, participation style, politeness, level of independence, student history (related by other staff members or passed along in cumulative folders), the reputation of previous school student attended or student's perceived "matching up" to the reputation of this school, family structure, family members' characteristics, sibling performance or behavior, group with which student identifies, or cultural patterns or choices. Biases can even be triggered by things as slight as student clothing, hairstyle, neatness or lack thereof, or body odors.

In addition to assessments of or implicit (or explicit) attitudes toward individuals, our stereotypes may generalize to groups with any of the above characteristics. **And most, if not all of these biases, inform and affect expectations about how intellectually capable students are and how they will perform in school.**

Frequently, implicit biases that lead to lower expectations of students and lowered instructional quality are racially based. Much of the research on teacher expectations shows that 50 years after *Brown v. Board of Education*, complex negative self-fulfilling prophecies still create educational inequities and unequal outcomes—with stigmatized minorities being at an intensified risk

> *The "soft bigotry of expectations" is just regular bigotry.*

of the negative expectancy effects. These effects are long-term, following students throughout their post-schooling histories (Weinstein et al., 2004).

According to researchers Starck, Riddle, Sinclair, and Warikoo (2020), attempts to address racial inequality in schools have been only minimally successful. They examined teachers' general attitudes and feelings toward racial groups in comparison to biases of a wider group of Americans. They did this with two studies: One included a sample of about 69,000 teachers and over 1.5 million non-teachers, using Project Implicit (a large-scale effort to evaluate implicit bias through web-based tests). The second used a sample of teachers and non-teachers from a smaller nationally representative data set (about 4,500). Results of **all** respondents indicated that about 30% expressed **explicit** pro-White/anti-Black bias and 77% expressed **implicit** pro-White/anti-Black bias. It was found that, on average, teachers hold levels of pro-White/anti-Black bias similar to those of the general population.

While the list of student characteristics that may activate bias is a long one (see the first paragraph of this section, above), the largest body of research affirms the widespread inequity of expectations for some particular groups of students: students who are Black, students who are in any other non-White group, and students who come from low socioeconomic status.

What follows in the list below are some key research results and conclusions to consider regarding the racial and socioeconomic biases. But know this: behaviors that flow from prejudiced expectations related to **any** characteristic will also be detrimental to a student's self-worth, general well-being, and the chance of flourishing educationally (revisit the earlier pages of this chapter to review the benefits and consequences of high and low teacher expectations).

- Teacher expectations differ by racial groups in a way that puts Black students at a disadvantage, exacerbating racial achievement gaps. A Black teacher and a White teacher are likely to have similar expectations regarding the future academic success of a White student. But if the student in question is Black, the Black teacher has far higher expectations of that student than does the White teacher (Johnston, 2017; Papageorge & Kang; 2020).

- The Center for American Progress Education Longitudinal Study (2014) followed 6,000 high school sophomores for 10 years. Teachers were asked whether they expected their students to complete a four-year college degree. The results showed that teachers expected 58% of White students and 37% of Black students to complete college.

- Many other studies have found that most White teachers had far lower expectations for Black students than similarly situated White students. In studying the effects of student-teacher demographic matches on teacher expectations, researchers found evidence that teachers' expectations are systematically biased. Specifically, "non-Black teachers have significantly lower expectations for Black students than do Black teachers. The effects are greater for Black male students and math teachers" (Gershenson et al., 2015, p. 1). The results from the study are particularly concerning because many students are taught by teachers of a different race. About 82 percent of teachers in the U.S. are White, compared to about 49 percent of students; only 6 percent are Black, although 15 percent of students are (Papageorge & Gershenson, 2017).

> *When we display our belief in the potential of students, it fortifies their belief in themselves and enhances their chances for success.*
>
> –The Master Teacher, Professional Development Services

- The researchers in the above study say their findings shouldn't be taken as a condemnation of White teachers. Instead, they see the findings as reminders of the power of implicit bias to shape our expectations and, eventually, reality (Papageorge & Gershenson, 2017).

- Teachers hold the highest expectations for Asian American students, and the expectations they hold for European American students are more positive than for Latino/a or African American students (Tenenbaum & Ruck, 2007).

- On average, teachers tend to have negatively biased expectations for the future academic performance of minority group students and students from less affluent families (Glock & Krolak-Schwerdt, 2013; Rubie-Davies et al., 2006; Speybroeck et al., 2012; Tenenbaum & Ruck, 2007).

- Low achievers and students from low-income families and minority groups are most susceptible to the detrimental effects of negatively biased teacher expectations (Hinnant et al., 2009; Johnston, 2017; Jussim et al., 1996; McKown & Weinstein, 2008; Sorhagen, 2013).

- "On average, Black students have lower test scores than White students, they attend schools with fewer resources, and they are less likely to graduate from high school and college. "The 'soft bigotry of low expectations' is just regular bigotry" (Nelson, L., 2015).

- Black students get punished more harshly than White students. Black students are suspended and expelled far more frequently than their White classmates, for the same or similar offenses. Many Black kids are missing weeks of school each year because of unfair discipline policies that lead to days of lost instruction due to suspension (Losen et al., 2017).

- In general, teachers are optimistic. But teachers are less optimistic about Black students' academic futures (Papageorge and Gershenson, 2016).

- Hua-Yu Sebastian Cherng's research (2017) analyzed data from the Education Longitudinal Study mentioned above. This followed 10,000 high school sophomores for 10 years to examine the effects of teacher expectations. After controlling for such factors as standardized test scores and homework completion, Cherng's evaluation found that both math and

English teachers were more likely to conclude their class as too difficult for students of color as compared to White students. Further, the research team concluded that teachers' underestimations of students' abilities created a negative impact on students' academic expectations of themselves—meaning that they would complete less school. This impact was particularly harmful among Latino/a and Black students.

- According to a 2014 Center for American Progress report, "The Power of the Pygmalion Effect," high school teachers believe that high-poverty, Black, and Hispanic students are 53, 47, and 42 percent less likely to graduate from college compared to their White peers (para. 5).

- Many educators are working from a "deficit model" (preconceptions about non-White students—their abilities and their work ethic). However, many educators' low expectations are nuanced to exclude (from high expectations) students who may not have the advantages of the middle class. These intangible middle-class advantages include such things as a computer with Internet access at home, a quiet place to study and complete homework, working parent(s) above the poverty line, no pressure to get a low-level job in high school to help pay the rent or support the family, and no fear of the streets upon which they live. (Lombardi, 2016).

- Teachers direct more positive and neutral speech (questions and encouragement) toward European American students than toward Latino/a and Black students and give more positive referrals and fewer negative referrals to the European American group (Tenenbaum & Ruck, 2007).

- Black students seem to perform better when they have Black teachers (Papageorge & Gershenson, 2016).

- Efforts to combat biases can prove helpful in reducing racial educational attainment gaps (Papageorge & Gershenson, 2016).

- "When teachers have confidence in the academic abilities of students of color, they (the students) reap even greater benefits than do their White peers" (Cherng, 2017).

Expectations Interventions

Clearly, there is a strong connection between expectations and a student's school experience. Just as clearly, biases exist—and they can lead to erroneous expectations and estimations of abilities. And the racial factor in expectations is repeatedly documented. However, the research on expectations does not stop with highlighting the discrepancies, inequities, and consequences. It goes on to look at solutions. And repeatedly, the findings show that we can learn to recognize our biases, diminish or banish them, change our expectations, and more fairly apply them to our students.

Researchers de Boer, Timmermans, and van der Werf (2018) reviewed the effects of 19 teacher expectation interventions to answer the question of whether it is possible to raise teacher expectations to prevent low expectations from having detrimental effects on student achievement. The interventions used involved creating awareness of the effects of one's expectations, addressing the beliefs underlying the expectations, and changing teacher behavior. Results showed that, when teachers were committed to the interventions, all three practices were effective in raising teacher expectations and subsequent student achievement.

In one experiment, Rubie-Davies, Peterson, Sibley, and Rosenthal (2016) examined the effectiveness of teacher expectation intervention across a variety of schools, grade levels, genders, socioeconomic levels, and ethnicity in terms of student achievement in math. The results showed that when teachers were trained in the practices of high-expectation teachers, student achievement markedly improved compared with that of students of untrained teachers (teachers in a control group). The specific practices involved training teachers to

- Organize and teach students within flexible grouping arrangements (as opposed to ability groupings).
- Build a positive classroom community climate where students work collaboratively and form supportive relationships.
- Use positive behavior management techniques.
- Develop and use classroom activities designed to show teacher care for students' emotional and academic development.
- Set specific goals with students and help students achieve them.

This study, called the Teacher Expectation Project (above), went on for three years, with effective results across all groups of students. The study suggests that when teachers are taught high-expectation practices, all teachers can raise student achievement.

When taught high-expectation practices—all teachers can raise student achievement.

The same researchers concluded that when teachers examined the ways they interact differently with students for whom they have low or high expectations and, with this training, adjusted their methods and body language to consistently express positive expectations to **all** students, student scores on academic achievement tests increased on average of three extra months of schooling (Rubie-Davies & Rosenthal, 2016).

In an article examining the racial bias of teachers, authors Starck, Riddle, Sinclair, and Warikoo (2020) concluded that the most promising approach for schools seeking to address bias is to better manage the bias we know exists in the teaching force. This means identifying how and when people's biases "leak out" and affect their judgments and behaviors (for example, when individuals are in ambiguous situations, cognitively taxing, distracting, or lacking in accountability). In addition, schools can realize their potential in educating all students of all backgrounds when staff members receive training in self-awareness, self-regulation, ways to avoid bias, and equity strategies to mitigate the impact of bias.

Longtime researchers of teacher expectations Gershenson and Papageorge (2015) contend, "Policies that would put Black students on the same footing as White students in terms of how teacher expectations are formed could narrow attainment gaps" (p. 22).

Analyzing the power of the Pygmalion Effect, Boser, Wilhelm, and Hanna (2014) make a strong plea for policymakers to implement strong, common college- and career-ready standards and see that teachers and teacher-preparation programs have training in examining stereotypes and having high expectations for all students. In addition, they recommend that teacher-training programs give students hands-on training in high-performing, high-poverty schools. And since non-White teachers are underrepresented in U.S. public schools, research provides additional support for the hiring of a more diverse and representative teaching force (Gershenson et al., 2016).

> *When students feel our doubts, we cripple their chances.*
>
> –The Master Teacher, Professional Development Services

Though some trends in the U.S. have suggested that racial prejudice has waned in the past 50 years, there is widespread evidence that great inequities, discrimination, and negative outcomes are widespread for Black people. It's possible, researchers point out, for people to act in prejudicial ways while rejecting prejudiced ideas. Patricia Devine and her colleagues (2012) developed a prejudice-habit-breaking intervention in hopes of facilitating long-term reductions in implicit race bias. The intervention combined awareness of implicit bias, concern about its effects, and specific strategies to reduce bias. In a longitudinal study, they found dramatic reductions in implicit race bias among people who completed the intervention.

In their paper, "Teacher Expectations Matter," Papageorge, Gershenson, and Kang (2020) delve into the distributions of biases in teacher expectations and the impact of those on student outcomes via self-fulfilling prophecies. They recommend these two actions to address the inequities of expectations:

- Hiring more teachers that look like the students (more non-White teachers).
- "De-biasing" of White teachers so that they are similarly optimistic about Black and White students.

Diane Bloom and her colleagues carried out a study in which student teachers spent a semester working in diverse classrooms. Results showed that experience in diverse settings influenced (and positively changed) the White student teachers' preconceptions about students of color and raised their own awareness of their heritage and privilege. The researchers recommend that teacher-training programs give prospective teachers a semester of immersive practice in a diverse classroom (Bloom et al., 2013).

Researcher Chloe Fitzgerald and her colleagues (2019) reviewed several interventions aimed at reducing implicit biases. They found some effective elements of several of the interventions, but caution that many interventions are ineffective and that the topic needs more study. A key finding was that successful interventions had this in common: the people involved strongly identified with the others in the scenarios used—including studies that examined the level of identification of self with the outgroup. In addition, a major factor in the success of an intervention to mitigate the effects of implicit bias is the person's willingness to work at it.

Nilanjana Dasgupta (2013), professor of Psychological and Brain Sciences, has researched implicit stereotypes or biases. Her work takes a particular interest in the plasticity of implicit bias—ways in which changes within social contexts (e.g., academic and professional settings) can change individuals' attitudes, beliefs, and behaviors. She notes that unconscious biases are not permanent. In fact, they are malleable; we can take steps to limit their impact on our thoughts and behaviors.

Dasgupta and her colleagues (2013) believe that implicit attitudes and beliefs mirror the environments and communities within which individuals are immersed—and that these are highly influenced by local media environments. They find that changes in environments lead to changes in people's implicit

Unconscious biases are not permanent. They are malleable. We can take steps to limit their impact on our thoughts and behaviors.

attitudes and beliefs. That is, when people are immersed in local environments (this would include schools, places of employment, families, social circles) where they see others with roles, behaviors, and abilities that defy the stereotypes, their own implicit beliefs are changed. And what's remarkable is that, often, these beliefs adapt without deliberation and intentional action. The "climate" of that local setting is that powerful! This is quite promising for schools! By changing the culture and attitudes in which we and our students are embedded, we can make strides toward bias reduction across the school community.

Reality and Hope—A Productive Partnership

Neuroscience and other research show us that **bias is real** and that **differing expectations for different students are clearly and broadly**

present in our schools. It also exposes the complexity of the topic of expectations and the attitudes and beliefs, many unconscious, that drive them. The research also provides hope and suggests solutions. We see that when we as educators

- **Are aware** that the bias and variance in expectations exist.
- **Are convinced** that students CAN attain higher achievement levels.
- **Are willing** to examine our behaviors and the beliefs of the wider school culture.
- **Embrace** interventions to understand and challenge differentiated expectations and implicit bias.
- **Collaborate** to design and operate an unbiased approach, we can create more equitable, brilliant schools where each student has a better chance of raising academic performance.

So here we are, realistically, in the presence of differing, often erroneous expectations, and powerful biases. But we don't run from the truth. Instead, we throw our hearts and energies into encouraging cross-cultural and human understandings and the empathy that can reduce bias-driven expectations. **We can do this.** We can examine our biases about each other, our students, their families, our leaders, the school's reputation, and the community. In our brilliant school, we can build a whole, unified culture that stands against bias and for high expectations that the whole school community will work tirelessly to help kids meet. This work takes honesty, humility, and work; but again, it is why we are here.

The next chapter contains steps, strategies, attitudes, and actions that contribute to crafting and communicating high, unbiased expectations and helping students meet them. As you read these suggestions, you will find that they are focused on expectations for students. But know that every good idea applies to all the expectations in a school community. The attitudes, beliefs, and practices that work to reduce biases about student abilities or raise expectations for all students—**all**

these apply to teachers, support staff members, administrators, and parents. We should all value and treat each other as we are striving to value and treat our students. Every strategy suggested by research (above) and suggested in Chapter 10 applies to and works with adults.

Chapter 10

How Do G.R.E.A.T. Leaders Get Results with Expectations?

You have to ignore it when a child says, 'I don't want to,' because what they're really saying is, 'I don't think I can and I need you to believe in me until I can believe in myself.'

—Shanna Peoples, 2015 National Teacher of the Year

The discussion of relationships in the Second Pillar began with an exploration of self-awareness as a foundation for gratitude, relationships, and all the other pillars of a brilliant school. This familiar factor—my insights into myself—ultimately affects how I see my neighbor, the guy passing me on the sidewalk, the clerk at the gas station, and certainly—any student, colleague, or parent in the school community.

In earlier parts of this book, I told some stories about how my assumptions about specific students impacted my expectations for them or my relationships with them. Brilliant schools are places that invite conversations about our subjectively-shaped expectations of individual students to raise our awareness of those expectations and how they influence us as their teachers. The schools create space for such reflective, hard conversations and use the plethora of research findings to educate, inform, and examine behavior. We need these conversations and exposure to the research to ensure that those filters do not impede student outcomes and achievement. It is the work of the entire school community to sift through the data to uncover the sources of biases and discuss how they affect the setting and maintaining high expectations for all. Beyond awareness and discussion, it is our absolute obligation to take action to de-bias our decisions and believe that all students are worthy of high expectations. When we give dedicated energy, belief, resources, practices, and

> *When we give dedicated energy, belief, good resources and practices, and persistence to reach students, they all CAN perform at higher levels.*

persistence to reach students, they all CAN perform at higher levels.

The research cited in Chapter 9, born out by the writings and experiences of many educators, gives us clues about how to move ahead with expectations. Based on those clues, along with my experiences, here are some suggestions for administrators and other leaders. These attitudes and practices get proven results! There are ways—big and small—to promote unbiased, accurate, high expectations for all students. I hope you'll understand that these approaches and strategies can be adapted to fit your purposes. I invite you to think about ways to implement these experiences with your teams, parents, students, and staff. Brilliant schools use such strategies to jumpstart the year and develop them into powerful habits throughout the year.

Keep These Discoveries in Mind

- Teacher expectations make a difference. This includes high expectations, low expectations, and everything in between.
- High expectations, when accompanied with action, raise achievement, self-concept, and overall positive school experience.

- Low expectations have tough consequences. Nobody deserves them.
- Most likely, many teachers are likely to have low expectations of some students—even if unconsciously.
- Most students are capable of more than we may think.
- We all have biases.
- Biases can be examined, questioned, and changed.
- Specific intervention practices can help teachers (and leaders) learn to raise expectations and to help students meet them.
- It's not enough to believe in high expectations. They must get communicated and demonstrated to the students. Then teachers must help students reach them.

Start With These Steps

Share knowledge with colleagues. You've just read a sampling of research findings of expectations in schools, as well as the effects of varying expectations on teacher behavior and students' self-belief and performance. Within these findings, you've caught a glimpse of some of the sources of expectations and the biases that underlie them. Start sharing this information with the school staff. This will not be a one-time event; the exploration of expectations will (should) be ongoing. But begin by getting information into the hands and minds of the entire staff. If it is already a topic of study in your school, share any new insights that you've read or that you can gain from other sources.

Acknowledge the existence of differing expectations. Starting with the leader and expanding to all the staff—acknowledge that you have preconceived conclusions about students and how they will learn or behave. We are all conditioned to expect certain behaviors and results; these conditionings vary from individual to individual. But all the adults in the school community must begin by noticing, naming, and owning the attitudes and beliefs they have about different students and their abilities to achieve.

Define and describe expectations. What do you mean by expectations? See that the whole staff is on the same page as you work on identifying and raising them. Keep in mind that the idea of expectations in the school setting is not to control people or tell them who they must be. The idea also is not to assume automatically that every student is the same or to try to make everyone learn and achieve in the same ways. The idea is to believe that all students can achieve at higher levels. The idea is to peel away the erroneous pre-assumptions about what people are or can do. Realize that the expectations for a student are not about pleasing the teacher; they are about giving students the help and tools so they can grow and learn to the best of their true abilities (not preconceived abilities). Remember that students are not locked in by a ceiling. Brains can grow. People can get smarter than they (or the teacher) might think.

Discuss the ways expectations are communicated. Teachers and others in the school may not be aware that they're giving different messages to different students about what they believe the student can accomplish. Delve into this topic: how do students find out how we think they will learn or behave? Identify words, phrases, facial expressions, body language, and actions that tell students what you expect and that signal differing or low expectations.

Examine expectations that are already in place. Begin the process of an up-close examination of expectations. Each teacher or other staff member must look closely at his or her own; each must do the work to notice the patterns in the way they view students. But social systems, such as a school, hold some group expectations. These are attitudes and beliefs that—conscious or unconscious, stated or unstated—permeate the school culture. Look at these together as a staff.

Review the benefits and consequences of teacher expectations. Re-scan Chapter 9. Pay attention to the bulleted lists; these summarize what research has to show us about what happens when students are on the receiving end of high expectations or low expectations (or subjected to underestimations of their true abilities). Also, review the lists of the teacher behaviors that flow (often unconsciously) from high and low expectations.

Begin the work of tuning into bias. Delve into the roots of expectations. Starting immediately, pay attention to bias. If you're a leader, start with yourself. Educate yourself about implicit bias. Investigate your own. Start teaching your colleagues about it. Get the conversation going about how to recognize and face it and how to spot the limits it places on some students' achievements. Explain that, often, implicit biases are opposed to stated beliefs—and that they are driven by deeply-buried unconscious assumptions.

> *Often, implicit biases are opposed to stated beliefs and are driven by deeply-buried unconscious assumptions.*

Start paying attention to mindsets and beliefs about the intellectual capacity of individual students or groups of students. Start noticing how students are affected by tracking policies. Start listening to the ways you and colleagues talk and think that may diminish certain students or their groups or families. Start paying attention to the patterns of discipline, that is, who gets consequences and for what. (See the next section of this chapter, "Include These Attitudes and Actions Throughout the School Year," for more help with this.)

Commit to working together to institutionalize fairness. Pledge to identify blind spots, undercut stereotypes, and make high standards for everyone the norm. Make a plan to learn more about how to combat bias and low expectations. As early as possible, starting planning for the school year, work on plans for comprehensive professional development related to expectations, bias, and equity. Plan for diversity training.

Use what you've already learned in previous chapters (the First and Second Pillars, Chapters 1-7). You've focused on gratitude and relationships. Continue gratitude practices. When you get in the habit of noticing people for who they are and for what they contribute to you or the wider group—and when you clearly state your gratitude, you'll be more likely to have accurate, fair expectations of them. Continue the work on caring, trusting relationships. It will be harder to hold biases or low expectations for a student that you know well and trust. And, when a student feels your belief and trust in that relationship, she or he is more likely to expect more of herself or himself. Continue to work on self-awareness; I've emphasized that from the beginning of this book. The entire staff will need all the self-awareness that can be mustered to honestly face biases and examine their expectations.

Be the model. As the leader—be sure that your day-to-day, moment-to-moment actions demonstrate what you've read, learned, and believe about expectations. Show that you believe all students, colleagues, and parents have the potential to meet high expectations. Set and strive toward high expectations for yourself.

Include These Attitudes and Actions Throughout the Year

BELIEVE that all your students can learn. Get into this mindset. Say it out loud to students. When we demonstrate belief in our students' potential, it bolsters their belief in themselves. Spread optimism to every student. Then follow up. Approach every day as a chance to show that you believe in them. Work to convince each student to have high expectations of herself or himself. Make it a mantra that every student in the school can reach high expectations. Show them that you will help them do it.

> *If my teacher doesn't believe in me, how can I believe in myself?*
>
> –The Master Teacher, Professional Development Services

Set high expectations from the beginning. Start with an attitude of high expectations. This begins with the school leader. Then all staff members should do this—not just from the beginning of the year—but at the beginning of each class, topic of study, project, or task. Don't let students ever begin to get any sense that they'll not do well because they've heard the class (or project, assignment, etc.) is hard. Make it clear that you expect all students to participate and contribute seriously to the learning.

Learn the language of expectations. It's hard for students to work toward something ambivalent. When expectations are not spoken, students can hardly get on board with them. So they won't be met! Unfortunately, many of the expectations for students are not clear to the students. Too many times, what the teacher expects is ambiguous. So **be explicit**. When expectations are explicit, students are less likely to be influenced by implicit biases. Take time to put expectations into words. Write them down. This holds for general expectations as well as expectations for specific tasks.

Assure students that they can meet the expectations. Then, let them know that you will work hard to help them achieve these goals. Knowing that will further help students believe they can succeed. This should help to drive an increase in standards and self-confidence.

Share expectations with parents. Get parents in on the process of high expectations for all students. Give them the same assurances that you gave students—you believe in their child's ability to reach high expectations, and you commit to helping their child succeed. Enlist parents' support in helping the child do the academic work and believe in herself or himself.

Differentiate the support, not the expectations. Too often, teachers hold differentiated expectations for different students or groups. As I've said before, students "pick up" on these differences. Nix the varying expectations. Instead, give students differentiated support to reach the high goals. For each individual's needs, design scaffolding that moves a student progressively through steps toward greater independence and higher achievement.

Differentiate the support, not the expectations.

Understand that it is not enough to speak your high expectations. Repeat this to yourself often! Yes, state the expectation and assure students that you'll be giving the support they need to reach it. But then, you must SHOW them they can succeed by providing what they need to reach high expectations. (See below.) Along the way, constantly inspire students' self-confidence, self-belief, and internalization of the expectations.

Help students reach the expectations. Good instruction is a critical partner with high expectations. If teachers and schools are to set and hold students to high expectations, the strategies for attainment must be in full force. Here are some of the practices used by what we refer to as "high-expectation teachers" –teachers who hold high expectations and apply them equitably to all students:

- Begin with dynamite instruction! This means activities, lessons, and learning of all forms that are engaging and relevant for students.
- Create realistic, reachable, intermediate acceleration goals— steppingstones ("chunks" of content or process) that give the student hope of reaching a goal and help her or him experience success.
- Provide tasks that are challenging for each student—just slightly higher than the actual skills. You want them to stretch, but to a place that's possible to reach (with work).
- Provide high-quality, plentiful resources for students getting to goals.
- Give constructive, frequent, quality feedback to each student.
- Help students lessen their fear of failure; teach them to weather and learn from failure experiences.
- Continually nurture a strong student-teacher relationship with each student.

- Develop lessons and activities designed to illuminate the importance of social and emotional learning, as well as academic growth.
- Group students in flexible groups, rather than designating them to groups "by ability."
- To promote autonomy and mastery learning, teach students goal-setting strategies.
- Create a caring classroom community—a warm, positive climate.

Treat all students the same. In addition to expecting the same of all students, relate to all students the same. That is, use the same behaviors with all students that you would use (or have used) with students for whom you have had the highest expectations: the same language, tone, level and kind of encouragement, smiles, amount of contact, amount of criticism (and way you criticize), discipline, consequences, kinds of questions, initiating contact with them, inviting/encouraging students to speak, soliciting and respecting their ideas, etc. Encourage your colleagues to experiment with this: Set a time (a week, perhaps). Commit to treating all students the same. Notice how students respond. Keep notes. Look for signs or patterns of the difference this makes.

Broaden efforts to challenge implicit (or explicit) bias. Awareness of biases and processes to examine and change them take time and practice. Taking clues from research, these are some recommended practices to move teachers and others away from the behaviors triggered by unconscious biases:

- Explore personal biases and assumptions. Take stock of beliefs you have about individual students, groups of students, colleagues, racial groups, genders, etc. Try to be honest and specific about what those beliefs are.
- Examine the biases (attitudes and beliefs) of the school environment in which you are immersed. Share and discuss the

personal and school-wide biases you notice. Also, as a staff, examine biases in your wider (beyond the school) community that affect the school climate or culture. Remember that the local cultural groups in which a person is embedded can affect beliefs and attitudes.

- Put concentrated effort into noticing behaviors that flow from your biases.
- Notice how behaviors around expectations transmit messages to students.
- Notice how your biases impact students.
- Practice unbiased behavior with colleagues.
- Invite colleagues to observe you and give feedback about any biased behavior they spot.

> *NEVER allow blame, shame, or judgment to creep into your efforts against bias.*

- Ask students for feedback on your behavior related to expectations and biases.
- Continually check your biases. Pay attention to your verbal expressions and tone, body language, expectations, and behaviors.
- Check what you say about students to other staff members.
- Check what you say and think about colleagues.
- Check what you say and think about students' family members.
- Look at each student as an individual. Envision what students are capable of when they're provided with positive expectations and support.
- Learn to express positive expectations of all students. Consciously practice this. Watch what happens when you do.

Never allow blame, shame, or judgment to creep into your efforts against bias. When teachers, leaders, and other staff members work to explore and discuss biases and expectations, it might get tempting for some to "rate" themselves in comparison to others. It is important to do the work of challenging bias in an environment of trust and care. We all have biases; they all flow from our past and present experiences and influences. **Acknowledging that we all have biases can help to reduce the shame levels in the group.** Don't let any conversations become loaded with assumptions about the attitudes of others, with comparisons, or with judgment. Seek to create safe situations where the school staff can help one another seek to act in ways that do **not** come out of our unexamined patterns.

Institute systemwide (school or district) procedures and programs to support equitable expectations and their attainment.

- Make the goals of reducing bias and schoolwide positive, high expectations for all students a systemwide priority.
- Plan professional development programs that address such topics as bias of many kinds (that is, for many students or "other" persons' characteristics), roots of bias and expectations, awareness of individual's own biases and group bias, disparate expectations, racial inequities, ways to combat implicit bias, high-quality teacher feedback, and building a culture of high expectations. Learn to spot non-verbal behaviors that belie expectations. Train staff in the practices of "high-expectations" teachers (See attributes early in Chapter 9. And later in Chapter 9, note some intervention high-expectation strategies.) Practice unbiased expectations and language on each other. When a comfort level is reached, film teachers teaching. They can analyze their practices or even join with a trusted colleague to give feedback to each other.
- Give teachers more time to plan and grade assignments that meet high standards.
- Set up a system to design and use rubrics that show students the criteria for meeting expectations on an assignment and reduce the extent to which teachers' biases might affect the grades on assignments.

- Improve teacher evaluation procedures to include growth in areas of "de-biasing" and expectations.
- Encourage cross-cultural understandings and reduction of bias-driven disparities in student achievement.
- Develop objective indicators for hiring, evaluation, and promotion to reduce stereotypes.
- Work to create more diversity in your teaching group, particularly racial diversity.
- Where possible, arrange for teachers to gain experience in diverse classrooms.
- Use whatever contacts and influences you have with local teacher-training programs to encourage training in these issues at the pre-service levels.

Resisting implicit bias is lifelong work. You have to constantly restart the process and look for new ways to improve.

–The AFM (An American Academy of Family Physicians Journal)

Look at other expectations in your school. The chapters to this point in the Third Pillar, Expectations (Chapters 8 through 10), focus mostly on the critical topic: teacher expectations of students' academic potential, behaviors, and accomplishments. The discussion so far has presented a good deal of research, benefits (or consequences), and effects of teacher's (or a school's) expectations on student success. But any school community is brimming with expectations beyond those that teachers hold for students:

- Students have expectations of their teachers and all other school staff.
- Students have expectations of each other.
- Adults in the school (staff members) have expectations of each other.

- Leaders have expectations of all other staff members.
- All staff members have expectations of their leaders.
- Parents have expectations of teachers, administrators, other staff members, and the school as a whole entity.
- School staff members have expectations of parents and families.
- Parents have expectations of their children, the students.
- Community members have expectations of school leaders, school staff, and students.
- School staff members have expectations of community support and involvement.

Whew! We educators function in a sea of expectations! And that "sea" will buoy us all best if we have clear, similar understandings of expectations and hold similar high expectations for our students and each other—and if we work passionately to uplift each other and help one another succeed. (The truth is, expectations are required for us to function in society. For example, it is expected that you put on pants when you leave your house. If you didn't, things might get a little weird. People might be uncomfortable!)

So, as I've noted before—understand that all the strategies and advice about accurate, equal, and high expectations for students, applies to all these other expectations as well.

Conclusion

The Third Pillar

Prejudice is a habit that can be broken.
—Dr. Patricia Devine, Social Psychologist, Researcher

In a fascinating *Atlantic* article, writer Jessica Nordell (2017) describes the work of Patricia Devine, a social psychologist from the University of Wisconsin. Dr. Devine's 1989 study on stereotypes and prejudice spurred decades of research on implicit bias and ways to combat it. In her interview with Nordell, Dr. Devine notes that this phenomenon (implicit bias) "has become so broad that it almost has no meaning." She now prefers to call this "unintentional bias" (Nordell, 2017, para. 28).

Recently, Dr. Devine has gone on to develop and refine a prejudice intervention that has been successful in combating unintentional bias. The basic intervention is based on this idea: if underlying beliefs and prejudices are the cause of biased behavior, then untethering those negative associations could help to eliminate bias. "Prejudice," Dr. Devine believes, "is a habit that can be broken" (Nordell, 2017, para. 33). People can believe and notice that they might be discriminating; they can identify and own their biases (not ignore or hide them); they can realize that discrimination is a problem; and they can grow confident that they can overcome their prejudicial habits. With this foundation of acceptance and belief, they can begin to break the habit.

After participating in Devine's training workshop, Nordell notes her own experience with recognizing how bias starts—and tells how she began to notice her spontaneous reactions to "an almost overwhelming degree." She recounts a brief story in which she saw two people at a upscale hotel where she was staying while at the workshop. Observing their clothing (worn and rumpled, with ragged holes in the knees), in seconds she formed a story about them in her mind. Her story was that they must be friends of the clerk but certainly not guests at this hotel. She explains:

> It was a tiny story, a minor assumption, but that's how bias starts: as a flicker—unseen, unchecked—that taps at behaviors, reactions, and thoughts. And this tiny story flitted through my mind for seconds before I caught it. *My God,* I thought, *is this how I've been living?*
>
> Afterward, I kept watching for that flutter, like a person with a net in hand waiting for a dragonfly. And I caught it, many times. Maybe this is the beginning of how my prejudice ends. Watching for it. Catching it and holding it up to the light. Releasing it. Watching for it again. (2017, para. 50-51).

This reminds me of the incident I described at the beginning of this pillar, before Chapter 8. I had that flutter—that quick judgment about Deshaun, the young Black man standing in our school office—a judgment I made after looking at him for a matter of a few seconds.

I repeatedly challenge myself, my staff, and all my readers to watch for "that flutter." Stop and think about this: In your school, how many times have you (or someone else you know) spoken or thought something judgmental, negative, or demeaning about a parent, colleague, administrator, visitor, or student—something that was triggered in some way by what you assumed, based on that person's looks, background, speech, marital status, family, education (how much and from where), level of experience, youth, older age, clothing, hobbies, rumors about relationships or previous jobs, physical condition, ethnicity, gender, friends or groups with whom the person associates, religious or spiritual beliefs, etc., etc.? Be honest. This happens all the time! Generally, we educators **do** believe in fairness, equality, and decency. We **do** want to help all the students succeed. It's our passion! It's why we're here. Nevertheless, those implicit biases **do** have some hold on each person.

You may have noticed that I've emphasized good instruction, engaging lessons, high standards, and personalized support as a part of helping students believe they can reach high expectations and a part of seeing that they reach them. This leads to the Fourth Pillar of a brilliant school: Achievement. As you read the following chapters on the Achievement Pillar, I think you'll notice the threads of gratitude, high-quality relationships, and high expectations woven through and fundamental to reaching your strong achievement goals for each student.

The Fourth Pillar of a
Brilliant School

Achievement

*Success doesn't come to you;
you've got to go to it.*

—Marva Collins, Influential
American Educator

At the beginning of the book, you learned that my roots are in Mississippi, a place I hold dear in my heart. Mississippi, like my mama and daddy, had a hand in raising me and has witnessed both my achievements and my failures. Although my personal and professional career has allowed me to crisscross much of the United States, I am now beginning to understand why I continue to return to her: so many pivotal moments and memories from my childhood to Hurricane Katrina happened here.

My daddy, too, was raised in Mississippi. His story began in the 1940s in Winston County, Mississippi. On fall, spring, and summer days, he walked barefooted on dirt, then gravel, roads to school. As I type this, I can hear him retelling stories about how he'd rush to get to school because he loved it so much. I must imagine he felt supported, cared for, and highly capable of achieving his goal—a hope that all of us who try to build brilliant schools have for our students. As time passed, he became more involved in school and the school's football team. Yet, as the ninth of eleven children, being a student was not his sole responsibility. Once his older brothers set out for life beyond Winston County, the duty to family and the work of sharecropping weighed heavily on him.

Like so many struggling families across the country, sometimes childhood is short-lived or interrupted due to the necessity of work. For much of his childhood, my daddy was tethered to work, but was able to divide his responsibilities to an extent that his father reluctantly allowed him to continue his studies. However, the pressure mounted. When he was in tenth grade, his father presented an ultimatum to forego school and help with farming. This led to a storm of verbal sparring, which later developed into physical altercations (so I'm told).

With those events in his mind, daddy went to school on a particular September day and found his teachers eating lunch in the classroom. He approached them with his news about quitting school. All these years later, I am deeply grateful for their response. The teachers laid down their forks, stopped eating, and said—almost in unison, "You most certainly will not quit school. You are too smart and you have too much going for you. We will speak to your daddy. You will be in school tomorrow, or we will come and get you. We will talk to him this afternoon."

The high school sophomore, who became my dad, turned and left the room to resume his day at school.

To this day, neither Daddy nor I know what those teachers said, but the father no longer pressured his son, and my dad was able to stay in school. Coincidentally, he became the only one out of those eleven children to graduate from high school. The teachers who pushed and prodded him to commit to his studies were not only his teachers; they were his advocates as well.

*As you read this, I am sure you can think of someone in your personal or professional life chapter who has been an unwavering cheerleader for you. On the other hand, **you** might be the one person who repeatedly demonstrates your support and belief in that student who, unbeknown to you, shoulders more than school-day responsibilities.*

It is often said that a teacher's impact is not known until long after a student leaves his or her classroom. My father's story and my family's story are evidence of that. I doubt that my dad's teachers in Winston County, Mississippi, calculated the risks associated with standing up for him in the manner that they did. Neither do I think that they understood the profound effect their collective belief in his capacity, as well as their actions and advocacy, would have on the trajectory of his life— and the trajectory of his children's lives and their children's lives that followed.

Chapter 11

What Is Achievement?

Success is the sum of small efforts,
repeated day in and day out.
—Robert Collier, American Author

Brilliant schools operate on the understanding that students attain both academic achievement and social and emotional well-being by addressing the needs of the whole student. Whether or not my father's teachers identified themselves as part of a "brilliant" school, his story shows the value of the relationships that the teachers formed with students and parents, as well as the power of the expectations they had for and communicated to the student and his parents.

While this chapter primarily refers to achievement in the sense of academic success, note how the earlier Pillars of Gratitude, Relationships, and Expectations have supported positive outcomes of all kinds—academic, social, and emotional—for students. Still, while schools across this country set intentions and high expectations before the first bell, many fail to adequately support students in academic growth and achievement. In rural, urban, public, and private schools, classrooms still hold students described as the "bubble kids" or "the bottom 25% academically." We lean on these terms to make sense of data, to strive toward growth, and to allow us to have hard conversations around how we move forward in service to our students. We examine what standards are taught, how effective or ineffective our instruction is, and what shifts we need to make to support understanding of the content that will lead to affect academic achievement for all students.

Achievement: A Working Definition ———————————

A basic definition of *achievement* is generally something like this: *a thing done successfully, typically by effort, courage, or skill* (Lexico, 2020).

But this denotation covers only a fraction of what we intend for students when we name *achievement* as a pillar of a brilliant school. Achievement is not just an end goal, as some dictionary definitions might imply. It goes beyond finishing a task, completing a project, or honing a skill to the place where it helps you do well on a test, write a good essay, design an experiment, or solve a series of problems. It is deeper than letter grades on a report card or the scores on the state tests. It includes learning and becoming competent at **the process** by which a goal is reached. Achievement includes, first, the desire to learn, know, or do something. It also includes the skills and satisfaction of setting a realistic goal, planning what you'll do to reach it, and going for it. When you reach a goal, part of the achievement process is reflecting on what you did, how you did it, what you learned from doing it, and what you might do differently—or even what you might try next. And when you DON'T reach the goal as you'd hoped, achievement encompasses another process: that of handling failure—embracing the setback, learning from it, and building the tenacity to try again.

Achievement includes every step of learning and growing. To get to any goal, a student will encounter many needs and chances for mini-achievements—small steps of learning. And a large part of "doing a thing successfully" is learning how to learn as a precursor to or as a part of the task completed or the skill grasped. Also, achievement is heavily laden with social and emotional factors. In particular, the process involves the extent to which the learner believes in his or her ability to learn and do the task. And in most cases, achievement involves the extent to which the learner knows that important others also believe in her or his ability.

So, for this book, let's define achievement this way:

Achievement: *the many steps and stages in a process—fueled by skill, effort, courage, belief in self, support from others, and tenacity— toward and culminating in successfully learning or doing something and in understanding what you did, how you got there, what you learned, and what more you need to learn.*

It's appropriate that the Achievement Pillar should follow the Expectations, Relationships, and Gratitude Pillars in this book. Any work on these first three pillars serves to create optimal conditions for learning and achievement across the student population.

Virtually every list of characteristics of effective schools (or successful schools or high-performing schools) includes high **expectations** and standards for all students. Lists also include practices to nurture and support achievement—such things as curriculum and instruction aligned with standards and ongoing assessment and monitoring of learning and teaching. You've seen, from the Third Pillar (in particular, Chapter 9) that students who perceive that their teachers have high expectations for their academic achievement are more motivated to try to meet those expectations and thus perform better academically than their peers who perceive low expectations from their teachers.

Furthermore, in the Second Pillar (in particular, Chapter 6), you've read the research about the impact that teacher-student **relationships** and other nurturing relationships in the school community have on the students' academic self-esteem and performance. That chapter showed such long-lasting effects of quality relationships as the greater confidence and self-efficacy students take into their adult lives and careers. In addition, it showed how the positive outcomes from supportive, trusting teacher-student relationships are particularly powerful for high-poverty students.

And the research in the First Pillar (in particular, Chapter 2) showed that regular **gratitude** practice not only strengthens quality relationships and increases social and emotional well-being, but increases satisfaction with school, goal accomplishment, motivation, engagement in school, and academic success.

The chapters in this pillar, Achievement, will explore the research findings on the benefits that follow when students see themselves reaching academic goals, the factors and practices that support achievement for all students, the obstacles that need to be overcome to close achievement and opportunity gaps, the part that a focus on achievement plays in the healthy culture of a brilliant school, and specific steps to take to make strong academic achievement a real and satisfying probability for all students.

Chapter 12

Why Achievement?

The value of achievement lies in the achieving.
—Albert Einstein, German Physicist, Nobel-Prize
Winner, Author of *Theory of Relativity*

What does a focus on achievement have to do with building a brilliant school? Why is the commitment to clarifying what achievement means, why it's important, and how to make it happen for all students a necessary foundation for a school? These may seem like outright ridiculous, no-brainer questions! After all, isn't this what school is for—to teach students to attain, by effort, the accomplishment of skills, the reaching of academic goals? Of course, this is a strong, central purpose of education! But this purpose is not accomplished in isolation from the other pillars of a brilliantly successful school. Already, the previous chapters of this book have drawn a broad picture of the personal, social, emotional, relational, and expectational setting in which students learn and grow academically.

Yet, gratitude, caring relationships, high expectations, and the good teaching and practice of social-emotional skills are not the whole picture either. Alone, they do not raise achievement. They must be combined with a wise understanding of how our students learn; a focused gathering of data about where a student is and how she or he learns; identification of relevant, engaging, and necessary content; honest, open acknowledgment of impediments to achievement that block progress for many individual students and groups of students—

and that must be eradicated; and downright excellent, personalized, skilled instruction and assessment, all with a healthy dose of growth mindset across the school community.

Benefits of a Focus on Achievement ──────────

Reams (literally mountains of reams!) of studies, books, articles, presentations, training manuals, and programs show how various practices (such as high expectations, quality relationships, etc.) help to raise achievement. So higher academic success is a benefit of many sound attitudes, structures, and practices. But something else happens in the partnership of the academic and the non-academic components of school culture. The very experience of achieving, itself, yields a wealth of benefits beyond academic accomplishments to students. **It is when our children (and even adult learners) see themselves as students having repeated successes with gaining the skills, processes, and content of learning (i.e., achieving) that self-belief, self-confidence, and fuller engagement with school all flourish and many other positive outcomes follow.**

> *The very experience of achieving, itself, yields a wealth of benefits to students.*

Perhaps the most highly touted benefits of successful academic experiences are the many positive outcomes for students' future lives, after the school years. Research shows that students with high achievement are more likely to be employed and are paid higher salaries than those with low academic success. Academic success in school is associated with many positive outcomes we value for students. It is connected to possessing a wider variety of skills and options for occupations, more stability in jobs, greater confidence in one's work, and higher work-related satisfaction. And academically successful students will have more employment opportunities than those with less education. In short, students who achieve well academically have a head start on an adult life that may not be as readily available to lower achievers (Brown, 1999; Fleetwood & Shelley, 2000; Frazier, 2009; Hearn, 2006; National Alliance of Business, Inc., 1998; National Center for Education Statistics, 2001; Rentner & Kober, 2001).

Just as important as post-school outcomes and possibilities are the extensive, significant benefits that take place **right now**, in every school, for all students who get that experience of tasting academic success. Most promising is this: a student's prior achievement is one of the single most powerful predictors of academic success (Hallikari et al.,2007; Kuncel et al., 2004). This means that, once students gain the fulfillment and knowledge of successful learning, **they are more likely to have continued academic success.** Those experiences of achievement not only add to the scope of students' knowledge and skills, but increase their academic self-view, giving them skills, confidence, and inspiration to keep doing well (Hallikari et al.,2007; Kuncel et al., 2004).

In addition, when schools hold all students to high expectations, have training in managing biases and stereotypes, and give students excellent instruction, scaffolding, support, and beliefs to reach those expectations, we see that students have greater

> *Nothing builds self-esteem and self-confidence like accomplishment.*
>
> –Thomas Carlyle, British Teacher, Essayist, and Historian

- Self-confidence and belief in their abilities as students
- Feelings of competence
- Self-motivation
- Self-expectations
- Pro-social inclinations and behavior
- Quality relationships with teachers and peers
- Self-control and self-regulation

- Sense of belonging
- Willingness to participate
- Engagement in collaborative activities
- Goal orientation and accomplishment
- Motivation and pride in their work
- Academic tenacity
- Overall sense of well-being and satisfaction in school (Boser et al., 2014; Cook et al., 2012; Filozof et al., 1998; Frenzel, Pekrun, & Goetz, 2007; Furrer et al., 2014; Furrer & Skinner; 2003; Rubie-Davies et al., 2015; Rubie-Davies & Rosenthal, 2016; Walton & Cohen, 2011).

Increases in achievement levels are also associated with lower levels of the following: student anxiety and depression, work avoidance, antisocial behavior, school dropout, and such poor behavior choices as substance abuse (Cicchetti & Toth 1998; Harackiewicz et al., 1997; Kasen et al., 1998; Liem, Dillon, & Gore, 2001; Nicholls, 1984).

Influences on Achievement

To answer the question of "Why focus on achievement?" our discussion must also consider the question of what it is that furthers academic achievement. Thousands of studies have tried to pinpoint just what conditions or approaches contribute to increased achievement for students. Many writers and educators have collected and examined decades of research—resulting in good meta-analyses of the topic. Brilliant schools pay attention to research in their quest for the best practices for their leaders, teachers, and students.

Education researcher John Hattie (2012) collected, compared, analyzed, and synthesized about 1,200 meta-analyses to examine influences on student achievement. The work from which he drew and reviewed in his book, *Visible Learning for Teachers: A Synthesis of over 800 Meta-Analyses Relating to Achievement*, involved over 80

Once students gain the fulfillment and knowledge of successful learning, they are more likely to have continued academic success.

million students from all kinds of locations and settings, learning with a variety of instructional strategies. His resulting report identifies 252 influences and the level of their effects (positive or negative) on achievement.

Learning Point Associates (2004), with the backing of the U.S. Department of Education's Institute of Education Services, promotes the use of scientifically based research to provide better direction and evidence for improving student achievement. Their guide outlines 11 research-based components for school reform aimed at raising achievement.

In a whitepaper, *How Schools Can Improve Student Achievement,* EL Education (2016) summarized research on strategies and conditions that it takes to increase student achievement.

And in the 2012 book, *Classroom Instruction that Works: Research-Based Strategies for Increasing Student Achievement,* authors Ceri B. Dean, Elizabeth Ross Hubbell, Howard Pitler, and Bj Stone synthesized years of research and practice to distill instructional strategies that have the greatest positive effects on student learning.

These four resources mentioned above are but a few of the many studies and meta-analyses that identify factors, practices, and commitments found to contribute positively to improving student achievement. Here are some of the factors that show up repeatedly as correlating positively with successful student achievement:

- High student involvement in and control over their learning
- Consistent encouragement of self-determination for students
- Strong emphasis on and support for student academic self-efficacy
- Student self-evaluation and self-reporting of their progress and processes

- A commitment to a culturally aware and culturally responsive climate, teaching practices, and behaviors
- Intentional practices and attitudes that culturally affirm students
- Regular examination of and diminishing of biases and stereotypes and their effects on individual students or groups of students in the academic processes (expectations, assignments, assessments, relationships, etc.)
- Regular, clear, and meaningful feedback given to students as they learn and work
- High, clear expectations with measurable goals and benchmarks for achievement
- Consistency in holding students to expectations
- Focused (and personalized) practices to help students reach expectations, including the state's challenging standards
- High-quality instruction, with a wide variety of proven instructional strategies and methods
- Skilled, passionate, culturally competent, effective teachers supported by good professional development
- Challenging and engaging content and active learning experiences that students see as having value, relevance, and connection to their lives

> *Education is not preparation for life; education is life itself.*
>
> –John Dewey, American Educator and Philosopher

- Curriculum and practices fit for the students' cognitive developmental levels
- Ongoing practices to improve curriculum and classroom instruction
- Focus on goal setting, goal management, and helping individual students reach goals
- Attention to developing conceptual understanding, metacognition, and creativity

- Strong teacher-student relationships and other trusting relationships within the school
- Positive relationships and experiences with peers
- Ongoing formative evaluation to inform instruction
- Extensive analysis and use of school data
- Data-driven decisions throughout the district, school, and classrooms
- Attention to increasing students' intrinsic motivation.
- Frequent use of cooperative learning
- Effective, proactive classroom management
- Intentional teaching of SEL skills.
- Meaningful involvement of parents and local community
- A safe (physical, social, emotional) environment for learning
- Courageous, collaborative leadership
- School-wide culture of trust, gratitude, and growth mindset
- High-quality technical support
- A school-wide action plan to raise achievement
  (Akey, 2006; Anderman, 2003; Ames, 1992; APA, 2009; Black & William, 2010; Blum et al., 2002; Bryk & Schneider, 2002; Caprara et al., 2000; CDC, 2009; Dean et al., 2012; Deci & Ryan, 2012; Eccles & Wigfield, 1995; EL Education, 2016; Hattie, 2018; Hanover Research, 2017; Hanushek et al., 2019; Learning Point, 2004; Leithwood et al., 2004; Martin & Collie, 2016; Martin & Dowson, 2009; McNeely et al., 2002; National Center on Safe Supportive Learning Environments, 2020; Reardon, 2016; Roeser et al., 1996; Ryan & Patrick, 2001; Safer & Fleishman, 2005; Saphier, 2016; Schunk & Swartz, 1993; Wentzel, 2010; Yin et al., 2008).

Barriers to Achievement

When we talk about school achievement, we must acknowledge the existing barriers to learning and achievement. If you re-read the bulleted list above, you'll realize that **the lack of any of the positive attributes described there can impede student achievement**.

In addition, we must recognize major hurdles that clearly and persistently depress the opportunity for thousands of students to achieve at higher levels: these are the long-term, deep-seated effects of poverty, of the mobility and many other difficulties that come with poverty, and of systemic racism and cultural bias. When we look at educational data, a consistent pattern emerges: race, culture, ethnicity, language, and economic status continue to be powerful predictors of school failure. Gary Howard (2002, 2004), who trains leaders in equity, inclusion, and excellence, says, "Whether the measure is grades, test scores, attendance, discipline referrals, drop-out or graduation rates, those students who differ most from mainstream White, middle/upper class, English-speaking America are also most vulnerable to being mis-served by our nation's schools" (p. 11).

Race, culture, ethnicity, language, and economic status continue to be powerful predictors of school failure.

In their recent study on the status of the achievement gap in the United States, researchers Eric A. Hanushek, Laura M. Tapley, Paul E. Peterson, and Ludger Woessmann (2019) found that social and economic disadvantages—poverty and many associated conditions—depress student performance. "The achievement gap between students at the highest and lowest socioeconomic levels is discouraging and fearful," they say, and "is equivalent to three to four years of learning" (cited in Downey, 2019, para. 8).

In their report, "The Achievement Gap Fails to Close" (2019), Hanushek and his colleagues state:

> Income inequality has soared in the United States over the past half-century. Has educational inequality increased alongside, in lockstep?

Of course, say public intellectuals from across the political spectrum. As Richard Rothstein of the liberal Economic Policy Institute puts it: 'Incomes have become more unequally distributed in the United States in the last generation, and this inequality contributes to the academic achievement gap.' Harvard political scientist Robert Putnam, citing research by Stanford sociologist Sean Reardon (2016), says, 'Rich Americans and poor Americans are living, learning, and raising children in increasingly separate and unequal worlds.' Another well-known political scientist, Charles Murray, argues that 'the United States is stuck with a large and growing lower class that can care for itself only sporadically and inconsistently . . .. The new upper class has continued to prosper as the dollar value of the talents they bring to the economy has continued to grow.' (para. 1, 2).

Sean F. Reardon (2016), professor of poverty and inequality in education at Stanford University, notes that the disparity between the rich and the middle class has increased dramatically over the past 30 years, so that "the rich now outperform the middle class by as much as the middle class outperform the poor" and "the academic gap is widening because rich students are increasingly entering kindergarten much better prepared to succeed in school than middle-class students" (cited in NAESP, 2013, para. 1). This means that the readiness gap handicaps students even before they get to school, where their achievement is measured. For example, at age three, there is a 30-million-word gap between children from the wealthiest and poorest families. Recent studies show that even by 18 months, children in different socio-economic groups display dramatic differences in their vocabularies (Fernald et al., 2013; Hart & Risley, 2003; Snow, 2013).

Another factor, strongly connected to and driven by socioeconomic factors, is the resulting racial segregation in schools. Sean Reardon (2016) has studied measures of segregation to understand how they are connected with gaps in academic achievement. He used data based on over 100 million test score records from all grade 3 through grade 8 students in public schools of over 300 metropolitan areas from 2009 to 2012. He shares this conclusion:

I find clear evidence that one aspect of segregation in particular—the disparity in average school poverty rates between White and Black students' schools—is consistently the single most powerful correlate of achievement gaps. This implies that high-poverty schools are, on average, much less effective than lower-poverty schools. (p. 1).

Reardon (2016) goes on to clarify that the strong association between racial segregation and depressed achievement—specifically of the kind that includes racial differences in exposure to poor schoolmates—is likely not caused by the segregation alone, but by a wide range of covariants that accompany it and affect the achievement. These are such factors as unemployment rates, racial disparities in family income, parental education levels, amount of racial discrimination in the community, and lack of access to affordable housing, safe passage to and from school, and parental jobs with livable wages. Other factors are those often found in high-poverty schools: lower quality of instruction, resources, and learning opportunities; higher teacher turnover; poorer facilities; fewer parental resources (economic, social, political); more disruptions and violence; and less exposure to higher-performing peers (pp. 47-51).

The circumstances into which people are born determine their opportunities in life ... not all people have anything close to equal chances to reach their highest potential.

Many educators have stopped referring to the disparity in academic performance between lower-income students (who are often students of color, non-native English speakers, or from rural settings) and more affluent students as the *achievement gap*. Organizations such as Teach for America instead use the term *opportunity gap*. Others use or add the terms *privilege gap* or *social justice gap*. They believe these terms define the circumstances more precisely. **These terms refer to the fact that the circumstances into which people are born (or find themselves through no choice of their own) determine their opportunities in life and that not all people have anything close to equal chances to reach their highest potential** (Mooney, 2018; Wexler, 2019). Such terms shine greater light on the obstacles students encounter in their school lives and "accurately place responsibility on an inequitable system that is not providing the opportunities for all kids to thrive and succeed" (Mooney, 2018, para. 3).

Another influence on academic performance for individuals comes from group stereotypes. A growing body of research finds that negative stereotypes raise doubts for students about their intellectual abilities or likelihood of doing well—because of their ethnicity or gender. This phenomenon is called *stereotype threat*. Researchers Claude Steele, Joshua Aronson, and Steven Spencer "have found that even passing reminders that someone belongs to one group or another, such as a group stereotyped as inferior in academics, can wreak havoc with test performance" (Cited in APA, 2006, para. 1). Stereotype threat saps mental energy, contributing to diminished motivation and sagging achievement. It contributes seriously to gender and racial gaps in academic performance (Aronson et al., 2002; Steele, 1997; Steele, 2010; Steele & Aronson, 1995; Steele et al., 2002).

And the stereotype threat does not stem from imaginary risks. The threat is real. Remember, back in the Third Pillar (Chapter 9), not only did we show the detrimental effects of long-term low expectations, but we shared substantial research showing that schools still house substantial bias related to students' ethnicity or socioeconomic status (and gender and many other student characteristics)—that profoundly affect achievement outcomes. Not only do these biases, many of them implicit, affect attitudes and lower expectations, but the behavior that flows from them results in unequal treatment of students, poorer instruction, and fewer learning opportunities or resources for certain students. This all works to depress chances for high achievement.

In his book, *Solving Disproportionality and Achieving Equity: A Leader's Guide to Using Data to Change Hearts and Minds,* Edward Fergus (2016, 2017) encourages leaders to "take a journey into disproportionality by engaging our hearts and minds on the presence of biases that create barriers to the success of students of color" (2017, para. 1). For one strategy, he suggests using data analysis (on such things as the rate of suspensions and expulsions, gifted program enrollment, special education referrals, progress rates) to become an equity-driven school.

A brilliant school must build awareness of these obstacles to individuals' achievement and many other obstacles that don't specifically fall within the category of racial, ethnic, or socioeconomic gaps. Though many of these are byproducts of racial and socioeconomic disparities, students of all backgrounds walk the school halls with characteristics that hinder their achievement possibilities. These are such factors as lack of belonging or acceptance; internalized lack of self-belief; fears for their safety; experiences of bullying about body features or appearance, clothing, disabilities, living circumstances, families, gender, sexual orientation, or gender identity; and a host of stresses or traumas from their lives inside or outside school.

Stereotype threat saps mental energy, contributing to diminished motivation and sagging achievement.

The Malleability of Ability ━━━━━━━━━━━━━

One of the most damaging, yet persistent, impediments to achievement is the concept that academic abilities are fixed. Until recently, a widespread theory suggested that a brain was hardwired at birth and that, thus, each person had a quantity of intelligence that was unchangeable. In addition, many believed that some racial and social groups are inherently more intelligent than others. Many still believe this, even if at a subtle or unconscious level. But neuroscience has shown us that the brain's capacity to learn, and even its structure, is not static. Indeed, the brain has plasticity; it can change based on experiences. According to intelligence expert Robert Sternberg, Cornell University psychologist, intelligence is not a set of innate capabilities. It's a set of skills we acquire (cited in Shenk, 2013, para. 1).

Neuroscience has shown us that the brain's capacity to learn, and its structure, are not static.

This is a complex topic—the subject of many studies and many theories. But in its simplest form, new research shows that the brain is more like a muscle that gets stronger and changes when you use it. Communication between neurons multiplies, and they make more connections, particularly when the brain is challenged or tackling new things. The brain actually changes in the presence of certain types of stimuli (Annenberg Learner, 2020; Kaufer, 2011). This means that we educators have the amazing position to help students "grow" their brains and their intelligence!

The reality that students can "get smarter" unfolds a myriad of possibilities for higher levels of achievement for all students. (And this is true for adults, too!) With the right kinds of nurturing and supportive conditions, acquiring new knowledge and understanding becomes more possible (Caine & Caine, 1994). Furthermore, researchers such as Carol Dweck and others have found that students who believe that intelligence is not innate can develop a growth mindset; and this growth mindset leads to greater improvement in academic tasks (APA, 2003; Blackwell et al., 2007; Dweck, 2007; 2017).

Educators need to understand these principles about how to help students grow their brain potential (no matter what their past academic performance has been). It is important to know, as well, how stress, boredom, or frustration block the brain from learning.

When teachers do not understand the neuroscience of learning and the power of a growth mindset—this becomes another obstacle to achievement. On the other hand, according to neurologist and classroom teacher Judy Willis, and author of several books including *Research-Based Strategies to Ignite Student Learning: Insights from a Neurologist and Classroom Teacher* (2006):

> There are no more critical life supports than passionate, informed teachers who can resuscitate students' joyful learning. When educators learn about how the brain appears to process, recognize, remember and transfer information at the level of neural circuits, synapses, and neurotransmitters, and when they share that knowledge with students, they share empowerment with their students. Informed teachers help students understand their ability to change their brains and experience success and renewed confidence. Students thrive in classrooms where teachers have the added tools from their neuroscience understanding. The result is nothing less than reigniting the joys of learning, even when they have been extinguished for years. (2012, para. 12).

Chapter 13

How Do G.R.E.A.T. Leaders
Get Results with Achievement?

Action is the fundamental key to success.

—Pablo Picasso, Influential Artist

Program outlines don't raise achievement. Promises won't do it.
Neither will elaborate plans. Raising achievement for all students
requires action. Yes, to raise achievement a school needs well-
informed, serious collaborative discussion and plans. But these aren't
what give all of our students the experience of setting and reaching
goals and standards. It's the every-hour, every-day, whole-community
patient and persistent actions that make the difference.

The research described in Chapter 12, born out by the writings and
experiences of many educators, gives us clues about how to move ahead
with building brilliant schools where achievement can soar for all
students. Based on that research, here are some suggestions for
administrators and other leaders. In action, these practices and attitudes
get proven results! I hope you'll understand that these suggestions can
be adapted to fit your purposes. I invite you to think about ways to
promote these mindsets and implement these experiences with your
students, teams, parents, and staff. Brilliant schools use such strategies
to jumpstart the year and develop them into powerful habits throughout
the year. These practices accumulate; they build upon each other to
increase academic confidence and improve achievement.

Keep These Discoveries in Mind —————————

- The brain has plasticity; intelligence can grow. It is not fixed.
- Students achieve better when they are involved in the direction, content, and evaluation of their learning.
- Academic self-belief is a strong, positive influence on a student's achievement.
- Cultural bias, implicit or explicit—and the behaviors (even subtle) that flow from it—severely depress achievement. To thrive academically, students must know that they are valued, accepted, and seen as able to meet high expectations—without cultural bias or bias toward any personal, family, or group characteristic.
- Achievement flourishes in the presence of high, clear, and consistent expectations that are accompanied by the school's action in helping each student meet the expectations.
- Positive interpersonal relationships with teachers, peers, and other adults in the school buffer stress and provide a basis for social-emotional development.
- The presence of high-quality, trusting teacher-student relationships is one of the strongest predictors of increased achievement.
- Students achieve better in an environment where they are comfortable with peers and where they feel safe physically, socially, and emotionally.
- When students set, manage, and reach goals, academic self-confidence and achievement are heightened.
- Over and over, the quality of teacher instruction is found to be one of the most important (if not the most important) influences on student achievement.
- Consistent, effective use of academic data—formative data as well as test scores—enables schools to improve practices so that students achieve more.

- Collection and use of data can enable schools to effectively examine disproportionality, identify and reduce biases, and achieve equity.
- The teaching of SEL skills boosts academic success.
- The consistent practice of gratitude boosts academic self-confidence and success.
- Strong, collaborative instructional leadership positively affects student academic success.

Start with These Steps

Believe in every student. So many facets of good education begin with belief. Achievement can only be a pillar to hold up a brilliant school if all the educators in the school believe that every single student can make progress—and that there are no pre-set limits on what that achievement can be. Remember that teacher estimates of a student's achievement are a strong factor in the actual achievement (Hattie, 2012). So, start the school year, your staff meetings, your communications with students by spreading and showing belief in **every** student's potential to achieve at higher levels.

When John Hattie (2018) completed an updated synthesis of 1200 meta-analyses related to achievement, he found the factor (out of 252 influences) that had the greatest positive influence on raising student achievement was something he called CTE or *collective teacher efficacy.* He defines this as "the collective belief of the staff of the school/faculty in their ability to positively affect students" (Hattie, 2021, para 3). This should help all of us as educators internalize the reality that our belief makes a difference!

Train teachers in the science of the brain. Neuroscience research has powerful implications for teaching. See that your professional development plans include instruction for teachers in the knowledge of the way the brain works so that they can apply this to their teaching and help all students grow their brain potential. Arm your staff with tested strategies that work for students. Get them collaborating and collecting data and experiences to share. Today, there are many good resources available for learning about how the brain learns and grows. And, once teachers become knowledgeable about how they can influence students' successful learning and behavior, encourage them to share the concepts with their students.

Set the bar high for everyone. We hear a lot about high expectations. You've finished a whole group of chapters in this book on the place of high expectations in a brilliant school. The idea of setting a high bar for every student flows directly from the previous step (above). If we believe that brains can change—that every student can achieve—then the call for high expectations is obvious! We believe in growth. Let's ask for it! Then let's get busy helping every student reach those high bars! Review the advice in the Third Pillar (Expectations), particularly Chapter 10, for setting and following through on expectations. Remember that expectations must be clear, reasonable, and reachable—but also that they must challenge students to reach a bit beyond where they can easily go.

Identify impediments to achievement that you can diminish. Chapter 12 addressed the topic of barriers to achievement and named many. Many of the circumstances that threaten achievement are indeed outside the control of school leaders and teachers. The crippling poverty, economic disparities, social inequities, cultural bias, family struggles, and other societal issues—schools cannot solve these alone. But schools can create safe climates for students while they are at school to diminish the effects of even the harshest circumstances. It's the work of the school to identify what barriers to achievement we can control—or at least chip away at significantly—and then to get busy doing so.

With your staff, start ferreting out those barriers. Go back to Chapter 12 and review the factors that influence achievement positively. Notice any that are present in your school. Review the barriers to achievement in that chapter. You might also review Chapter 9 (in the Third Pillar), which addressed the topic of implicit bias. List the impediments to achievement that you find in your school. Look for threats of stereotype that depress motivation and achievement (and sap students' mental energies). Discuss them. Make a plan. Act—to diminish (or better yet, eradicate) biases and stereotypes, erroneous beliefs about achievement, disparities in expectations, inequities in quality of instruction and support for students, implicit biases about individual students or groups of students, unchecked student-to-student discrimination and bullying—that might flow from these biases. Act to ban cultural insensitivities and all other barriers that interfere with students thriving.

Make teacher competence and self-belief professional development goals. Multiple research studies find teacher competence and instructional excellence, as well as teacher confidence in their abilities to help students succeed, at the top of the list of factors that raise student achievement. Revisit your PD goals, plans, and budgets to see that you're doing your best to hire and develop excellence in teaching. Research tells us that teachers who are skilled with a wide variety of relevant, engaging, and challenging instructional strategies and approaches are the most successful at helping students achieve at higher levels. Brilliant schools provide all the training they possibly can to help raise teachers' level of instruction. Be sure, as well,

> *You never want to get on a plane where the pilot learned to fly from worksheets.*
>
> –Todd Whitaker, Author, Speaker, and Professor of Educational Leadership

that part of this competence includes culturally aware and culturally responsive classroom management, relationships, and instruction.

Be reminded of the relationship-achievement connection. The role of teacher-student relationships in academic success can't be repeated too many times. Yes, an entire group of chapters in the Second Pillar detailed the benefits of trusting, supportive relationships and offered dozens of strategies and descriptions of what they look like and how to build them. But still, this is so important for achievement that it's getting another mention. Such relationships yield a load of positive outcomes for students. Greater academic self-belief and success are some of those outcomes to keep in mind constantly.

Remember, too, that it is not only teacher-student connections that affect achievement. The relationships among peers or even lack of relationships have powerful effects on each student's academic performance. If a student feels ignored, teased, excluded, stereotyped, frightened, inferior to, or in any other way uncomfortable with classmates—achievement may take a dive. Efforts to help a child achieve can be futile in the face of miserable peer contacts. On the other hand, healthy, cooperative, and positive contacts with peers can provide comfort and even positive examples to contribute positively to academic achievement. Don't forget these relationship lessons. As individuals and as colleagues, make frequent relationship checkups a habit.

Establish a safe environment for achievement. Many students feel unsafe at school. High numbers perceive or experience physical or emotional threats at school. Any lack of safety interferes with students' academic performance, as well as with feelings of belonging, satisfaction, or confidence. Take some time to examine the safety level of your school and classrooms—not just physical safety, but all manners of social and emotional safety as well. Identify places and situations that need safety improvement. Here are some conditions that **threaten** students' safety as well as their likelihood to perform at their best academically:

- Chaotic climate
- Poor classroom management
- Unclear expectations
- Inconsistent expectations or consequences
- Inconsistently enforced expectations or consequences
- Explicit or implicit bias for or against any personal or group characteristic

- Lack of cultural equity, sensitivity, or response
- Comparison to other students or other family members
- Lack of adult supervision in hallways, on playgrounds, and other corners of the school
- The atmosphere of frequent misbehavior or violence
- Unchecked lack of self-regulation by other students
- Threats or bullying in any form
- Lack of adult response to bullying
- No reliable advocates
- Inequitable treatment by adults; teacher favoritism of certain students
- Feelings of isolation
- Feeling that no one has your back

Get into the data-gathering habit. We're all tuned into the standardized tests! Plenty of data is collected and stored—and hopefully, shared with teachers, students, and parents. But assessment is not a once-a-year phenomenon. Or shouldn't be! Start every year with expectations and plans for ongoing formative data. Encourage teachers to regularly gather information from observations, mini-lessons, daily assignments, group learning experiences, and many other classroom activities. The pieces of information teachers gather daily are like golden gems to let them know how students are learning, what they know, and what they need.

Later in this chapter, there's some advice about using the data you collect. But first, you need a commitment to paying attention to all the signals students continually give about their achievement processes, accomplishments, struggles, or gaps.

Teachers can work together in teams or grade-level groupings to build a toolbox of formative assessment strategies. The more they pay attention to what can be learned from students as they work, the more effective teachers will become at using the information to adjust instruction and build bridges for higher achievement.

Collect and pay attention to data that may expose inequity. This is such data as those on suspensions, expulsions, opportunities for enrichment, academic coaching—checking to see if biases or inequitable expectations by ethnicity or SES contribute to inequity in students' chances for higher achievement.

Include These Attitudes and Actions Throughout the Year

Start with the leader's role in achievement. In a 2010 study, researchers Karen Seashore Louis, Kenneth Leithwood, Kyla L. Wahlstrom, and Stephen E. Anderson, examined the connections between school leadership and student achievement. The largest study of its kind, this drew from states across the nation, sampled 180 schools within 43 school districts to assure variation in school size, level, type, and student demographics, and collected data over two years. The study found that when principals shared leadership with teachers and built strong collaborative relationships with them, student achievement was higher. The researchers noted that they were unable to find any cases of a school with overall improved student achievement in the absence of talented leadership.

> *Researchers were unable to find any cases of a school with improved student achievement in the absence of talented leadership.*

Raising achievement takes strong, courageous, collaborative, trustworthy leadership. Though the effects of leadership on student achievement are **indirect**, they are powerful. This is because a leader **directly** influences the climate and conditions throughout the school, the relationships across the school and community, every teacher and his or her instruction, and all the policies, programs, practices, and attitudes that affect student learning.

The school leader sets the tone and heads the parade for the school staff to take collective responsibility for student achievement. According to the Wallace Foundation, which funded the study described above (2020), "Principals are most effective when they envision themselves working with district personnel, teachers, and other principals towards clear, common goals" (para. 4). And "In schools that perform well, teachers and principals tend to establish high expectations for students and pay attention to multiple measures of student success" (para. 1).

In all of the steps, strategies, and attitudes described in this chapter (previously, as well as to follow), the principal's influence is clear and strong. As the school head, she or he spreads an unshakable belief that all

> *Know that the leader's influence does not diminish when it is shared.*

students can achieve, and also acknowledges and takes on the battle against barriers to achievement. The leader sets the example for and honoring and celebrating the diversity of the student body and the community. She leads the charge against bias. He works with students, parents, and staff to make decisions and take steps toward academic excellence and improvement. The school leader gathers good data, shares and discusses the data, and makes data-driven decisions in collaboration with school personnel and other school and district leaders.

As a school or district leader, arm yourself with a positive, passionate commitment to these tasks. Know that the leader's influence does not diminish when it is shared; indeed, it becomes more productive and leads to greater growth for students and staff.

Strengthen students' academic self-efficacy. This is another one of the top factors demonstrated to improve student achievement. We must convince learners that they can learn and will succeed. As shown in the Third Pillar of this book, expectations that teachers, other school personnel, and parents have for students have striking significance on student progress. But that is mostly true because those expectations fuel and support students' self-beliefs. The expectations students hold for themselves are critical to building and sustaining a brilliant school. What I think I can do, I do. What I think I can't do, I don't. What I believe I can achieve impacts my daily actions and decisions and adds up to achievement.

I imagine that, when you think about self-belief, certain names and images come to mind. We all know people who make amazing strides because someone helped her or him grow an "I can do this" mindset. For myself, I conjure up athletes who, with practice, tenacity, and grace—along with belief and skill, continually exceed what peers or critics may have imagined possible. Perhaps you see characters pulled from the pages of history books or current leaders in business or civil service. Or you may call on examples in your own life—times when you defied what you thought possible for yourself, only to learn that through some inner trust of yourself, along with hard work, you grew more adept at some undertaking. These images all remind us that people can "beat the odds" and reach higher goals—with a mindset of self-belief and the effort that such belief sparks.

Michael Jordan is one global icon who displayed his confidence in his capacities on a worldwide stage. I can't forget the oft-repeated clip of his 20-footer in game 6 of the 1998 NBA finals when the Chicago Bulls played the Utah Jazz. With a little more than 5 seconds remaining, Jordan hit a 3-point shot to give the Bulls an 87-86 lead. I remember screaming at the TV, being on the edge of my seat during the whole game—wrapped in nervous energy. Yet Jordan, the practitioner, did not appear nervous. He came onto the court that night for this moment. He had practiced for it. In a YouTube interview, he said,

> I practice as if I am playing the game, so when the game comes it's not new to me. Every day in practice was a competition. So when the game comes, there's nothing I haven't already practiced. It's a routine. Whatever happens in the game now— okay, I've done this before. I never feared about my skills

because I put in the work. Work ethic eliminates fear. (Jordan, 2013).

As you recall Jordan's accomplishments—and certainly when you use him as an example of self-belief for your students—remember to include these facts about Michael: (1) As a sophomore, when Jordan tried out for his high school basketball team, he failed to get a spot. (2) From that failure, he developed a work ethic that did not stop—even long after he was a star.

> *Specific, clear, challenging goals lead to greater effort and achievement than easy or vague goals do.*
>
> –Ken Blanchard Leadership Consultant, Author of *The One-Minute Manager*

Understand students' belief in their academic abilities and possibilities as the positive force that it is. Then, think about the moments we create with students, colleagues, teachers, and families—and realize how the content and environment contribute to their belief in themselves. From anchor charts on the wall to the words we choose as we work with students, to the level of trust among classmates and teacher, to the biases we eliminate, to the support and hope we demonstrate, to the choices and uses of assessment (summative and formative) and the data they yield—we need to have a fervor to propel our students toward experiences of proficiency and success. We want ALL students to mutter to themselves, "I can do this!" with a fervor that makes achievement reachable and palpable.

Academic self-belief grows from experiences of academic success with consistent support and feedback. Encourage teachers to

- Constantly affirm students in the belief that, with effort, they can grow in the ability to do well academically.
- Set a safe, low-stress, non-chaotic learning environment.
- Aim for every student to taste moments of success every day.

- Teach students about growth mindset and neuroplasticity.
- Teach students skills and tools for learning, including independent learning.
- Help students set personalized, meaningful goals.
- Make sure the goals are achievable by the individual child.
- Give students plenty of positive, constructive feedback.

Increase students' ownership of goals and expectations for their learning. When John Hattie (2018) completed his synthesis of 1,200 meta-analyses related to achievement, he found that out of 252 factors, one of the most successful at enhancing achievement was what he described as "self-reported grades." (He says that now he would call it "Student Expectations.") He went on to describe this as the process of students predicting how they will perform and self-assessing what they've done. He claimed that students are their own best critics. Once students have stated their expectations for their performance, the teacher can push each student to exceed those expectations. When a student accomplishes that, the result is a huge boost in her or his academic self-confidence.

You know that the processes of students setting their own goals and stating self-expectations bolster achievement. Apply this knowledge to the classroom. See to it that students

1. Set their own goals for a lesson, unit, or project.
   - The teacher teaches students how to identify and state reachable goals.
   - The teacher learns the student's expectations.
   - The teacher understands the relevance and emotional connection of the student to the goals.
   - The teacher understands the student's goals and shows the student that the goals matter to her or him (the teacher).
   - The teacher can challenge and push the learner to meet and go beyond their expectations.

2. Predict performance on any upcoming tests or quizzes.
   - Students compare their predictions to their performances.
   - Students discuss the results of the comparisons.
   - Together the teacher and student set a plan for catching up on what was missed and preparing for future assessments.

3. Reflect after completion of the lesson, unit, or project.
   - The student and teacher review the goal performance.
   - The student self-assesses with scoring guides, checklists, or rubrics that have clear benchmarks for progress or performance.
   - The student reflects on how she or he did at meeting their goals.
   - The student and teacher discuss the outcomes and how the student feels about the performance.
   - The student identifies what was hard and what went well, describes what surprised them, and thinks about what they could do to improve.
   - The teacher gives feedback and guidance on what the student might do next.
   - The student lets the teacher know what help is needed to meet the goal.

John Hattie, author of *Visible Learning for Teachers* (2012), emphasizes that when students set realistic goals for themselves, they'll want to achieve the goals—and this process builds their confidence as learners. In addition, he points out that teachers need to raise the bar and nudge students to exceed the expectations they set for themselves. You might consider using the SMART Goals approach from Project SMART (Eby, 2019; Haughey, 2014; MindTools, 2021; O'Neill, 2003).

Increase students' ownership of their data. When students measure their achievement or are presented with measures of their achievement which they can understand, they gain recognition and confidence that their goals can be reached. They see themselves as students—as persons who can achieve. So often this data is hidden from students. It is their right to see exactly what they got right, where they were weak, and what they need to do for better outcomes.

Aside from the year-end IOWA Test of Basic Skills, no one ever spoke to me about my performance on a state test. (And sadly, even today, most students are never invited to a discussion about their state test scores and what they mean.) I had more anxiety about my mathematical abilities than about what I could or couldn't do on the end-of-the-year test. Of course, my anxiety about this grew as math became more complex and my confidence waned. Although my need for support and coaching in math increased as the content became more complex, my teachers rarely spoke to me about my misconceptions or my low test scores. Nor did any attempt to show me how to tackle the math in a way that helped me grow my understanding and confidence. I don't blame them. Math was transactional, and I had no desire to ask why I was always coming up short.

> *Some teachers taught the curriculum today. Other teachers taught students today. And there's a big difference.*
>
> –Dr. Justin Tarte

The first time a teacher sat with me to talk about my failing math grade was during my freshman year in Algebra I. The teacher, Coach Rivers, would tout, "Positive Mental Attitude" as he'd tutor me, and I'd find setback after setback as I tried to understand quadratic equations. He'd use my work within the problems as data and talk to me about my misunderstandings. With his help, I was beginning to understand aspects of algebra because I had an instant feedback loop, data readily available to me, and the opportunity to discuss how I could become a better algebra student. After that, I never looked at math the same. Coach Rivers used his "PMA" approach (which was another way to say he had high expectations for me and let me know I should have them too) and formative data to coach me into owning my data and putting it to good use.

Armed with data, I felt more comfortable making mistakes and setting reasonable goals for myself. Knowing that my teacher was a supportive cheerleader in my progress toward becoming a more proficient algebra student gave me a new relationship with math achievement. Coach Rivers was a partner in my work toward understanding the math content and creating meaningful goals. He was on my team. Because the conditions were supportive, I gained a better grasp of my content. In *Academic Tenacity: Mindsets and Skills that Support Long-Term Learning,* Carol Dweck and her team of researchers found that students who endorse learning goals tend to seek out academic challenges, persist on difficult academic tasks more, and develop their abilities more readily. Setting and going for their own learning goals promotes academic tenacity in students (Dweck, Walton, & Cohen, 2014).

Until I sat with Coach Rivers, I avoided discussions about my performance in math. I took no real responsibility for my learning because I had this idea that I simply couldn't do math. I was unmotivated because my performance told me I was a failure. Coach Rivers knew that his performance as a teacher was linked to my success or failure. I'd like to think that my daddy's teachers back in Winston County, Mississippi understood that, too.

Earlier, I referred to Michael Jordan and the self-belief and work ethic that he developed, even in the face of disappointment and failure. I believe that the harder he worked, the more his belief grew. But also, Michael was gaining something as he worked—much that our students, too, can gain as they work. His practices **gave him data** about his performance. This informed his decisions and actions on the court during games. He understood how to make the data—including both successes and setbacks—work for himself. You can use his story with students to show that kind of step-by-step path to achievement. When we practice something, we can anticipate obstacles and become curious about barriers that arise; we can try again or try new approaches; we can reflect on our performance and then adapt and move forward.

Make effective use of data. Earlier in this chapter, I made the plea for schools to carefully collect data—formative as well as summative. But all the data in the world won't do us any good unless we know how to use it and use it well.

When discussing achievement, many resist the picture the data creates for us. Perhaps we pile the classroom roster report into groupings of mastery and failure, having lapsed back into a fixed mindset. Maybe we are called to teach to our middle kids, those "3's" who allow us to teach to a subset of students, the middle; but then we miss the kids at each end of the learning continuum.

Let's face it, the pressure to increase achievement forces us to examine our beliefs about achievement and success. And rightly so. Brilliant schools tackle such questions as:

- *What does high achievement look and sound and feel like?*
- *What feelings and beliefs do we have around failure?*
- *How will we discuss both success and failure with my teachers and students?*
- *What are we doing well?*
- *What should we do differently?*

In the past, I have also failed colleagues with the ways I have approached data and achievement (while in leadership positions). One cannot live in the land of assumption when building a brilliant school. Again and again, effective teachers arm themselves with class and student data to uncover understandings and misconceptions. It is hard work to be both a teacher and a researcher, but effective teachers wear both hats simultaneously. And when we do, we expect successes, setbacks, and failure—because these are all part of achievement. At any data review meeting in a brilliant school, you will find teams of teachers and leaders with worried brows asking,

- *Did we teach to the depth and breadth of that standard?*
- *Did we teach to make sense of the text? Or of the problem?*
- *Did we teach for understanding?*
- *Or did we teach for coverage because we were running out of time?*
- *Did we customize instruction for those students performing at the outer spectrums of our data?*

Good data make for good decisions.

In school teams, we ask these questions because we are tethered to the achievement of our students. Achievement requires these check-ins. It takes a certain mindset to embrace a setback. In any arena—in school, in our personal lives, in business—setbacks are often opportunities to reflect and improve. Our most effective teachers examine and re-examine their instructional practices on a repeated loop. They repeatedly ask: *How can I improve my teaching to impact student understanding and achievement?*

Good data makes for good decisions. How student achievement data are collected and implemented will determine how well that data supports the instructional decision-making by principals and teachers. The guidelines are clear: data must be made part of the ongoing cycle of instructional improvement; students must be taught to examine their data and set their own learning goals; teachers must examine their classroom data and set their own teaching goals; principals must establish a clear vision for schoolwide data use; schools need to foster a data-driven culture, and school districts must develop and maintain district-wide data systems.

Yet, there is perpetual pressure on schools to perform at the highest levels at every benchmark each quarter—well before the state test. The pressure can cause us to disregard the formative data we gather each day from our students.

If you fell down yesterday, stand up today.

–H. G. Wells,
American Author

Perhaps we see a lack of participation or an incomplete essay as an indication of student apathy or reading ability. Maybe we reflect on our teaching practices only to become discouraged by the barrage of data hoops we have to jump through—before appreciating how we might incorporate such practices into our classrooms. After all, we use the "A" through "F" scale to communicate success and failure when discussing school performance. Data conversations can become heated and overwhelming if given the chance. High-performing schools wear that "A" as a badge of honor. Lower performing schools carry the extra pressure to bring up the scores. Many of us carry the pressure to perform into parent meetings, after-school meetings, and our classrooms. School leaders and teams of teachers do their best to make sense of this pressure because we all want to feel and be successful. Often, our experiences with disappointment and failure are our greatest teachers, so we work diligently to create environments that support success.

Whatever struggles we may have with data use, it's a critical component of our mission to raise achievement. We must share and discuss data with all the affected parties. We must think outside the box of the infrequent data-analysis meeting—usually, a review of the state tests after the results are in. We must

- Start from a place of understanding what it is we believe students should learn and be able to do. This topic centers around a clear embracing and knowledge of our state standards. And that needs to be expanded to include other needs of our society and community.

- Outline the curriculum that will enable students to meet the standards.
- Decide how we will measure progress on the standards along the way (formative assessment).
- Agree on how we will be able to tell if students have learned and can meet the standards we've set.
- Have a plan for reviewing ongoing and summative data to find out how we've fared in teaching our students.
- Be clear about what we'll do to increase achievement when the data shows us what students are not learning well.
- Make data-based decisions to adapt the curriculum or parts of it.
- Make data-driven decisions to strengthen instruction and instructional materials.
- Use individual student data to adapt content, instructional practices, and materials for individual students or groups.

And we must do this all in the spirit of collaboration and a shared goal to improve student achievement.

Jan O'Neill (2003), the co-author of *Building Shared Responsibility for Student Learning* and cofounder of Quality Leadership by Design, writes

> When applied with knowledge and integrity, using data heightens our ability to make informed and reasoned decisions about our work; it is what distinguishes the professional practitioner from the technician. In other professions—such as medicine, law, athletics, and the arts—shared learning, research, public scrutiny, feedback on performance, and peer review are characteristic of professional practice. Why wouldn't we expect the same level of professional rigor from ourselves as educators? Teaching is not just about methods and textbooks. Teaching is about learning and being able to demonstrate through the performance of the learners that real teaching and learning have occurred. (para.13).

As we decide the *what, how,* and *why* of our data, it is the actions and decisions of educators in our school that allow us to monitor progress toward student goals. We determine *what* data we use (which

> *Consider data a goldmine of information that can help improve teaching and raise achievement.*

means we need to be sure that our materials, practices, and programs support student goals), and we decide the *how* and *why* as we monitor progress and adjust based on what the data tells us. Do not be afraid of your data or overwhelmed by it. Consider it a goldmine of information that can help improve teaching and raise achievement for all your students.

Rethink mastery. Embrace struggle and failure. In school, failure is a major source of fear and frustration for students and teachers alike. Our attitude toward failure may well be the result of a ladder metaphor for learning. This is the notion that successful learning (along with good teaching) is defined by steady progress forward toward mastery. (Let's note here that *mastery* is generally defined somewhat like this: *control over something* or *comprehensive knowledge or skill at something.*)

Many schools, districts, or states look at academic performance in such categories as *basic, proficient, mastery, advanced,* or *excelling.* In considering how educators should look at mastery in the context of our mission to raise achievement, I find a definition of mastery that has altered my previous thinking. In her article, *"Five Musts for Mastery,"* high school teacher Catlin Tucker (2013-2014) notes that she has studied topics for years without "mastering" them. She adds,

> The term *mastery* creates this illusion that we can master a concept or skill—when, in reality, mastery isn't an endpoint but rather an elusive goal that remains forever out of reach. This may dishearten some, but I prefer this definition (See Daniel Pink's definition below). There is no dead end in learning.

> *Absolute* mastery of a subject may remain out of reach, but
> there are *degrees* of mastery. In that sense, students can master
> a subject—to a degree. This is broadly recognized, as in the
> ancient game of chess, which confers titles of chess master and
> grandmaster on players with varying degrees of expertise.
> In his book *Drive,* Daniel Pink writes that mastery is 'the desire
> to get better and better at something that matters.' When I
> dissect this definition in the context of the classroom, I'm struck
> by two elements. First, students must have a *desire* to get better.
> Second, they must feel that what they're learning or doing
> *matters*. (para. 2-4).

I think what appeals to me about Tucker's discussion on mastery (and Pink's definition) is the idea that learning is a progression and not a finite goal. It's how we defined *achievement* back in Chapter 11. Instead of thinking they must learn everything about a subject, speak a new language flawlessly, never fail to solve a two-step equation accurately, or get an A on every test they ever take, students can set and succeed with many steps in the process of learning a process, concept, or skill. For students to master things by degrees, they must become key players in their learning. When we think back to the rows of desks that greet us each day, we have students who already have the tenacity to move increasingly toward degrees of mastery of a subject or content area. They have defined the purpose for their work, set and adjusted their goals based on the data they received, met a setback, and then practiced some more. People who perform at high levels of achievement have or acquire a relentless drive to practice, adjust, and reflect on their performance in a given area because they hold a set of goals in their mind and keep a path that has overall forward progress.

This alternate look at mastery as getting better and better leaves students more nurtured and allows for more creativity in the forward path. Instead of a straight line, progress toward achieving inevitably includes some side trails, interruptions, restarts, and backward steps.

This way of understanding mastery embraces failure as part of the process. It gives us room and reason to discuss failure; shows students how it is an intricate part of life, learning, and achievement; and provides them with tools to handle and learn from it. When students see their work as challenging in an exciting way—with

> *Mastery is the desire to get better and better at something that matters.*
>
> –Daniel Pink, Author of the book, *Drive*

decisions to make and problems to solve along the way and with glitches that are a normal part of the process—they'll be more likely to be willing to keep trying.

The Fourth Pillar in this book opened with a story from my father's school life. Daddy wanted to be in school. His desire likely influenced his behavior and his use of time in school. He had the **desire** to be in school. For me, progress toward mastery in math didn't come until I **wanted** to become a better math student. I think we can take a lesson from Caitlin Tucker's definition of mastery, along with many experiences we've had and seen (such as my dad's and mine) to remember that, first, students must have a *desire* to get better. Second, they must feel that what they're learning or doing *matters*. This means we'd better be inspiring that desire and then making sure that they have access to curricula and resources for lessons on things that matter.

Honor and support the rhythms of learning. Earlier in this chapter, I mentioned findings in neuroscience that show that learning involves changing the brain. We also recognized that, for optimal learning to occur, the brain needs certain conditions to be able to grow and change. Here are some key learning principles that can help us understand some things about the brain that will help us optimize learning for our students. According to Daniela Kaufer (2011), Berkeley professor of integrative biology and author of an article, "Neuroscience and How Students Learn,"

- Moderate stress is beneficial for learning. This includes such factors as introducing minor change in an activity, adding participation, discussion, music, or movement to an activity.
- Extreme stress hinders learning.
- The brain learns best when a person has adequate exercise, nutrition, and sleep.
- Active learning stimulates several areas of the brain and promotes memory. These are learning experiences that involve higher-level cognitive functions and engaging techniques such as debates, simulations, group learning, peer teaching, or role-playing.

To develop meaningful, internalized skills, learners must actively build neural networks, a time-consuming process that results from the effort required for repeated trips over the same ground—to lay out the routes, mark them, clear them, create foundations, pave them, roll them several times, connect them, and add the signs, lines, and railings that will guide us when we revisit them. Each time we cover this ground, each time we rethink our way through the Civil War or try to write a paragraph or interpret the graph of an equation, the network becomes more defined. Sometimes, progress is slowed by obstacles—a new idea or an old idea we thought we understood but didn't, or an inability to focus; but, over time, our understanding or skill deepens and improves. And because we are building these neural paths, these abilities, in our own brains, we must be active and persevere. No one can think or act for us (which further suggests the need for the goal to matter to us—to be emotionally relevant). Being told is not a substitute for learning (Annenberg Learner, 2020).

For optimal learning, the brain needs supportive conditions in which to build new networks. The success of the brain's work is heavily dependent upon the context in which the student learns. Students need social and emotional supports, an environment free of chaos, fear, or excess stress, the right amount of challenge and active learning experiences, and patient teachers who understand how the brain learns. When school conditions are right, acquiring new knowledge and understanding becomes *more* possible (Neuroscience, 2020).

Yet, even when teachers sustain or successfully create highly supportive conditions, their students' performance will fluctuate, showing signs of improvement and regression—two steps forward, one step back. That's the rhythm of learning, the rhythm of constructing new neural networks. It's a process of building and rebuilding that allows us to continue to improve, each time advancing a bit further from a more solid base. Integrating skills into increasingly complex systems of representations and then abstractions is difficult work, involving considerable trial, success, and error. Each success brings us closer to the limit of our ability or understanding until we stumble, go back a bit, and start again—learning from both our progress and regression and slowly building stable neural networks (Kaufer, 2011).

Be persistent. Our students come to us with a collection of stories about their school experiences. Those stories are likely connected to feelings and attitudes about their success or failure. We know some factors influence achievement and sit outside our locus of control. For our students who arrive with empty bellies, breakfast is a more pressing concern than passing a math test. A student can't concentrate on learning or achieving if he or she is hungry.

Teachers and administrators have their own stories about the demands of school. Many teachers have multiple content areas for which to prepare with class lists that extend well beyond their arms. I have had colleagues who had five or more classes of 32 students each period. I am sad to say that monitoring progress and fully knowing each student's strengths and challenges was not the first thing on this teacher's mind. Acknowledging limitations and realities is critical to our work because it allows us to say: "OK, well within these given parameters (whatever you identify them to be)—what can we do to ensure achievement for all students? "

Who spends himself in a worthy cause; who at the best knows in the end the triumph of high achievement, and who at the worst, if he fails, at least fails while daring greatly.

–Theodore Roosevelt, 1910, from "Citizenship in a Republic"

Let it not only be our duty but also our passion and mission, to believe in every student's right and ability to achieve and to act to make this a reality. Let us give the gift of our energy and care to help each child enjoy the fruits of higher achievement. Let us work feverishly to lessen those burdens carried by many of our students and their parents—the burdens that intensify the already painful barriers to achievement.

While schools recognize the need to challenge every student to reach higher and to catch students up, learning and achievement may well be the last thing on a student's mind. Given that many of our students have much to contend with, monitoring progress, setting goals, and prompting students to own their data can be challenging. While we recognize we have students like Michael Jordan who understand the purpose of practice, whose choices and behaviors mirror the high expectations we set, and who works diligently to practice, revise, and reflect on his or her learning, we have some students who struggle to define the purpose for learning and their lack of practice or stick-to-it-witness demonstrates just that.

I know that many schools work tirelessly to address and create supports to lessen the burdens exacerbated and tolerated by our social, economic, and political systems. We feel those burdens too. Let's take the actions that we can take, solve the problems over which we have control, and at the same time work long and hard to improve those widespread, deep-seated societal problems that depress achievement.

To mount any obstacle or achieve the goals we set to raise achievement, we understand that to achieve ourselves we must be proactive, vulnerable, and brave. And we must work together. Brilliant schools understand that. Brilliance is intense light. Let's keep the lights illuminating the pathway for all our students to achieve.

Conclusion

The Fourth Pillar

There's no elevator to success.
You have to take the stairs.

—Zig Ziglar, American Author

Consciously or unconsciously, all students are asking themselves several critical questions related to identity, inclusion, and success: *Who am I? What is my worth? Do I belong? Am I safe? Is school my place? Am I smart? Can I be successful? Who cares about me and who decides whether I succeed?* These questions form the implicit curriculum that functions beneath the surface of schooling. (Gary Howard, 2002, p. 3).

How we answer these questions and many similar ones will influence our level of success in helping all students achieve well and in contributing in a significant way toward closing the gap that we call the achievement gap or the opportunity gap.

Halfway into the first semester of my seventh year of teaching, a virus stole my voice during a lesson on the theme of insults and revenge. This unit and its topic were inspired by Edgar Allen Poe's short story, "The Cask of Amontillado." I had been reading the story to them, but since I couldn't read, twenty-two young teenage students sat in desks too small to be comfortable and took turns reading from the literature text. One by one, they labored through the paragraphs, many of them stumbling over words they didn't know and stopping only at my whispered cues to pronounce the difficult words or to ask a question. At the end of the class period, I collected students' written work as they filed past giving me a high-five or a "Get well, Parker—we like **you** to read to **us**."

There was no high-five from Jamie. Her lips pursed in more of a frown than a smile. She handed me her work along with a folded letter and cocked her hip to the right as she popped the letter out toward me. As I took the letter; she flipped her braids and walked out of class, saying, "See you tomorrow, Mr. P. Be sure to read my letter."

When the room cleared, I opened Jamie's letter, expecting to find it brimming with teenage angst and attitude, similar to what I had seen in Jamie's exit from class. However, what I got wasn't that at all. It read:

> *Dear Andy, please do not call on me to read out loud in your class because other students will laugh at me. I do not read very well, and if they laugh at me, I will fight them, and I do not want to fight in your classroom. Thank you. – Love, Jamie.*

Guilt and incompetence flooded me. Jamie's body language and facial expression made sense now. I had come very close to delivering her a great insult. I berated myself, "How could I have put her in that position? How terrified she must have been as her turn inched closer!" I wondered, "What will I do next to help her? And "oh-oh"—what about all those kids who **did** read but did so with difficulty? How did I not get that I was putting them into an embarrassing position?" (And ironically, I did it during a lesson about insults!)

The *Dear Andy* letter was a tool I used each year for students to communicate troubles to me, something that they needed, or a tidbit they needed me to know. Jaime's message taught me more than one invaluable lesson that day. And luckily, since Jamie never got a turn to read, the class escaped what might have been a real-life lesson on insults and revenge right there in the classroom.

While I didn't fully realize it at the time, the assumptions I held for Jamie and the class influenced my expectations, and my expectations affected the teacher-student relationships, the students' self-belief, and ultimately, the students' chances for achievement. I assumed that all these students could read fluently, or at least passably. I expected that they'd all feel confident enough to read out loud to the class. The letter sent me on a quest to understand how to support students like Jamie to realize their potential and reach their goals without humiliating them in the process.

Before this, I had certainly worked with students who struggled. But something about Jamie's letter shook me up and forced me to commit to doing better. I started investigating the statistics and information on at-risk students. Since the 1983 publication of *A Nation at Risk*, the awareness of the critical need for education reform has been in the spotlight. And all educators have been more acutely aware of the gaps in opportunity, achievement, and school quality. With increased attention to school reform, many studies are showing large gains for students in at-risk categories. But still, low income, poverty, substandard schools, and several other societal and personal or family factors contribute to high numbers of at-risk students. Millions of teachers lead classrooms where students either feel supported by a nurturing adult, or they don't; where they learn math, English, art, science, PE, music, or history, or they don't; where they are supported with social and emotional coping mechanisms, or they are not.

The opening message of *A Nation at Risk* is:

> All, regardless of race or class, or economic status, are entitled to a fair chance and to the tools for developing their individual powers of mind and spirit to the utmost. This promise means that all children by virtue of their own efforts, competently guided, can hope to attain the mature and informed judgment needed to secure gainful employment, and to manage their own lives, thereby serving not only their own interests but also the progress of society itself. (United States. 1983, p. 1).

After reading Jamie's letter, I started looking at every one of my students differently. Jamie was a kid who appeared to have a strong sense of self. She certainly was honest and could communicate straightforwardly. But even I (her teacher!) did not know her well enough to realize the depth of her reading problems! Looking down the roster at each student's name, I began to realize that there were probably academic, social, or emotional needs directly tied to learning in my classroom about which I had no clues. That one letter taught me that I needed to pay attention to who my students are and what works for each one. It helped me see that I needed to start doing a far better job of listening to my students.

Decades later, I still have that *Dear Andy* letter. Over the years and today, it has kept me more fully awake to the situations and needs of individual students. Though I do not want to minimize the work to be done for at-risk students as identified in the categories mentioned above, I want to note that many students (at all levels of academic performance, socioeconomic status, and ethnic group) can be at risk of underperformance or other school difficulties—for long or short periods of time. A host of personal, family, social, emotional, physical, school, and societal factors contribute to this.

Jamie's letter was the catalyst that inspired me to assemble and hone the concepts, strategies, and messages describing the five pillars of a brilliant school presented in this book—the foundation that supports all of the Jamies and other students in reaching their potential.

Any brilliant school understands the critical role of achievement in its fabric, mission, and success. The task of doing right academically by all our students is a huge one. The challenges are great. It will take all the courage, care, and bold action we have. But we must be up to it. Our students and their families—and our society—are counting on us to do this.

The first three pillars in this book—Gratitude, Relationships, and Expectations—all join together with Achievement to lend a strong structure to support this brave work of doing right academically by all our students. The pillar that comes next completes the image of the brilliant school. This Fifth Pillar is Tenacity—a component that infuses and cements all the other pillars. Certainly, it is fundamental to achievement. Our students need tenacity to meet the kinds of high expectations we have discussed and enjoy the benefits of increased achievement we've noted. And educators—all of us who work in schools and lead them—we, too, must pool our growth mindsets, passions, and persistence of spirit and of action to build and maintain the schools our students need.

The Fifth Pillar of a Brilliant School

Tenacity

Success is often not a matter of talent, but a matter of tenacity.

—Nathaniel Brommer,
American Entrepreneur

You may remember my story about Jamie from the conclusion of the previous pillar (Achievement). She's the student who wrote me a "Dear Andy" letter, begging me to spare her the humiliation of reading in front of the class—something I had insensitively and cluelessly asked other students (some of them stumbling readers) to do. Her courage to trust me with her secret—that she could not read well—sent me on a journey to help students like her over my 30-year career. I've thought of her often for years, wondering where her bravery and tenacity had led her after her middle- and high-school experiences. About five years ago, I went to social media to track her down. I located her with just a couple of clicks, and I wrote my own version of a "Dear Jamie" letter—one that trusted her with the outcome of that earlier interchange.

Dear Jamie,

I have retired from working in Mississippi, and now live and work in New Orleans. I am so happy that Katisha and I connected on Facebook; this enabled me to find you. I wanted you to know how much I appreciated being your teacher. I'm not sure if you remember or not, but you wrote me a *Dear Andy* letter asking me not to call on you to read aloud in class because you didn't think you could read that well. You feared that people might laugh at you and you would have to fight them if they did. You didn't want to fight, so you asked me not to call on you to read out loud.

I still have that letter, and I have used it over my career to teach principals and teachers about the importance of knowing their students and providing them the compassionate support that they need to succeed. I also want you to know that because of you and your letter, I became a great principal who was able to impact a lot of kids' lives. Thank you so much for that. Tell me about you! How are you? Where are you? Tell me about your life.

Here is the response I received from Jamie:

OOMMGG, Mr. Parker, I do remember you! OOOMMGGG! I can't believe it's really you! Woooowwww! OMG, because of you, I'm where I am in my life. I work at the casino here as a supervisor in the reservations department. I'll be going back to college for my social work degree, and I am doing more writing because of you. OMG, it's so great to hear from you! My God, you made my night. I now have three kids: 17,16, and 7. I've told my oldest daughter about you soooooo many times. Because I knew my reading wasn't that great, I found a love in teaching myself, and I now own over 300 books that I've read more than once. I remember you telling me to take my time in everything I did and because of that, reading is one of my favorite things to do. A friend of mine wants me to finish writing a book I started. Wow! You've always been my hero. Thank you.

Biggest. Smile. Ever. And a trail of tears on my face.

I've reread Jamie's message dozens of times. It reminds me, first, that we can never know today what impact our interactions with students will have on their lives in the future. Sometimes we may take the small moments for granted and fail to recognize that they can expand into meaningful memories that shift someone's outlook on just what is possible. Second, when the pressures of school success and performance overwhelm me, Jamie's message gives just the pause I need to reflect on the reality that students are at the heart of our work. This renews my commitment to ensuring that they—the students—are the top priority in any decision I make. Lastly, the news from Jamie was highlighted by her persistence over the years to become an avid reader even when she hadn't felt confident in her reading ability early on. Way back then, this girl had some grit to let the teacher know his methods needed changing. Today, her story reminds that same teacher of the beauty of tenacity. I'm so honored to have been a small part of igniting the fortitude within her that led her to keep pushing on with self-belief and hope! She is the very picture of tenacity.

Chapter 14

What Is Tenacity?

When you've exhausted all possibilities,
remember this: You haven't.

—Thomas Edison, American Inventor

If we make it into adulthood, each of us likely has a collection of stories about setbacks and challenges. Many of us can recall that shared rite of passage that undoubtedly included obstacles, stumbles, and usually, tumbles: learning to ride a bike. I remember the mix of fear and excitement lodged deep in my belly as I watched Daddy, crescent wrench in one hand and pieces of the training wheels in another, install training wheels on my new bicycle. In my five-year-old eyes, that shiny red and white bike was huge. How intimidated I was!

The search to find a rhythm in the ride was challenging enough. My little feet tried to clamp down on metal pedals as my shoes did an awkward dance to make contact. More often than not, the pedals spun and each little foot swam in circles, unable to connect to a pedal. As my five-year-old feet slipped off the pedals and the bike wove and bobbed across the yard, my insides churned. With one of the whirls caused by my panicked oversteering, I was ready for a fall. Then, by some small amount of grit, I gripped the handlebars and calmed myself enough to avoid a crash. The unbalanced cantor of the front wheel required that I adjust my bottom, so I wiggled in the seat to steady the wheel. The mix of nausea and excitement meant I was learning a new skill. I soldiered on, but soon the scraping of the pedals that greeted the hard summer ground told me I had made another mistake. I couldn't get my balance back and soon toppled off the bike.

So, now I had a choice: dust myself off and either quit or try again. I did what lots of kids do, and what most adults encourage them to do: got up (maybe with some tears) and tried again. While successfully riding the bike on my own was the goal, this would not have been possible without practice, failure, adjustment to correct my balance or strategy, and humility. Oh, and also some downright patient parent guidance. And practice, guidance, failure, adaptation, and humility— again and again and again! Learning a new skill, process, concept, or task requires that we believe we can improve. When we try, fail, figure out what might be tweaked or adapted, and try again at any endeavor, we're getting practice in tenacity.

Academic Tenacity

Tenacity is often used interchangeably with such other words as *persistence, perseverance, determination, grit, mettle,* and even *courage.* Indeed, tenacity is an overarching concept that encompasses all of these components. Let's take a look at some common denotations of *tenacity* and these other words associated with it:

Tenacity: the quality of persistence in maintaining, adhering, or sticking to, or going after something valued; determination to keep doing what you're doing (Merriam-Webster, 2021a).

Persistence: keeping going in a course, despite interference; continuing firmly or obstinately in spite of difficulty; continuing without change of course (Merriam-Webster, 2021b).

Perseverance: going on resolutely or stubbornly in spite of obstacles; insistently and unrelentingly repeating a task or process (Merriam-Webster, 2021c). Perseverance implies strong persistence over a long period of time (Lucas & Spencer; 2018, p. 11).

Determination: acting with definite decision and firmness of purpose and willpower (Merriam-Webster, 2021d).

Mettle: capacity for meeting difficulty or challenge with fortitude and resilience (Merriam-Webster, 2021e).

Grit: firmness of mind or spirit; unyielding courage in the face of hardship or danger; courage and resolve; strength of character (Merriam-Webster, 2021f; Lexico, 2021).

Courage: mental or moral strength to venture, persevere, and withstand danger, fear, or difficulty (Merriam-Webster, 2021g).

Resilience: the ability to recoil, or jump back—a mental toughness that enables a person to recover quickly from misfortune or disadvantage (Merriam-Webster, 2021h).

These definitions are given in a general context—applying to all ventures, paths, and decisions. In this book, we're concerned primarily with *academic tenacity*. Yes, all the terms used above certainly are components of academic tenacity. But I want to zero in specifically on tenacity in the context of learning at school. Of course, we want our students to stick to a venture, to weather interference or difficulty, to have a firm spirit and strong character to keep on a course for a long time. We want them to do this in all ventures—academic or otherwise. But academic tenacity draws from these characteristics in a unique way, and its definition has some other components. The term *academic tenacity* is said to have been coined by researchers Carol Dweck, Gregory Walton, and Geoffrey Cohen (2014) as explained in their publication, *Academic Tenacity: Mindsets and Skills that Promote Long-Term Learning.*

Academic Tenacity: A Working Definition

For this book, the discussions and research presented here, and our work together as educators, I'll be speaking of tenacity in the context of *academic tenacity*. For this, I'll borrow the definition crafted by Dweck and her colleagues (2014):

> **Academic tenacity:** *the mindsets and skills that allow students to:*
> *(1) look beyond short-term concerns to longer-term or higher-order goals, and*
> *(2) withstand challenges and setbacks to persevere toward these goals.*
> *The non-cognitive factors that promote long-term learning and achievement can be brought together under the label 'academic tenacity.' At its most basic level, academic tenacity is about working hard, and working smart, for a long time.* (Dweck et al., 2014, p. 4).

I've already mentioned above that *tenacity* includes *grit.* This is a trait so key to tenacity, that I want to fold it into the definition. Angela Duckworth, who has done many studies on grit, defines it this way: Grit is *perseverance and passion for long-term goals; resolve with courage and strength of character added.*

Note that these definitions of *academic tenacity* and one of its components, *grit,* include these concepts:

Mindsets—Tenacity presumes, or certainly encompasses, the attitudes and beliefs a person holds about herself or himself. Academic tenacity would presumably then include attitudes and beliefs a person has about self as a student—about the ability to learn and achieve at a high level.

Skills—The definition shows that its authors believe academic tenacity includes a set of skills. I'll say right now that these skills are not necessarily inborn—but they can be learned and developed. Research that follows in the next chapter will affirm this.

Non-cognitive factors—Wow! Academic tenacity is not about intelligence or ability level. It has something to do with things not involving conscious reasoning or remembering.

Long-term, higher-order goals—Academic tenacity is not just about stubbornly repeating something just for the sake of holding on. It's about determination to continue following meaningful goals that are bigger (perhaps further away and more important) than immediate gratification or immediately "finishing the task." Long-term and higher-order goals are always a part of the discussion of academic tenacity.

Withstand challenges and setbacks—As with the other associated terms, academic tenacity includes the idea of resilience—carrying on in the face of obstacles or even failures.

Working hard—Ahh! Yes, all the terms and characteristics associated with academic tenacity do include this element of rigor.

Working smart—Here's something unique to the definition of *academic tenacity*; that is, it is not specifically stated (though it might be implied) in all definitions of *tenacity*. You might have noticed that the dictionary definitions of *persistence* and *perseverance* include the idea of doggedly continuing on the same course, steadfastly and repeatedly doing the same thing. Academic tenacity, on the other hand, includes the elements of strategy, creativity, adaptation, and resilience. The use of the phrase "working smart" implies that if one way to a goal isn't working, we examine why, learn from it, and try a different way. We use our experience, judgment, and insights to figure out what to do: pay attention to what is ineffective, pay attention to what is effective, amend the approach, or start over.

Hard work alone does not necessarily lead to or measure success. Academic tenacity demands an open mind and willingness to change. It demands "smartly" staying in touch with the importance and the meaning of your goal, so that you can be resilient in setbacks, changing course where needed. This is all part of succeeding in the face of challenge.

Long time—Definitions of *tenacity*, as of words associated with it, all include this attribute: the tenacious person keeps showing up, doesn't give up. The added idea of working smart makes it more possible to carry on. When you have the flexibility to change course, try a new approach, and use a different strategy—the possibility of sticking it out for the long haul is more likely!

Passion—I included the definition of grit because academic tenacity is at its most potent when it encompasses the passion for learning that is a key component of grit. In her book, *Grit: The Power of Passion and Perseverance,* Angela Duckworth (2018) is careful to define passion as enthusiasm that has endurance—not something that is there for just a brief moment. It involves a long-term interest in and enjoyment of the work you're doing—as well as a belief that the work matters.

Courage and strength of character—From the definition of *grit,* I see these as two aspects of tenacity that play a part in the academic capacity we hope to nurture and help build for our students. Being tenacious takes courage. Practice with academic tenacity builds character strength.

In the next chapter of this pillar (Chapter 15), you'll learn about the benefits of building students' academic tenacity and explore research findings of the underpinnings and effects of academic tenacity. Then Chapter 16 will focus on attitudes, practices, and strategies to teach, nurture, and sustain tenacity across your school community.

> *Perseverance is not a long race. It is many short races one after the other.*
>
> –Walter Elliot, British Naturalist, Archaeologist, Politician

As you continue through chapters 15 and 16, you will realize—not only how tenacity is a strong pillar of a brilliant school—but also how it works in partnership with the other pillars (Gratitude, Relationships, Expectations, and Achievement) to complete the solid, safe foundation for the structure that is home to all our students and staff.

Please take a minute to reread the Thomas Edison quote at the beginning of this chapter. Then reflect on Edison's observation and how it embraces the spirit, mindset, and content of the meanings of academic tenacity! And don't fail to share (and discuss) the quote with the educators and students in your school.

Chapter 15

Why Tenacity?

Let me tell you the secret that has led me to my goal. My strength lies solely in my tenacity.

—Louis Pasteur, French Chemist and Important Founder of Medical Microbiology

Any of us who have been in education for longer than a few minutes know that the measurement of intelligence leaves a lot unexplained when it comes to academic achievement. There are plenty of smart kids who don't achieve at a high level. And there are plenty of students who, with IQ scores not in the top ranges, achieve brilliantly. Here is something all of you educators have probably seen, because it happens often: A highly talented, smart student does well on a project, test, or even through weeks of a class. Then, she or he stops working—maybe after acing the test or getting an A for the quarter, or maybe because the work starts to get harder. Lots of high-achieving or gifted students don't know how to struggle or deal with something that doesn't come easily. Angela Duckworth, who has done groundbreaking research on grit, states "Being intelligent does not guarantee being hardworking or passionate" (Cited in Perkins-Gough, 2013, p. 18).

Obviously, intelligence still correlates with academic success. But it is not enough. According to many researchers, traits other than cognitive ability—such traits as tenacity and some of its component attributes—are higher predictors than intelligence of achievement and success in school and beyond. This is because someone who works hard and works smart can exceed another who has more talent but doesn't work hard and smart.

Tenacity is not about intelligence. It is a personal quality (or a set of combined qualities) that is positively associated with high achievement. A tenacious learner persists despite obstacles. This is not only about a student's tenacity getting him or her past problems; it's that tenacious learners are aware of their knowledge and level of understanding; they are tuned in to how they are working and how they are thinking. Tenacious learners recognize a need to develop and follow a strategy or change to a different one. They realize when they need help; they can ask for feedback. They have confidence that they are capable of working out a problem—even if it is giving them fits at the moment (Lucas & Spencer, 2018).

Why does tenacity matter? In an educational setting, it is deeply entwined with many aspects of each student's academic, social, and personal success or failure. Bill Lucas and Ellen Spenser (2018), both of the Centre for Real-World Learning at the University of Winchester (England), address the question of "Why does tenacity matter?" with four answers, all of which are of importance to educators:

1. Tenacity leads to higher performance.
2. Tenacity underpins social mobility.
3. Tenacity is valued across societies and cultures.
4. Tenacity is part of what it is to be employable. (p. 13).

A growing body of research examines the many facets of tenacity, its value to individuals, how it (or the lack of it) affects the school climate and the school experience of students, and what interventions or practices can influence its development in educational settings. As you review some of these findings, you'll begin to notice the interconnections among academic tenacity and the key ideas and goals of previous pillars. I believe you'll recognize the critical need for attention to tenacity as its links to achievement, expectations, relationships, and gratitude unfold through chapters 14-16.

Benefits of Academic Tenacity

When students increase in tenacity as learners, benefits abound. Here are some accomplishments, attitudes, behaviors, and characteristics that blossom as tenacity develops. Tenacious learners (in comparison to those who are less so) more likely

> *Grit predicts success over and beyond talent.*
>
> –Angela Duckworth, Researcher on Grit

- Achieve academically to their best potential.
- Believe in themselves to take on the tasks (higher academic self-efficacy).
- Demonstrate a growth mindset.
- See difficulties and setbacks as opportunities to learn rather than as signs of failure or their lack of ability.
- Can set and pursue long-term goals.
- Are willing to work hard.
- Are not looking for the easy way out.
- Use long-term self-regulation strategies to keep motivated and stay committed.
- Use self-control to avoid distractions (external and internal).
- Have coping skills to handle normal stressors.
- Keep pressing on (rather than give up) due to difficulties.
- See the value in their contributions.
- Believe that effort is worthwhile—that their persistence will get them to their goals.
- See school as relevant to their future.
- Have a sense of connectedness (belonging) at school.
- Are not afraid of self-evaluation.
- Seek input and feedback from others.
- Are open to considering new ideas and taking academic risks.
- Seek academic challenges.
- See beyond the immediate rewards to longer-term rewards.
- Are learning-oriented rather than performance-oriented.

- Stay engaged and motivated over the long term.
- Know when to quit a quest or change strategies.
  (Bashant, 2014; CDC, 2009; Duckworth, 2018; Duckworth et al., 2007; Dweck et al., 2014; Duckworth & Seligman, 2005; Education Northwest, 2015; Elmore, 2014a; Elmore, 2014b; Headden & McKay, 2015; Kaufman, 2014; Lucas & Spencer, 2018; SRI International, 2018; Wingspread, 2004).

The list above gives us an idea of the positive outcomes—gifts we can offer students when we teach and live with them in a school culture that conscientiously nurtures tenacity. Those attributes and attitudes flow from tenacity. But it's not a simple cause-effect relationship! Instead, the connection between each of the characteristics and tenacity is more of a circular current! As each grows, it, in turn, feeds and strengthens tenacity. It's more of a cause-effect-cause relationship.

Influences on Academic Tenacity

We'd like for all of our students to be academically tenacious—right? Yet speeches about working harder, staying on task, staying with a project, not giving up (i.e., being tenacious) don't necessarily work to develop tenacity in students! **The good news is that tenacity can be learned.** Yes, perhaps some of your students walk into your classrooms already armed with a good measure of tenacity. But all is not lost for the others.

Research points clearly to a path: What works is not talking longer and louder, telling kids repeatedly to "stick with it." Tenacity grows out of a schoolwide culture that models, teaches, and strengthens the many attitudes, beliefs, skills, and behaviors that make up the "personal quality" of tenacity. We must look at the many building blocks that work together to get a student to the place where the academic tenacity develops.

Here are some of the factors that researchers find most influence the development of academic tenacity:

Mindset

Earlier in this book, you read about how our minds, unconscious and conscious, affect our behavior and our expectations. We develop stories about ourselves—about who we are and what we can do. These stories can be true and thus helpful, or they may be false and harmful narratives. Students' mindsets about their academic abilities stem from these stories. Research shows that "students' belief in their ability to learn and perform well—their self-efficacy—can predict their level of academic performance above and beyond their measured level of ability and prior performance" (Bandura, 1997).

> *We are finding that the brain has more plasticity than we ever imagined.*
> –Carol Dweck,
> Mindset Researcher

Back in Chapters 12 and 13 of the Fourth Pillar: Achievement, discussions included the power of the "growth mindset" and its connection to expectations and achievement. These days, most educators have an understanding of the power of mindsets. The basic concept is that core beliefs (mindsets) can set up different patterns in the way a person responds to academic work, challenges, and setbacks (as well as to many non-academic situations).

Students with **fixed mindsets** believe that their capabilities are static—that each individual was bestowed with ability at birth and is stuck with it. Such a student may be full of doubts and embarrassment about her academic abilities and might avoid challenges (so as not to do poorly), believe that effort is not worthwhile because she can't achieve anything beyond her fixed ability, give up readily when facing setbacks, ignore or be offended by feedback that is in any way negative, and feel "less than" in the presence of others who are successful. Or a fixed mindset may lead a high achiever to believe "they've got it" and are "smarter than." This student might then also avoid taking any risks on harder tasks or seeking any feedback because he doesn't want to fall below the level of perfection he expects of himself.

With a **growth mindset**, the person believes that intelligence and other abilities can be developed with work and practice. This student is more likely to welcome challenges, believe that effort is worthwhile and will lead to meeting goals, persevere through obstacles or failures, welcome feedback from others, and not feel threatened when others do well.

Dweck's identification of the concept of growth mindset and the expanding research on mindset has given new life to the notion of academic tenacity. Near the beginning of their paper, *Academic Tenacity: Mindsets and Skills that Promote Long-Term Learning*, backed by the Gates Foundation, Carol Dweck and her fellow researchers Gregory Walton and Geoffrey Cohen (2014) state: "Students' beliefs about their academic ability influence their academic tenacity (p. 7)."

Here's how it works: students who think their ability is fixed (either at a high or low level) play safe. The students who think they have good ability want to keep proving that they are smart; they don't want to take on anything too challenging that could lead to anything but a top grade. The students who think they have lower ability certainly don't want to take on anything hard that will make them look worse than they think they already are. For both groups, their goals may focus on **proving the ability they think they have rather than improving their ability**. There is little motivation to persist in meeting challenging goals.

But, as motivation researchers Susan Headden and Sarah McKay (2015) explain, "When students know that their abilities can be developed, they seek out tougher challenges, make greater effort, persist longer at tasks, and achieve at higher levels" (p. 32).

Researchers Lisa Blackwell, Kali Trzesniewski, and Carol Dweck (2007) conducted two studies exploring theories of intelligence in adolescents' math achievement. They followed hundreds of students just entering junior high school, grade seven, and tracked their progress in math. All the students were struggling in math. A growth-mindset seminar was given to one half of the students. The other half served as a control group. Students who received a growth-mindset intervention were more motivated to learn and outperformed those with fixed mindsets. The gap continued to grow over two years.

Étienne Denoël and his research colleagues (2017) used data from PISA (the Program for International Student Assessment) to examine factors that drive the performance of students around the world. This data covered more than half a million students in 72 countries. They found students' mindsets (their beliefs and attitudes) to be twice as predictive of students' PISA scores as their home environment or demographics. Students with strong growth mindsets outperformed students with fixed mindsets. This was particularly true for students of low socioeconomic status and those from poorly performing schools. The researchers identified **academic tenacity** as a key component of a growth mindset contributing to these academic outcomes.

Mindsets can be changed; this is good news! The truth that intelligence is not static comes to us out of neuroscientific research and experience. In an article about praising students for effort (rather than ability), Carol Dweck (2007) says,

> More and more research in psychology and neuroscience supports the growth mindset. We are discovering that the brain has more plasticity than we ever imagined; that fundamental aspects of intelligence can be enhanced through learning; and that dedication and persistence in the face of obstacles are key ingredients in outstanding achievement. (p. 35).

When students are taught that their brains can grow new connections and that they can "get smarter," **and when they are taught how to do it (introduced to the skills, beliefs, attitudes, and strategies of a growth mindset),** their academic tenacity and academic experiences can change drastically. Teachers and researchers report impressive gains for students who complete various growth-mindset classes or interventions—gains in their grades and tenacity. (Blackwell et al., 2007; Dweck, 2017a; Dweck, 2017b; Dweck et al., 2014; Eccles et al., 1998; Good et al., 2003; West, 2016).

Go back and read the bold phrase in the paragraph above. Just explaining to students that they can get smarter—just getting them to understand that ability is not static—is great! But it is not enough to produce academic tenacity or raise achievement. Once students understand that they **can** "get smarter," we have to take the next steps. We have to show them how to do it and work with them as they learn **and practice** habits and strategies for getting smarter!

> *Just explaining to students that they can get smarter—that their abilities are not static—is not enough to produce tenacity or raise achievement . . . we have to show them how to do it.*

In an article titled, "Mindsets Matter—But That's Only Half the Story," James Anderson (2018a), author of *The Mindset Continuum,* puts it this way: "The strategies that work best do not focus on teaching **about** a growth mindset. Rather, they focus on teaching **for** a growth mindset" (para.9).

Anderson goes on to explain that students must be taught strategies "to overcome what they are stuck on" (para.8). Students can put a lot of time and energy into something and can be praised for their effort. But if their energies are spent in ways that are ineffective in reaching goals—they'll just sink deeper into a fixed mindset. So, along with telling kids that their brains can rewire themselves and develop new skills—teach them the strategies of trying to tackle difficulties, learning from mistakes, and correcting the mistakes. Anderson notes that many have "lost sight of growth" (2018b, para. 7). We tell students to change the thought "I can't do this" to "I can't do this—*yet!*" This is a good thing. But we must help students identify what the "yet" implies—what they can do to achieve the goal.

The gains in achievement connected to mindset come with time and clear teaching of how to build their self-efficacy. These gains take accumulated experiences of success and competence. This is the path for the growth of academic tenacity. Self-efficacy is at the heart of tenacity. The factors below are all partners in that journey.

> *Academic self-efficacy is at the heart of academic tenacity.*

Self-Efficacy and Self-Regulation

Over and over, research links tenacity to self-efficacy and self-regulation. Both of these abilities are driving forces in tenacity (Bandura, 1997; Duckworth, 2011; Duckworth & Kern, 2011; Duckworth & Seligman, 2005; Dweck et al., 2014; Farrington et al., 2012; Lucas & Spencer, 2018).

Self-efficacy is one's belief in his or her ability to reach a goal or achieve something. The greater one's self-efficacy, the greater is that person's confidence that she or he can exert control over her or his behavior, motivation, and social environment to attain these goals.

Self-regulation is knowing how to manage one's thoughts, emotions, and behaviors acceptably in a variety of settings and situations. This involves stress management, self-motivation, self-discipline, delaying gratification, and setting and working toward goals. Self-regulatory skills also allow students to rise above immediate distractions and to plan their behavior to help them reach their goals.

Both of these traits (with their many components) work together as part of the foundation for academic tenacity. Programs that work at increasing students' sense of control and capacity as learners, that teach strategies for managing stress, and that practice managing anxiety and negative thoughts yield results of greater tenacity and higher test scores (Villares et al., 2011; Lemberger & Clemens, 2012).

Belonging at school is one of the most protective factors against every form of adolescent risk and distress.

It makes sense that skills of self-regulation would be critical in academic tenacity. Our students these days live in a maelstrom of distractions! Beyond the anxieties and busyness of their school and out-of-school social environments, they have a host of interruptions from electronic devices. There is so much more for them to put aside in the short term to work for long-term goals.

Belonging

Part of tenacity is weathering, getting around, or rising above difficulties and distractions to persist at long-term goals. When a student is consumed with feelings of isolation, exclusion, or inferiority, it's difficult to focus on anything. According to researchers Carol Dweck, Gregory Walton, and Geoffrey Cohen (2014), "an important predictor of academic tenacity is students' feelings of social belonging in school . . ." (p. 11). Simply put, a student who feels little sense of belonging will have little energy for academic tenacity.

When students feel that they belong, emotionally and socially, they are less fearful about their academic performance, and they have less stress, in general, at school (Kaufman, 2014). In a meta-analysis of 82 studies between 2000 and 2018, researchers found positive correlations between school belonging and such social, emotional, and academic outcomes as goal orientation, self-efficacy, engagement, and higher achievement (Korpershoek et al., 2020).

In a national study of over 12,000 adolescents, "students' belonging in school emerged as one of the two most powerful protective factors against every measured form of adolescent risk and distress" (Cook et al., 2012). (The other factor was family connectedness.) Many other research studies show that a strong sense of belonging is a powerful force to help students with long-term motivation and success in school. This is true for all students but is particularly true for adolescents and other students in low-performing schools, low socioeconomic backgrounds, or groups that are often marginalized (Cohen & Garcia, 2008; Cohen & Sherman, 2014; Furrer & Skinner, 2003; Goodenow, 1991; Walton & Cohen, 2007; Walton & Cohen, 2011).

All the outcomes of increased belonging mentioned above—goal orientation, self-efficacy, engagement, achievement, motivation, less stress, and fear—enable students to be more committed to and more tenacious in their work. Researchers have tried belonging interventions using such practices as helping students understand that worry about social belonging is normal, asking students to write essays about their personal belonging experiences, and having students examine their values in light of how school could play a part in helping them achieve what was most important to them. These interventions had the positive results of greater initiative in the classroom, better grades, and taking more advantage of learning opportunities (Kaufman, 2014).

Relationships and Social Skills

Closely associated with belonging is the presence and quality of relationships a student experiences in school. As is true with emotional skills, social skills strongly influence academic tenacity. These skills include the ability to take the perspective of others, feel and show empathy, value others and show respect and care, welcome and appreciate differences, and empathize with others. They also include the ability to establish and sustain meaningful, positive relationships and show skills of clear communication, conflict resolution, cooperation, listening, mutual support, and avoidance of negative pressure. Giving students opportunities to engage with others, share their opinions and seek ideas from others, and practice a variety of other social skills—all these actions help them to build tenacity (Lucas & Spencer, 2018).

The Second Pillar of a brilliant school focused on relationships in the school, showing multiple research-supported benefits of trusting, high-quality relationships between students and teachers (and other school staff members) and among students. If you look back at Chapters 5 and 6, you'll notice that among the research-backed benefits to students are such factors as increased academic resilience and tenacity; higher levels of motivation and engagement; greater student sense of belonging; enhanced autonomy, self-direction, and self-confidence; less isolation, stress and depression; overall satisfaction with school; and better academic performance. Now think about the components of tenacity (such things as engagement, self-motivation, ability to work hard for long-term goals, ability to see obstacles or difficulties as learning opportunities, etc.)! When you make these connections, you'll understand why many researchers find that students who have better relationships with teachers and peers are more likely to develop academic tenacity. Indeed, it is hard to build academic tenacity at all in the absence of secure, trusting relationships.

Long-Term and Higher-Order Goals

In 2018 SRI International (an American nonprofit scientific research institute formerly known as the Stanford Research Institute) released a research brief, *Promoting Grit, Tenacity, and Perseverance: Critical Factors for Success in the 21st Century*. The research identified one of the major aspects of a learning environment that promotes grit, tenacity, and perseverance as this: "students need to have the opportunity to take on worthwhile long-term or higher-order goals" (p. 31).

These goals should be

- Relevant to the student's life and interests. (The goal has intrinsic value; the student will get some enjoyment from pursuing it.) (SRI, p. 33).

- Worthwhile. (It is important to the individual to reach the goal). (SRI, p. 33).
- Optimally challenging. (Goals require work and persistence to achieve, but do not overwhelm or seem impossible.) (SRI, p. 33).
- Centered around tasks that relate to other current and future goals. (The pursuit and tasks will help the student with something needed now and will also contribute toward something desired in the future.) (SRI, p. 33).
- Realistic. (The goal is something the student can believe she or he can achieve in the time allotted.) (SRI, p. 33; Dweck et al., 2014, p. 10).

Students are more likely to strive toward a goal when it meets these criteria. According to researchers Carol Dweck, Gregory Walton, and Geoffrey Cohen (2014):

Even when the school environment promotes goals for learning and provides opportunities for cooperation, students still may think, 'What's the point?' That is, students may not enthusiastically seek to learn or grow their intelligence if they do not see learning as serving a purpose that means something to them. Students' higher-order or long-term goals—or purposes—contribute to their engagement and tenacity. This is because students who are working with purpose feel that they are learning so that they can become the kind of person they would like to be and contribute something of value to the world. They are not simply memorizing material (that they will soon forget) to pass a test. (p. 10).

Numerous other research studies have linked students' higher-order or long-term goals to their academic tenacity (Damon, 2008; Kaplan & Flum, 2009; McKnight & Kashdan, 2009). In one study examining the many facets of goals of students, researchers found that a group of

> *When it comes to equity in education, developing academic tenacity has the potential to go a long way toward closing achievement and outcome gaps.*
>
> –Shannon Davidson, Researcher, Education Northwest

African American eighth-grade students who began to focus on their long-term aims (aims that they understood would be related to schoolwork) showed significant benefits in the form of higher grades, better standardized test scores, and higher ratings in tenacity (as observed by their teachers (Oyserman, Gant, & Ager, 1995).

We can't expect students to be tenacious on goals that do not have worth, meaning, or personal value. (Yet, unfortunately, educators often keep doing just that!)

Rigorous and Supportive Learning Environment

The previous section (on goals) described **one** aspect of a learning environment that promotes grit, tenacity, and perseverance that was identified by the SRI researchers (2018)—higher-order and long-term goals. The second identified aspect—**interdependent with the first**—is this: "they (students) need a rigorous and supportive learning environment to help them pursue these goals" (p. 31).

According to the SRI report, "a rigorous and supportive learning environment" has these qualities and principles:

- **Care and respect:** Students will persist more when they perceive that they are treated fairly and with respect and adults show they care about them.
- **High expectations; high standards:** Students will persist more when teachers, administrators, and others in the school environment have high expectations for their success and hold them to high standards. These expectations can be conveyed explicitly or implicitly.

- **Caring, positive academic help:** When remedial support is necessary, it is provided in ways that do not feel punitive or interfere with opportunities to engage in other interest-driven activities.
- **Teaching of learning strategies and tactics:** Provide students with opportunities to develop clarity about what their goals are, why they are important to them, and what they will to face challenges; develop general study skills to deal with cognitive demands; building a robust set of cognitive and emotional skills for success; develop content-specific metacognitive skills.

> *Helping students cultivate positive academic mindsets and effective learning strategies are the best ways to foster academic perseverance.*
>
> –University of Chicago Consortium on School Research

- **Thoughtful evaluation:** Evaluation of student performance should be carefully designed not to undermine perceptions of competence and future expectations.
- **Wise, meaningful feedback:** Rather than indiscriminately meting out unearned praise, those giving feedback should base it on clearly defined criteria, provide specific and useful comments, and ensure that students have opportunities to demonstrate competence in different ways.
- **Intrinsic, not extrinsic motivation:** "Extrinsic rewards and punishments that undermine intrinsic motivation should be avoided. (Direct quotations as cited in SRI, 2018, p. 35 and 67-69.)

In other words, to gain academic tenacity, students need excellent teaching and the best possible resources. They need mentoring, guidance, scaffolding, practice, good feedback, and specific strategies for all the aspects of tenacity. We need to teach them **how** to set goals, break tasks into small chunks, work toward goals, evaluate their progress and processes, meet and deal with challenges. We must teach them specific tactics to handle setbacks. We need to guarantee that every student has repeated experiences with feeling competent—with reaching goals successfully. **Students who don't have broad instructional, relational, and cognitive support will not be able to build academic tenacity.** Students who are not inspired or allowed to pursue relevant and worthwhile goals will not have a chance or motivation to tenaciously strive for them.

We must be careful not to press for tenacity without high-quality goals and superb support. Just as kids vary in their readiness for learning to ride a bike, they vary in their readiness and confidence to take on risks and challenges. If students are not ready or supported adequately, they are less likely to work hard or know how to work smart over a long period of time. It's up to the adult to attend to each student's readiness, and give the

> *Students who don't have broad instructional, relational, and cognitive support will not be able to build academic tenacity.*

right amount of support in building skills and confidence—just as you would support them a little or a lot as they mount, tip, and tumble from the bike. Don't push a student to be tenacious until you've helped her or him gain intrinsic investment in learning.

In her article, "How to Foster Grit, Tenacity, and Perseverance: An Educator's Guide," Tina Barseghian (2013), editor of *Mindshift*, explores "the dark side of grit." She says:

> Persevering in the face of challenges or setbacks to accomplish goals that are extrinsically motivated, unimportant to the student, or in some way inappropriate for the student can

potentially induce stress, anxiety, and distraction, and have detrimental impacts on students' long-term retention, conceptual learning, and psychological well-being.

As grit becomes a more popular notion in education, there is a risk that poorly informed educators or parents could misuse the idea and introduce what psychologists call the "fundamental attribution error"—the tendency to overvalue personality-based explanations for observed behaviors and undervalue situational explanations. In other words, there is a risk that individuals could over-attribute students' poor performance to a lack of "grittiness" (or tenacity) without considering that critical supports are lacking in the environment.

The University of Chicago's Consortium on School Research has examined the role of noncognitive factors in shaping school performance. They found these five categories of noncognitive factors associated with academic performance:

1. Academic behaviors (going to class, doing homework, organizing materials, participating, studying).
2. Perseverance (tenacity, grit, delayed gratification, self-discipline, self-control).
3. Mindsets (sense of belonging, belief in one's ability to grow and succeed with effort, belief in the value of academic work).
4. Learning strategies (study skills, metacognitive strategies, self-regulated learning, goal setting).
5. Social skills (interpersonal skills, cooperating, empathy). (Farrington et al., 2012, pp. 1-2).

In their investigation of what fosters these factors, the University of Chicago researchers note that "Students with poor academic behaviors or a lack of perseverance (tenacity) may be misperceived as students who are not motivated or students who do not care, when in fact they lack strategies or mindsets that would help them learn" (Farrington et al., 2012, p. 3). They conclude that students are more likely to show tenacity if the learning context helps them learn these (growth mindsets and learning strategies) along with self-regulatory skills and metacognitive skills. To increase academic tenacity and improve academic behavior, they emphasize that each student must be able to say and believe

- *I belong in this academic community.*
- *My ability and competence grow with effort.*
- *I can succeed at this.*
- *This work has value for me.* (Farrington et al., 2012).

> ***Gratitude practice unshackles people from toxic emotions, such as self-doubt, resentment, and envy.***
>
> –Joshua Brown and Joel Wong, of the *Greater Good Magazine*

Note that this reaffirms the point that Barseghian made in her statements (above)—**if kids are not showing tenacity, don't assume it's because they don't want to learn, grow, succeed or even work hard**. It may be that they have not been given the right tools. And even a growth mindset is not enough, without the classroom instruction that teaches them learning strategies.

But when all the elements are there—the mindset, the instruction, the ongoing support, the positive environment, and the strategies—wow! It's wonderful to see. Just realize that, while we may be excited to see tenacity grow, our joy will not be nearly at the level or have nearly the power as the students' excitement.

Gratitude

The regular practice of gratitude fuels tenacity. It helps people to keep going through tough times, allowing them to see possibilities for healing and reaching goals in the future—enabling them to believe that they will "make it." Gratitude is about noticing and appreciating what is meaningful and valuable to yourself and **in** yourself. So it makes sense that gratitude would contribute to tenacity: you're more likely to work long, hard, and smart for something that has value and meaning (Lucas & Spenser, 2018; Sansone & Sansone, 2010).

Neuroscientist Glenn Fox has dedicated his life to studying gratitude. He put his research to practical use to help him manage and recover from grief during the long illness of his mother and after her death. His mother's gratitude practice had a profound effect on the quality of her remaining life, and his gratitude practices were therapeutic for him. He knew from his research that grateful people have greater tenacity—handling difficulties better and recovering faster from trauma, illness, injury, and other setbacks. But his own experience of that gratitude-supported tenacity made all the knowledge deeply personal. As you learned from the First Pillar of this book, gratitude, practiced regularly, actually changes the brain. Fox says, "It's a regular practice that shores up our reserves and changes how we perceive the bad times." (Cited in Tung, 2019).

Obstacles to Academic Tenacity

Some obstacles to developing tenacity have been mentioned or inferred above and in previous chapters: fixed mindset; lack of self-regulatory skills and practices; experiences of not belonging; the absence of trusting, supportive relationships; poor social skills; goals that are irrelevant, unrealistic, unchallenging, or not meaningful; bias; stereotype threat; and lack of any number of kinds of support needed (support such as good instruction, learning strategies, caring personal remediation, quality resources—both material and human, etc.).

In addition, we all can identify, acknowledge, and relate to these impediments that threaten our students' tenacity noted by Tim Elmore (2014b), CEO of Founder of Growing Leaders and international speaker:

- These days, in this society, we make life convenient for kids.

- Many adults work to remove or minimize difficulties. They do too much "saving the day."
- Media (everything from TV to social media to Internet sites and videos) gives kids a false idea of what it takes to achieve. Often the great achievements are shown—but not the work, the many setbacks, the time, the practice, the tenacity.
- Kids can find anything they want to "know" in an instant with Google. They don't have to struggle with research or with figuring things out.

There are other impediments to developing tenacity, perhaps even more difficult to surmount than those already mentioned. These are such obstacles as

- Family trauma
- Social alienation
- Racism
- Family mobility
- Dangerous neighborhoods
- Poverty

> *Many of life's failures are people who did not realize how close they were to success when they gave up.*
>
> –Thomas Edison, American Inventor

Even with the toughest of roadblocks, we educators need to draw on all our creativity, resources, skills, and care to identify and work on those we can affect.

Back in Chapter 13, I admitted that for much of my school life I labeled myself as bad at math. Setbacks in many math classes had multiplied over the years; I attributed these struggles, poor grades, and gaps in understanding to my limited ability. Talk about a fixed mindset! When it came to math, I had it in spades. The list of failures or near-failures, combined with my belief that the lack of understanding was inherent, dampened any possibility of success I could have in math. I was just plain convinced that I had no math ability; I could not do it.

Any shreds of confidence evaporated as math became more complex. Tenacity in math studies? I had none. I couldn't even risk trying. It was different in my high school English or History classes. There, I wasn't wracked by self-sabotaging thoughts in the presence of a challenging text or task. I could push myself and work long and hard because I believed I could succeed there. There, I could exercise my tenacity muscle.

Enter, Coach Rivers. Through the entire class that preceded algebra, the anxiety would build. My stomach would turn in fits of nausea in anticipation of the math class. But this algebra teacher had me figured out. He may not have had the terms *fixed mindset* and *growth mindset* in his vocabulary. But he certainly lived, breathed, and shared a growth mindset. He scheduled those one-on-one sessions with me and gradually added mindset work to the math remediation. Covertly, he chipped away at my mathematics fixed mindset while he presented math concepts in small chunks that led me to little successes. I slowly gained experience with competence. Without knowing exactly what was happening, I began to become more tenacious in my approach to math. I was able to stick with it for longer periods to work on problems. When I stumbled, he helped me reflect on my error, figure out what went wrong, or try a different approach.

Little by little, Coach challenged me more, but with plenty of what we now call "scaffolding" and support. He kept adding to my repertoire of skills and tools to tackle evermore difficult problems. I began to accumulate more successes and feel the joy and hope that accompanied them. His confidence in my progress led him to show me that I could rejoin with other students to continue the work on problems. One day I realized that I was beginning to become one of those math students that I secretly envied; I was belonging to a cohort of kids and a learning environment that I'd never envisioned I could be part of. And this felt great!

As I've learned about tenacity and the influences that help it develop, I now realize that Coach Rivers knew plenty about it and what to do to build it in students—even if *academic tenacity* wasn't the latest educational buzzword in his world at the time. He knew to use the tools of mindset, self-efficacy, scaffolding, teaching specific strategies, challenge, relationships, relevance, and belonging (all now proven to be influences on tenacity) to change me from a math phobic to a kid who felt like a real math student. Thank you, Coach Rivers. I am forever grateful and far more tenacious around challenges.

Chapter 16

How Do G.R.E.A.T. Leaders Get Results with Tenacity?

It's not that I'm so smart. It's just that I stay with problems longer.
—Albert Einstein, German Physicist, Nobel Prize Winner, Author of *Theory of Relativity*

The definition of *tenacity* that I used back in Chapter 14 (borrowed from researchers Carol Dweck, Gregory Walton, and Geoffrey Cohen) referred to academic tenacity as a group of non-cognitive factors. Most discussions of tenacity in an academic setting identify tenacity as "non-cognitive." However, before suggesting ideas of ways to get results in developing academic tenacity (or more of it) in your school, I want to offer a caution: We can step into a bit of a morass when we make too-sharp distinctions between *cognitive* and *non-cognitive* factors in our work in a learning setting. I won't get into a detailed look at the

> *The most difficult thing is the decision to act. The rest is mere tenacity.*
> —Amelia Earhart, American Aviator

discussions/arguments on this here, but I will remind all readers that these two kinds of "ingredients" are rarely separate. Cognitive and non-cognitive factors are intertwined tightly and with much complexity. They both influence and are influenced by one another. This is very much true of each component of tenacity and its relationship to academic performance and academic processes.

The research cited in Chapter 15, as well as the everyday experiences of many educators, gives us clues about how to move ahead with addressing academic tenacity. Based on that research, here are some suggestions for administrators and other leaders. These attitudes and practices get proven results! There are ways—big and small—to promote all the facets of academic tenacity for all students. I hope you'll understand that these ideas can be adapted to fit your purposes. I invite you to think about ways to implement these experiences with your teams, parents, students, and staff. Brilliant schools use such strategies to jumpstart the year, and then develop them into powerful habits throughout the year.

Keep These Discoveries in Mind

- Students who understand the concept of a growth mindset and are shown how to gain it are more academically tenacious.
- Students' self-beliefs about their academic abilities are foundational to the possibility of building tenacity.
- Teachers, as well as students, must believe that each student can learn tenacity.
- The factors of self-regulation are essential to tenacity.
- The more a student feels a sense of belonging to the class and school, the more readily she or he will be able to grow in tenacity.
- Healthy, trusting, caring relationships—with teachers and with peers—are essential to tenacity.
- Students are not likely to put forth long-term, passionate, risk-taking work (i.e., tenacity) unless the experiences/activities of their learning are relevant, worthwhile, and realistic.

- Tenacity is fueled by realistic long-term goals—along with training on how to achieve them and plans to work toward them.
- Tenacity grows in the context of high standards and challenging ventures.
- Tenacity cannot grow without a planned, rigorous, respectful, expertly delivered support system of instruction, interventions, and evaluation/feedback.
- Students need to be taught learning strategies specific to all facets of tenacity.
- Intrinsic motivation is a partner with tenacity.
- Being aware of obstacles to tenacity enables us to address those we can control.
- Gratitude fuels tenacity.

Start with These Steps

Start talking about tenacity. Start conversations across the school community. Talk with students about the factors that make up tenacity—such things as persistence, grit, resilience (rising above setbacks), attitudes and beliefs you hold about yourself, your passions as a student, long-term goals, working hard, working smart, and courage.

- Talk with staff and students about academic tenacity. Define the term. Look at the attitudes and actions that are explicit and implied in the definition of tenacity. (Refer back to Chapter 14). Engage them in sharing (in discussions or writing) examples they've seen and experiences they have had with any of those factors that are part of tenacity. Underscore ways that tenacity is about more than just working hard. Get them brainstorming about the difference between working hard and working smart.

- Emphasize to staff and students how valuable this trait is for academic success. Talk about the power of attitude and persistence.

Include tenacity in your professional development plans. Make sure all the adults in the school understand the nuances and components of tenacity. Emphasize the absolute necessity of believing that every student can develop this tool. Commit the leadership and staff to make plans for teaching tenacity throughout the school. You've just read a chapter of research findings on tenacity. Share these with your teachers. Track down some of the articles to read together. Be sure to point out the positive outcomes of tenacity listed in Chapter 15.

Brains are like rubber bands— they are most useful when they are stretched.

Review, repeat, and strengthen information about mindset. If your school has not focused on this, get your staff up to speed on the concept of growth mindset and its powerful impact on students. (Don't forget to review the negative impact of fixed mindsets.) Ask staff members to do personal checks on their mindsets—about their abilities and the possibilities for **all** the students.

Start (or keep) talking with students about mindset. Help kids understand how their brains can flex and grow (somewhat like plastic). Teach them the meaning of *neuroplasticity*. Help them learn about a *neuroplasticity* and *growth mindset*—and how their brains grow new neural connections and "get smarter" when they are challenged. Tell students that this continues to happen as they work hard and use learning strategies to handle tasks that stretch their brains. You can tell them: their brains are like rubber bands—they are most useful when they are stretched.

Plan for mindset instruction and get it rolling. Talking about mindset is important. But the discussion must be followed with teaching and practice. Set goals for instruction/intervention across the grades, offering strategies that help students internalize the truth about growth mindset and repeatedly practicing the strategies. Identify grade-level materials so students can read about neuroplasticity and mindset in language they can understand. Trust the students to digest, understand, and discuss the research. Find and share some articles, books, or posters about this concept. Provide grade-level materials so students can read, understand, and discuss some of the research. You can visit the website MindsetWorks.com to learn about Carol Dweck's programs for schools and parents, or find a variety of books, posters, and programs at online sites where teachers share ideas and materials.

In her article, "The Perils and Promises of Praise," Carol Dweck (2007) describes a mindset intervention that she and her colleague Lisa Blackwell did in an urban junior high school where many students were struggling with the transition from elementary school, showing disengagement and grades on a downslide. They offered an eight-week workshop to students divided into two groups. Both groups were taught study skills, time management strategies, and memory strategies. But the intervention group was also taught about how their brains worked and **what they could do to make their intelligence grow** (Blackwell et al., 2007). Students were taught that the brain is like a muscle that can get stronger. They learned about the brain making new neural connections. Here are comments from some of the students:

- *You mean I don't have to be dumb?*
- *If you do not give up and you keep studying, you can find your way through.*
- *I can actually picture the neurons growing bigger as they make more connections.* (Dweck, 2007, pp. 37-39).

Not only were students in this group riveted by what they learned, but students with this training showed significant improvement in their grades. (In comparison, students in the control group continued to show declining performance, even with the study skills training.) Dweck and other researchers have found similar results in other schools with students at varying levels. I recommend that you read this entire article. It would be good reading/discussion material for your students too—maybe as low as fourth grade. You can find it in the reference list for the Fifth Pillar (Tenacity) at the end of this book (under Dweck, 2007).

"When students believe they can develop their intelligence, they focus on doing just that," writes Dweck (2007), "Not worrying about how smart they will appear, they take on challenges and stick to them" (p. 34). She goes on to say that students who believe they can develop their intellectual ability through hard work and education "don't necessarily believe that anyone can become an Einstein or a Mozart, (but) they do understand that even Einstein and Mozart had to put in years of effort to become who they were" (p. 34).

Revisit the benefits of and strategies for building gratitude, quality relationships, high expectations, and greater achievement. Previous chapters in the First, Second, Third, and Fourth Pillars address these key foundations of a brilliant school. **Each one of these factors influences the development of academic tenacity.** So, you might scan through earlier chapters again to double-check the status of your work in those areas. Remind teachers that their already-in-progress work on these pillars will benefit students trying to expand their tenacity.

Model belief in tenacity and the practice of tenacity. As a leader, or teacher, attend to your own tenacity. Reread the characteristics of tenacious learners near the beginning of Chapter 15. Do these describe you in your work? Do you live and demonstrate tenacity to those who watch you? And do your actions show that you believe all your fellow staff members and all your students can develop tenacity? Can you spot and affirm examples of tenacity in the work of your colleagues?

Model a growth mindset and belief in neuroplasticity. Revisit the sections that address these topics in chapter 15 of this pillar (as well as chapters 12 and 13 of the Fourth Pillar). Does the definition of a growth mindset fit you? Would your colleagues and students say that you have and live a growth mindset? Do you believe (and act on the belief) that

all students (and adults) in your school **can** "get smarter"—that they can develop and apply a growth mindset? Make sure this shows to everyone around you. Your growth mindset can inspire others' belief and hope in the possibilities that flow from a growth mindset. If you are a school leader, lead the way in spreading the belief in the possibility of academic growth for everyone. It's a major way you set the groundwork for tenacity.

Include These Attitudes and Actions Throughout the Year

Establish a safe environment for tenacity. We want to ask students to work hard and work smart on long-term goals. We want them to grow to a place where they can embrace setbacks, learn from them, and keep going. But all these actions that are part of academic tenacity won't happen unless students are in an environment where they are respected and treated fairly. They must know that teachers and others around them will "show up" to be their supporters and advocates. They need to feel protected from threats and bias. This means attending to the relationships built in the school, expectations for behavior, proactive and effective classroom management, and follow-through with our goals of a safe setting.

> *Quitting wrinkles the soul.*
>
> –Douglas MacArthur, American World War II General

Intentionally work to strengthen academic self-efficacy. Along with growth mindsets, this component of tenacity is one with the most power to propel tenacity forward (or in its absence, derail tenacity). Make self-efficacy for every student a priority. Yes, teaching students that their brains can get smarter is a start. But there is more to building students' belief that **they can do** academic tasks and attain certain levels or goals. We must see to it that they DO achieve goals. Plan with your teaching staff for practices that allow every student to experience competence every day in every class. Get into habits of breaking challenges into small steps so kids can feel the satisfaction of having wins under their belts. No child should go home on any school day without having had some credible academic success. (By credible, I mean something that the student KNOWS is an accomplishment—not just having done something easy.) Other practices detailed in this chapter will contribute to this.

Identify impediments to tenacity in your context. As we work to build any of the foundational pillars for a brilliant school, we must acknowledge that obstacles will challenge our work. As you move forward with plans to increase academic tenacity, take some time to identify those factors. They may be attitudes, biases, fears, lack of resources, instructional trends, community characteristics, demographics. Try to get a handle on what obstacles are present in your situation, so that they won't surprise you in your efforts. Once you identify obstacles, you'll be able to take stock of which ones you have the power and capability to combat (or work around or embrace) and those that are out of your control.

Set the bar high for everyone. High expectations and challenging goals—these values have shown up before in this book. We know that they are critical to raising achievement and developing successful learners. Again, they are on the list in this pillar; **high expectations and challenging goals have powerful influences on the teaching and growth of tenacity.** Continue to work to embed these into all classes and ingrain them into the culture of the whole school. When I say everyone—here is another chance for the adults in the school (leaders, teachers, support staff) to model for each other, students, and parents that these are non-negotiable practices in your school. With respect, care, and support, hold each other to high expectations and honor each other with challenges that will help develop tenacity.

Boost Belonging. You've seen that a student who feels a sense of belonging in her classes and school is more likely to be tenacious in her learning processes and goals. When we consider what tenacity is—

working hard and smart for a long time, withstanding challenges and setbacks, and persevering for/toward long-term goals—it makes sense that the odds would be against tenacity for a kid who is constantly worried about whether she or he is accepted, valued, or "fits in" with the class and school. Make belonging a focus in your school and every class, at every grade level, every day. Here are some of the circumstances and practices that help to boost belonging for all students:

- A safe environment that continually communicates safety, trust, equality, worth, and inclusion for everyone; effective classroom management to guarantee these conditions (and effective management in other places—playgrounds, buses, halls, cafeterias, etc.)
- Clearly communicated behavioral expectations enforced equitably
- Strong, respectful, and caring teacher-student relationships
- Intentional teaching of social skills needed for quality peer-to-peer relationships
- Experiences of self-efficacy and autonomy
- Teaching goal setting (and goal accomplishment) skills and processes
- Zero tolerance for stereotyping, exclusion, or harassment of any kind
- Teaching strategies for self-management and for coping with various emotion-laden situations
- Teaching and practicing learning strategies applicable to many school situations
- Regular inclusion of collaborative group work in the context of a well-managed group work process; for solving problems, making decisions, completing academic tasks, or planning or evaluating nonacademic procedures

- Many opportunities for students to speak their ideas, opinions, and thought processes—along with opportunities to listen and respond to others'
- Training in specific, kind, and helpful feedback (giving and receiving it)
- Talking about belonging

Be honest about the struggles encompassed by tenacity. Many people think of tenacity in terms of just having the will to grit your teeth, bear down, and **do it**! But tenacity (academic or otherwise) is not that simple. As I imagine you are beginning to see—even from the definition of it back in Chapter 14—the trait of *academic tenacity* is complex. And it has plenty of emotions and glitches involved in its execution! Hold conversations about these facets of the tenacity efforts.

> *Success is the ability to go from one failure to another with no loss of enthusiasm.*
>
> –Winston Churchill, Prime Minister of the United Kingdom during WW II

For example, let students know that you know that practice is not easy. Sometimes they will find it boring. Sometimes they'll make mistakes or misunderstand something. When this happens, they can say, "I knew this would be part of the process" because they've been taught to expect it. Talk about how a goal might be exciting at first, and you're all jazzed to get started. Gathering materials might be exciting, but then you have to actually get to work. Sometimes that drags you down a bit!

Persisting at something—working hard toward a goal—includes struggle. Identify and talk about these struggles. Share actual experiences with each other. Talk about the emotions involved in working toward a goal. Name them. Identify the obstacles that may come up as you work. What gets in the way of your tenacity? OR what might get in the way? When you are open about the hard stuff, and when students get a chance to share their emotional experiences that are part of the process of working toward a goal, they'll know that struggle is normal and that they are not alone.

> *The next mile is the only one a person really has to make.*
>
> –A Danish Fur Trapper's Principle

Talk with students about failure and what to do about it. Get their ideas. Ask for ideas about what they can do instead of being afraid of failing and giving up. Let them brainstorm about how a student could readjust strategies in a situation rather than giving up. Ask for their ideas about how they can support and encourage each other through setbacks. Arm them with strategies for getting around obstacles. Repeat—again and again, that failure is a part of getting better. No one succeeds without a lot of failures.

Teach them that it's okay to take minor steps. Pass on this mantra to students: "I may not be there yet. "But I'm closer than I was yesterday."

You hear a lot about helping kids identify and emphasize their strengths. In developing tenacity, it's most helpful to discuss strengths **concerning the task at hand**. This helps when they're discouraged. Ask a student to think about and name a strength that she already has (or something she already knows or can do) that will help with the problem or assignment in front of her. Once that ability is identified, have her get started so she can see that it's true—she does have the ability to do that part! That removes an obstacle and gets the tenacity rolling. It's more effective to assure a student of his strengths when he can put them to use right away than to assure him generally that he has a lot of strengths or ask him to name his strengths in the absence of a situation for applying them.

It would be rare to find a student who does not encounter some sort of struggle in her or his school life. They all have situations in which they feel uncomfortable, disappointed, scared, or helpless. Let them know that, though they can't control some circumstances at school or in their lives or the attitudes and behaviors of others—they still have some control, some power. Remind them to be tuned in to **what they can control**. Their mindset is one of their great sources of power. No one can take that away from them. Suggest that they use this trick: whenever they start to feel the weight or challenge of a situation or task—they should stop and think, "What can I control in this situation?" When they act on that, they will feel less overwhelmed or helpless.

Strengthen SEL Skills. You've seen that self-regulation (or lack thereof) has a major influence on tenacity (or lack thereof). The same is true of social skills. See that students at all levels have intentional instruction in social and emotional skills (mini-lessons, or SEL skills embedded into content) regularly. In addition, see that the schoolwide practices and policies further the skills. The Collaborative for Academic, Social, and Emotional Learning (CASEL, 2020a) defines social and emotional learning (SEL) this way:

> Social and emotional learning (SEL) is an integral part of education and human development. SEL is the process through which all young people and adults acquire and apply the knowledge, skills, and attitudes to develop healthy identities, manage emotions and achieve personal and collective goals, feel and show empathy for others, establish and maintain supportive relationships, and make responsible and caring decisions.
>
> SEL advances educational equity and excellence through authentic school-family-community partnerships to establish learning environments and experiences that feature trusting and collaborative relationships, rigorous and meaningful curriculum and instruction, and ongoing evaluation. SEL can help address various forms of inequity and empower young people and adults to co-create thriving schools and contribute to safe, healthy, just communities. (para. 3-4).

In addition to the definition of SEL, CASEL (2020b) identifies five broad (and interconnected) areas of core competence. CASEL's framework of SEL competencies includes

1. Self-awareness
2. Self-management
3. Social awareness
4. Relationship skills
5. Responsible decision-making

Classes should regularly offer strategies and practice in skills related to these competencies. Teachers can plan mini-lessons or discussions to teach and practice a skill or can imbed the concepts and practices within content areas. Much of the time, teaching SEL skills does not have to be an added lesson; so many of the skills are intrinsic to ongoing academic processes and procedures of the classroom. See CASEL's website for specific skills within the above competency categories. Use the links from the website (casel.org) to download the complete competency framework. Note that any of the capabilities listed there are topics for teaching students of all ages.

Broaden Use of True Cooperative Learning. Cooperative group work is a means of teaching and strengthening both self-regulatory skills and social-relationship skills. This is any task in which two or more students work together, equally contributing to meet the goals of the group. Cooperative learning is **interdependent**—all students work together to maximize their own learning and each other's learning. The success of the group depends on the successful contribution of each member. Well-planned and well-managed cooperative group work also contributes heartily to the blossoming of belonging. Furthermore, it is a great booster for tenacity.

The phrase *positive interdependence* is used to describe effective cooperative work. This means that individual members meet their own goals **only** when others meet their goals and the group as a whole meets its goals. As students work together cooperatively, particularly within diverse groups (academically and socially), the interactions help to break down barriers. Students get to know one another better, appreciate and value each other more, have more empathy for others, rethink previous conclusions about someone's abilities or social desirability, and treat each other more respectfully. All these kinds of changes make it far safer and motivating for students to be academically tenacious. (It has a great positive effect on belonging, too!)

Set a standard goal-setting process for the school. At the center of tenacity is its purpose—to persevere toward longer-term and higher-order goals. At all grade levels, students work toward goals. Most assignments and projects have goals, even if they are not stated or labeled as *goals*. It's helpful to learners if they understand what a goal is, what the difference is between a short-term goal and a longer-term goal, and (as age-appropriate) what a higher-order goal is.

> *When obstacles arise, you change your direction to reach your goal. You do not change your decision to get there.*
>
> –Zig Ziglar, American Author

For the sake of continuity of learning, it's a good idea to design a common approach to goals. Work together as a staff to craft a plan for selecting and setting goals, working toward their accomplishment, and identifying and handling obstacles or changes along the way, and evaluating the outcomes. A general overall structure gives all teachers a framework. Be sure to include in the framework a list of "musts" for goals: they must be realistic, relevant to students, worthwhile, appropriately challenging, connected to current needs and/or future goals.

Teachers can collaborate in grade-level or subject-area committees to fine-tune the specifics for their students. The specifics of the exact steps to follow will vary and grow with complexity at different grades—but, as students move through the grades, they will be familiar with what it means to set goals, what kinds of goals to set (or kinds that will be set for them), how to work toward goals, and how to know when you've reached them. You might follow the SMART elements for your common goal-setting guide. These are readily available on the Internet. (See Eby, 2019; Haughey, 2014; O'Neill, 2003; MindTools, 2021). Or you might create a template for a goal-planning and work guide that can be adapted to different projects, tasks, or grade levels.

Revere relevance. It's been said herein (more than once) that learning goals must be relevant to students. This doesn't mean that every child can choose work of his or her interest in every lesson or task of every school day. Many topics, processes, and assignments are given because educators believe they are endeavors students need as part of a good education. What I'm saying is to value relevance and keep it in mind all the time. Though this, too, has been said, I'll repeat it: we can't expect students to be tenacious about a goal that has no meaning or value in their eyes. A good way to address this constantly is to—always—tell students the *WHY* before the *WHAT*. Get into the school-wide habit of explaining (with a passion) the reasons and value for a skill, process, or concept that students are about to tackle. Better yet, get students involved in extrapolating the **WHY** and giving examples of when such a skill or idea is needed or shows up in their lives. Good leaders know that this works well with their teachers and other staff members. When they're being asked to work for something, adults too need to know the *WHY*!

Always tell students the WHY before the WHAT.

Teach strategies that support tenacity. This is the "working smart" part of academic tenacity. In the research review (Chapter 15), you encountered the phrase *learning strategies* several times. It is one of the prime categories associated with tenacity. Students need strategies to use as they work hard on tasks and goals. These are strategies that are not content specific—but that make it possible for kids to plan their work, know where they are going, get past difficulties, and move forward. They need to be taught these "smart" strategies as integral parts of any subject. Each of these strategies will be a set of specific steps or actions to take. To foster positive academic behaviors and be successful, students need strategies for such things as (but certainly not limited to)

- Setting goals and going after them
- Thinking about how you are thinking (i.e., *metacognition*); understanding how you approach a task—how you work, how your mind works
- Reflecting on (evaluating) your progress as you're working
- Reflecting on (evaluating) performance or outcomes
- Planning for obstacles or setbacks that may arise and gathering ideas for how to deal with them
- Creating an alternate plan when one plan isn't working
- Identifying your own "trouble spots" with tenacity and gathering ideas for what to do when they crop up
- Identifying what you already know that will help with this task or assignment
- Breaking goals or tasks into chunks or steps—sub-goals or sub-tasks; looking at a task as a series of minor steps
- Working with a partner or group
- Organizing your work or your findings/results; managing your work time
- Keeping records or taking notes to keep track of important facts or concepts
- Reading, understanding, and solving a problem
- Examining/monitoring your comprehension when reading (i.e., getting the most out of what you read)
- Finding evidence to support claims (made in writing, speaking, or other presentations)
- Checking your understanding or progress (self-monitoring, self-questioning)
- Recalling information

- Practicing in ways that help the mind remember (i.e., spaced practice in smaller chunks)
- Finding/choosing resources (including human) to clear up confusion or fix mistakes
- Keeping track of parts completed and parts yet to be completed
- Participating effectively and meaningfully in class
- Listening to and learning from others
- Asking questions
- Coping with stress
- Dealing with distractions
- Asking for help
- Preparing for tests
- Giving and receiving (and making use of) feedback; handling criticism
- Dealing with and learning from failure when it happens

Many tactics can fit into this list—tactics that help students in the work of learning, thinking, understanding, and remembering. Remember that mindset, belonging, challenging work, and high standards are not enough. **Students must have the skills to tackle the challenges, or they won't be able to stay with them.** *Note: The aforementioned skills are general to all topics and subject areas. However, there are learning skills and strategies that **are specific** to particular content. Students need training in these, too.*

Continue to practice gratitude. Gratitude ignites tenacity and empowers learners. It spotlights opportunities that you're fortunate to have. Tenacity gives a person hope; it is freedom from helplessness. In two studies, Charlotte Witvliet (2019) and her research colleagues found that the trait of gratitude exceeded other traits and practices (such as patience, forgiveness, and self-control) in predicting and bolstering present happiness and hope for the future.

Just think about that! For that student who realizes he truly does have the ability to reach a goal if he works hard and uses the right strategies, that feeling of expectation and trust (aka hope) propels him forward with excitement. So many of our students feel hopeless about school or their prospects beyond school. **As tenacity increases, the hopelessness wanes, and it wanes because a student knows she has the power to change things.** Remind students to practice gratitude for their self-agency (yes—teach them that word—*Self-agency is your ability to take action to contribute to the outcome of an event or the meeting of a goal*) as well as gratitude for the people and circumstances that helped them gain tenacity.

To conclude this chapter, I leave you with a thought shared by a student:

> *When I didn't believe I could, I didn't start. Then I started slowly—by showing up. I started tracking my setbacks. I saw patterns in my mistakes. I started to pay attention to this. I used the patterns to decide what to do differently. Then, when I practiced and kept on practicing, I got better. Skills got better and the problems or assignments got better and I could do them with more confidence. I'm trying harder things. I'm watching this happen. I get it now. My effort is a big deal. It works. And what I'm doing matters to me more now. I'm starting to stretch myself outside of where I'm comfortable. I'm seeing that my effort is paying off.*

> **Tenacity gives a person hope; it is freedom from helplessness.**

CONCLUSION

THE FIFTH PILLAR

Without tenacity, there is no hope.
—Dr. Andy Parker

The more I investigate academic tenacity and learn about how it develops and about what its growth does for students, the more excited I am to be a tenacity advocate! I hope you've caught some of the fever and see the truth that tenacity is indeed an essential supporting pillar for a brilliant school. I hope you are inspired to spread enthusiasm for a focus on tenacity throughout your school. All the good information and strategies lead to improved academic tenacity **only when they are embedded in the culture of the entire school**. Students may not keep working hard and smart over the long haul if next year's class (or 4th-period class) does not value and continue to teach tenacity in the same way. The outlook on tenacity has to continue and build class after class and year after year.

It has taken the entirety of my adult life to understand that perfection is an illusion and that some level of tenacity is a necessity, even when—especially when—I'd rather throw in the towel. The *I-want-to-give-up* moments in life are many for most people. If we've learned tenacity and practiced it, again and again, these moments allow us to keep pushing forward. Brilliant schools intentionally ensure that students have teachers, coaches, and a safe, trustworthy, nurturing environment to nudge us forward.

Regardless of whether the setting is the hard cement of a driveway, on the neighbor's once-manicured lawn, or inside the school halls or classroom—all of us must understand (and teach our students) that missteps, failures, and disengagement are not the result of some inherent intellectual or conceptual deficiency. Instead, they are steps along a journey that can move forward, instead of stalling or sliding backward. We must invite our students to be tenacious, show them the value of being so, model repeated examples of our own tenacity, and work hard to carry out the brilliant teaching and programs that teach them HOW to grow tenacity. Then we must keep on supporting them as they try to do it.

Tenacity is a partner with hope. It both inspires hope and is, in turn, fueled by it. Tenacity is a whole set of outlooks and actions that comprise a brilliant beacon of hope. When we teach our students the skills and attitudes of tenacity, we give them this precious gift of hope.

The Culture of a Brilliant School

A school's culture has more influence on life and learning in the schoolhouse than the president of the country, the state department of education, the school board, or even the principal, teachers, and parents can have.

—Roland Barth, Author and Founding Director
of Harvard University's Principals Center

Chapter 17

Connecting the Pillars

The concept *of school culture shows* up in every article, book, video, presentation, and discussion about successful schools. *School culture* is the personality of a school—the underlying pervasive beliefs, values, assumptions, and attitudes that shape every aspect of a school, the relationships within it, and the way things are done. Written or unwritten, the culture influences the behaviors and experiences of every member of the school community.

Often, you can feel the school's culture within a few minutes of walking through the doors (or even setting foot on the school property). It's that overall sense of cohesion, passion, collaboration, safety, and shared purpose. You can see it in the faces and the brightness and cleanliness of the building. You can hear it in the welcoming voices and the language of "our" school. Or, of course, you could feel, see, and hear the absence of the mentioned qualities. For school culture may be positive or it may be less so.

Many wise and thoughtful experts offer excellent insights into school culture, the effects of both positive and negative school cultures, and practices to improve your school's culture. Through the information, examples, and advice I've included in this book—in the structure of the G.R.E.A.T. pillars—I've shared beliefs, assumptions, attitudes, and behaviors that I've watched enhance the success of schools and turn them into brilliant schools. I have seen how focused work on these five components of infrastructure can transform struggling schools in all kinds of communities into thriving, engaging, student-centered places of learning. As well, I have seen how focused work on these compoents can transform pretty good schools into brilliant schools.

Here's why I've described the five components as **pillars**: I want you to envision them as strong, solid, and foundational. The described work on Gratitude, Relationships, Expectations, Achievement, and Tenacity is not a set of "programs" or "procedures" or "processes" to be Googled, cut, and pasted on top of an existing school culture. **Each pillar and all that it includes must be thoroughly embedded in the school culture.** Success in any one of these areas—or others your school chooses as missions—is tied to your school culture. You cannot just impose practices (no matter how worthy the goals) on top of a culture that does not wholly embrace and "live" a mission. If you try this, whatever improvements you make **will not stick**. Gratitude, growth mindset, trust and care for one another, high expectations, grit, tenacity, belief that abilities can grow—**these must all be felt in the bones of the humans who inhabit the school and its wider community.** They must be agreed upon, embraced, understood, learned, practiced (over and over, with hard work), fought for, and demonstrated repeatedly in daily attitudes and actions!

> *You cannot just impose practices on top of a culture that does not wholly embrace and live the beliefs of a mission.*

So how do we know when a mission (or school improvement endeavor) is enmeshed in culture? It doesn't happen overnight! It's an ongoing, growth process that develops with belief, attention, and consistent work. Here are some of the signs that show any one of the pillars described in this book to be embedded in the school culture:

- Shared values, beliefs, and attitudes (related to the pillar) across the school community
- Crystal clear communication and understanding—across the building—of what the pillar means, why it's a priority, and what the expectations are for practicing the traits

- Modeling of the pillar's values, attitudes, and practices by all the adults in the school
- A leader whose actions show compassion and openness, caring, benevolence, a positive outlook, and high regard for every student, staff member, parent, and visitor (The leader listens more than she or he speaks, communicates kindly and honestly, supports the teachers, and shares leadership.)
- The use of common language—shared vocabulary around the traits of the pillar
- Planned, explicit teaching and practicing of the skills (of the pillar and its components) in the classroom
- Support for this teaching intentionally practiced outside of the classrooms (Think hallways, cafeteria, playground, buses, after-school sports and events, and communications with parents and community members.)
- Shared routines, rituals, and traditions around the traits and practices of the pillar
- Demonstration of trust among school leaders, teachers, students, support staff, and families
- Indications that the school is a safe, supportive space for the improvements to be taught and practiced
- Evidence that no one is left out of the efforts to cultivate traits [Everyone knows that this goal (for example, high expectations) is central to the ethos of the school.]
- Recognition that students play a key role in the growth and practice of the pillar's traits (Everyone understands that this is not a "policy" to be imposed on the students.)

School culture (or any aspect of it) should not be assumed. It should not be implicit. It must be explicit. Put it in writing. In every chapter of this book, you'll find repeated research, advice, and practices that support the deep infusion of the values and practices of each pillar into the fabric of the entire school community. We want these five foundations to become integral parts of the soul of the brilliant school. This is when our efforts work best to make a difference for our students and all those who care about, teach, and support them.

Five Pillars Intricately Woven Together ────────────

I have watched leaders model and maintain the practice of gratitude and seen how this profoundly continues to impact collegial and student relationships in service of academic achievement and student social-emotional well-being. I've been awed by the growth in trust and belonging that comes out of hard work on quality relationships, and particularly on reducing or wiping out bias. I've seen the "light come on" when teachers start honest examinations of their expectations for individual students or groups of students and realize how those expectations enhance or sabotage student achievement and self-belief. I've been honored to be a part of schools where kids have come to believe in themselves as students and have reached levels of achievement that they hadn't thought possible. I have listened in on student and teacher feedback about the stamina,

Every pillar both bolsters and is fortified by each of the others.

reflection, and setbacks that come with academic tenacity—followed by the joy of accomplishment that accompanies its growth.

Every pillar both bolsters and is fortified by each of the others. Let's summarize and reiterate some of the primary connections among these pillars to remember how they work together as a solid structure for a brilliant school:

The Gratitude-Relationships Partnership

Gratitude practices, along with the *Yes-Brain* approach behind them, propel people to act proactively and positively toward peers, colleagues, and others. They inspire collaboration and cooperation—

creating a culture of active gratitude. A focus on gratitude positively affects prosocial relationships among students. The conscious and genuine practices of gratitude make relationships richer and more meaningful. When any member of the school community receives an expression of gratitude, she or he gains a boost in trust, value, and sense of belonging. This calls forth a relationship and deepens it.

In turn, any satisfying relationship triggers gratitude. Our work on caring and supportive relationships gives us more reasons to feel and express gratitude to others. As we examine a relationship in preparation to offer gratitude, we shine a spotlight on the value of the person and the relationship to us. This gives rise to even deeper gratitude and more impetus to keep expressing it.

The Gratitude-Expectations Partnership

When we practice gratitude in a school, we can open our minds and hearts to the truth of our expectations for one another (including inequities and biases in those expectations). Being regularly grateful opens our eyes to each student and to the possibilities for their academic and personal growth. When others receive gratitude, their self-expectations rise. As we act on our higher expectations—working to help our students or colleagues reach them—our gratitude for them as humans, for their hard work, and for the gifts they share with us deepens.

In turn, as students (or others) rise to meet expectations, gratitude blossoms. They may feel grateful for their abilities or their hard work. They may feel grateful for the teachers, peers, parents, or others who believed in them and who supported them in reaching their goals.

The Gratitude-Achievement Partnership

Gratefulness in youth is a high predictor of school achievement. With regular gratitude practice, we see an increase in motivation, connectedness to school, ability to set and pursue meaningful goals, self-regulation, and academic performance level (higher GPAs).

In turn, as students enjoy experiences of competence or other joys of learning and as they learn more about their capabilities—there are many occasions for gratitude. They can notice and express gratitude for opportunities, self-regulation, their hard work, or for many small or large gifts of help, encouragement, and celebration from peers or adults.

The Gratitude-Tenacity Partnership

As students learn to express gratitude for their values and skills, for the many consistent ways others help them, and for the many values they notice in others, they are more likely to work longer, harder, and smarter. Gratitude supports academic tenacity! It shores up reserves and helps people have hope during tough tasks or situations. And when anyone receives gratitude from others, that, too, inspires tenacity.

In turn, as academic tenacity grows and pays off in greater self-belief, ability to survive setbacks and work around obstacles, success with meeting challenges, and higher performance—there are many reasons for gratitude. The reaching of a goal after hard, smart work is a great occasion for some gratitude practice.

The Relationships-Expectations Partnership

One of the most effective interventions to combat low teacher expectations (and students' low self-expectations) is to work on quality relationships in the school. This includes teacher-student relationships, peer relationships, and individuals' relationships with themselves (self-belief, self-esteem, self-confidence). And it includes work on getting to know students better as individuals. For when people get to know one another's qualities, value, and abilities through learning about each other and working together—they are far more likely to see each other accurately. Within a caring relationship, they are more able to have accurate expectations for one another. When a teacher pays close attention to who a student is, it will be hard to hinder the student with low expectations. Negative biases are less likely to thrive in the presence of close, caring relationships.

In turn, when students are held to high expectations and have success reaching them, their trust in the teacher grows. This process just strengthens the relationships! When a student is trusted with high expectations and works hard to meet them, peers notice. The student feels more a part of the group of "students who succeed." This improves relationships among peers.

The Relationships-Achievement Partnership

Relationships at school—teacher-student relationships, peer relationships, and students' feelings about themselves—affect academic performance. The way a student feels about his or her school abilities and achievement has an impact on achievement. Students who are attuned to their strengths and abilities, who believe they can "get smarter" with hard work, and who see themselves as one of the "students who can succeed" will perform better. Students who have the benefit of trusting, caring relationships with teachers have increased academic performance and resiliency. They also gain motivation, engagement, self-direction, and tenacity. Students with a strong sense of social belonging at school have greater classroom engagement, self-motivation, belief in themselves as students, positive attitudes toward learning, and academic achievement. When students are safe with and supported by each other, they contribute significantly to one another's academic, social, and emotional development. From each other, students can learn academic and strengthen concepts as well as many skills such as collaboration, communication, and self-regulation.

In turn, a student's experience of achievement contributes to self-confidence, prosocial behavior, and trust. This strengthens relationships with self, peers, and teachers.

The Relationships-Tenacity Partnership

When we look for the strong influences on academic tenacity, we find relationships, belonging, and social skills high on the list. Growth mindset, self-efficacy, and value affirmations are strong influences also. All these traits are relationship-based. For tenacity to grow, humans need affirmation and skills for building secure relationships with themselves (self-belief, esteem, sense of control over their actions and environment). A self-relationship is bolstered by caring relationships with others and by a growth mindset. We've learned that a sense of belonging is an important predictor of academic tenacity. We've seen that quality teacher-student and peer relationships affect a host of traits and conditions that are components of academic tenacity; these are such factors as self-direction, motivation, resilience, and engagement.

In turn, tenacity offers benefits that enrich relationships. The same traits and skills that work for academic tenacity can be applied to the challenges and benefits of building and sustaining relationships (such traits as self-belief, self-regulation, growth mindset, refusal to give up, handling setbacks, and willingness to work hard and smart).

The Expectations-Achievement Partnership

Teacher expectations (often informed by implicit biases) have a major impact on student achievement as well as on students' academic self-beliefs and their attitudes toward school. It's been found that teacher expectations translate into how the teacher articulates expectations, provides support, relates to the students, praises the students, communicates, and evaluates students' work. The differences in teacher behaviors (associated with expectations) either contribute to or detract from students' achievement. Teacher expectations of a student or group of students also influence peer expectations of one another. When a student picks up on the teacher's low expectations, the student often internalizes those expectations for herself or himself and performs accordingly. Conversely, when teachers expect a student to show intellectual or academic growth, the students **do** show growth. In addition, a teacher's beliefs in a student's academic capabilities positively affect the student's self-beliefs and the student's achievement. Students' academic struggles or failures affect their expectations of themselves.

In turn, when students are helped to succeed (achieve hat higher levels), their self-belief and confidence increase, and the achievement successes enable them to raise their expectations for their performance.

The Expectations-Tenacity Partnership

Expectations (high expectations, that is) are central to tenacity. Academic tenacity can only grow within the environment of the challenge of high expectations (including self-expectations) that are realistic and attainable, along with the skilled teacher support to reach the goals.

In turn, the traits of academic tenacity are what enable students to care about and reach those expectations. To be attained, appropriately challenging expectations need the growth mindset, hard work, flexibility, and problem-solving skills (the ability to work smart), risk taking, and grit that are components of tenacity.

The Achievement-Tenacity Partnership

These two themes are so intricately entangled with each other that it can be hard to speak of them separately! We see that tenacity is a huge part of academic achievement. It transcends intelligence, socioeconomic challenges, school quality, and sometimes even family influence in leading to success. It affects and is affected by mindset, self-worth, risk taking (academically), motivation, and engagement.

In turn, the experience of achievement is a major boost to tenacity. Once a student (or adult) feels the accomplishment—especially an accomplishment that involves some challenge—that achievement can inspire greater self-belief, confidence, and motivation to do more. The reaching of relevant, meaningful, and challenging goals breeds coping, self-control, the ability to work around difficulties, and long-term persistence that are marks of academic tenacity.

Keep the Light Shining ━━━━━━━━━━━━━━━━━━━━━━━━

The work of building a brilliant school is our charge as educators. It is humbling, at times exhausting, but more often exhilarating. When you work to create a culture that is ongoing and consistently growing more positive, the outcomes are purpose, power, and the strong belief that you, your co-leaders, your staff, your students, their families, and the supporting community are all part of something great. This work is not a burden you must impose. It is what you, your colleagues, and your students, parents, and community want anyway, isn't it? It's that experience of being needed, collaborating, working hard as a team, having someone's back, everyone having yours, and belonging to something important and life-changing—and knowing that you are better together.

Upon the foundation of the pillars described here in my G.R.E.A.T. Leadership Philosophy™—pillars deeply embedded in a dynamic, positive culture—you can build a brilliant school. Keep the acronym in mind. Focus on each underpinning, keeping in mind how it works in harmony with the other pillars to fire up and let out the brilliant light that will flood your school.

References

References

First Pillar—Gratitude

Abblett, M. (2019). *Tame reactive emotions by naming them.* Mindful. https://www.mindful.org/labels-help-tame-reactive-emotions-naming/

Allen, S. (2018). *The science of gratitude.* Greater Good Science Center UC Berkley for the John Templeton Foundation. https://ggsc.berkeley.edu/ images/uploads/GGSC-JTF_White_Paper-Gratitude-FINAL.pdf

Appleton, J. J., Christenson, S., & Furlong, M. J. (2008). Student engagement with school: Critical conceptual and methodological issues of the construct. *Psychology in the Schools, 45,* 369-386.

Bartlett. M. Y., & DeSteno, D. (2006) Gratitude and prosocial behavior: Helping when it costs you. *Psychological Science, 17*(4), 319-2-325.

Bartlett, M. Y., Condon, P., Crus, J., Baumann, J., & DeSteno, D. (2012). Gratitude: Prompting behaviours that build relationships. *Cognition and Emotion, 26*(1), 2-13.

Bono, G., & Emmons, R. A. (2010). Being grateful is beyond good manners: Gratitude and motivation to contribute to society among early adolescents. *Motivation and Emotion, 34*(2), 144-157.

Bono, G., Emmons, R. A., & McCullough, M. (2012). Gratitude in practice and the practice of gratitude. In P. A. Linley & S. Joseph (Eds.), *Positive Psychology in Practice* (pp. 464-481). Wiley.

Bono, G., Froh, J.J., Disabato, D., Blalock, D., McKnight, P., & Bausert, S. (2017). Gratitude's role in adolescent antisocial and prosocial behavior: A 4-year longitudinal investigation. *The Journal of Positive Psychology, 14*(3), 1-13.

Bono, G., Krakauer, M., & Froh, J. J. (2015) The power and practice of gratitude. In Joseph, S., (Ed)., *Positive psychology in practice: Promoting human flourishing in work, health, education, and everyday life* (2nd ed., pp. 559-576). John Wiley & Sons, Inc. https://onlinelibrary.wiley.com/doi/10.1002/ 9781118996874.ch33

Bono, G., & Sender, J. T. (2018). How gratitude connects humans to the best in themselves and in others. *Research in Human Development, 15,* 224-237.

Brown, J., & Wong, J. (2017). *How gratitude changes you and your brain.* Greater Good Magazine. https://greatergood.berkeley.edu/article/item/how_gratitude_changes_you_and_your_brain

Childre, D., & Cryer, B. (2000). *From chaos to coherence: The power to change performance.* Planetary.

Chowdhury, M. R. (2020). *The neuroscience of gratitude and how it affects anxiety and grief.* PositivePsychology.com. https://positivepsychology.com/neuroscience-of-gratitude/

DeSteno, D., Duong, F., Lim, D., & Kates, S. (2019) The grateful don't cheat: Gratitude as a fount of virtue. *Psychological Science, 30*(7), 978-988.

Dickens, L., & DeSteno, D. (2016). The grateful are patient: Heightened daily gratitude is associated with attenuated temporal discounting. *Semantic Scholar.* DOI:10.1037/emo0000176

Emmons, R. A., & Crumpler, C. A. (2000). Gratitude as a human strength: appraising the evidence. *Journal of Social and Clinical Psychology, 19*(1), 56-70.

Emmons, R. A., & McCullough, M. (2003). Counting blessings versus burdens: An experimental investigation of gratitude and subjective well-being in daily life. *Journal of Personality and Social Psychology, 84,* 377-389.

Emmons, R. A., & McCullough, M. (2004). *The psychology of gratitude.* Oxford University Press.

Emmons, R. A., & Mishra, A. (2011) Why gratitude enhances well-being: What we know, what we need to know. In K. M. Sheldon, T. B. Kashdan, & M. F. Steger (Eds.), *Designating positive psychology: Taking stock and moving forward* (pp. 246-262). Oxford University Press.

Fauteux, M. (2018). *Building school culture with gratitude.* GettingSmart. https://www.gettingsmart.com/2018/12/building-school-culture-with-gratitude/

Froh, J. J., & Bono, G. (2008). The gratitude of youth. In Lopez, S. J. (Ed.), *Praeger perspectives: Positive psychology: Exploring the best in people, Vol. 2. Capitalizing on emotional experiences* (pp. 55-78). Prager Publishers.

Froh, J. J., & Bono, G. (2009). Gratitude in school: Benefits to students and schools. In R. Gilman, E. S. Huebner, & M. J. Furlong (Eds.), *Handbook of Positive Psychology in Schools* (pp. 77-88). Routledge/Taylor & Francis Group.

Froh, J. J., & Bono, G. (2011). *Gratitude in youth: A review of gratitude interventions and some ideas for applications.* Semantic Scholar. https://www.semanticscholar.org/paper/Gratitude-in-Youth%3A-A-Review-of-Gratitude-and-Some-Froh-Bono/21da509a924dda8375ad6d19eaef8e9e735561c7

Froh, J. J., & Bono, G. (2012). *How to foster gratitude in schools.* Greater Good Magazine. https://greatergood.berkeley.edu/article/item/how_to_foster_gratitude_in_schools

Froh, J. J., & Bono, G. (2014). *Making Grateful Kids: A Scientific Approach to Help Youth Thrive.* Templeton Press.

Froh, J. J., Bono, G., & Emmons, R.A. (2010). Being grateful is beyond good manners: Gratitude and motivation to contribute to society among early adolescents. *Motivation and Emotion, 34,* 144-157.

Froh, J. J., Bono, G., Fan, J., Emmons, R. A., Henderson, K., Harris, C., Leggio, H., & Wood, A. M. (2014). Nice thinking! An educational intervention that teaches children to think gratefully. *School Psychology Review, 43*(2), 132-152.

Froh, J. J., Emmons, R. A., Card, N., Bono, G., & Wilson, J. A. (2011). Gratitude and the reduced costs of materialism in adolescents. *Journal of Happiness Studies, 12*(2), 289-302.

Froh, J. J., Kashdan, T. B., Ozimkowski, K. M., & Miller, N. (2009). Who benefits the most from a gratitude intervention in children and adolescents? Examining positive affect as a moderator. *The Journal of Positive Psychology, 4,* 408-422.

Froh, J. J., Miller, D., & Snyder, S. (2007). Gratitude in children and adolescents: Development, assessment, and school-based intervention. *School Psychology Forum: Research in Practice, 2*(1), 1-13.

Froh, J. J., Sefick, W. J., & Emmons, R. A. (2008). Counting blessings in early adolescents: An experimental study of gratitude and subjective well-being. *Journal of School Psychology, 46,* 213-233.

George, J. (1995). Positive mood and group performance: The case of customer service. *Journal of Applied Social Psychology, 25*(9), 778-794.

Good Therapy. (2018) *Dan Siegel.* https://www.goodtherapy.org/famous-psychologists/daniel-siegel.html

Greater Good Science Center. (2020). *Gratitude.* https://greatergood.berkeley.edu/topic/gratitude

Hanessian, L. (2018). *Dr. Dan Siegel: What hearing "Yes" does to your child's brain.* Mindful. https://www.mindful.org/dr-dan-siegel-hearing-yes-childs-brain/

Hill, P., Allemand, M., & Roberts, B. (2013). Examining the pathways between gratitude and self-rated physical health across adulthood. *Personality and Individual Differences, 54*(1), 92-96.

Howells, K. (2007). Practicing gratitude to enhance learning and teaching. *Education Connect, 5*, 2-7.

Howells, K. (2009). Strengthening relationships and resilience through practices of gratitude. *Principal Matters, 80*, 2-6.

Howells, K. (2012). *Gratitude in education: A radical view.* Sense Publishers.

Howells, K. (2013) *Enhancing teacher relationships and effectiveness through the practice of gratitude.* Teachers Matter. http://www.kerryhowells.com/wp-content/uploads/2013/11/58-Enhancing-teacher-relationships-and-effectiveness-through-the-practice-of-gratitude.pdf

Howells, K. (2014). An exploration of the role of gratitude in enhancing teacher-student relationships. *Teaching and Teacher Education, 42,* 58-67.

Huebner, E. S., Drane, W., & Valois, R. F. (2000). Levels and demographic correlates of adolescent life satisfaction reports. *School Psychology International, 21,* 281–292.

Jarrett, C. (2016). *How expressing gratitude might change your brain.* The Cut. https://www.thecut.com/2016/01/how-expressing-gratitude-change-your-brain.html

Kini, P., Wong, J., McInnis, S., Gabana, N., & Brown, J. W. (2015). The effects of gratitude expression on neural activity. *NeuroImage, 128.* DOI: 10.1016/j.neuroimage.2015.12.040

Lin, C., & Yeh, Y. (2014). How gratitude influences well-being: A structural equation modeling. *Social Indicators Research, 118*(1), 205-217.

McCanlies, E., Gu, J., Andrew, M., & Violanti, J. (2018). The effect of social support, gratitude, resilience and satisfaction with life on depressive symptoms among police officers following Hurricane Katrina. *International Journal of Social Psychiatry, 64*(1), 63-72.

McCraty, R., & Childre, D. (2004). The grateful heart: The psychophysiology of appreciation. In R. A. Emmons & M. E. McCullough (Eds.), *The psychology of gratitude* (pp. 230-255). Oxford University Press.

McCullough, M., Emmons, R. A., & Tsang, J. (2002). The grateful disposition: A conceptual and empirical topography. *Journal of Personality and Social Psychology, 82*(1), 112-127.

McKibben, S. (2013). Tapping into the power of gratitude. *ASCD Education Update, 55*(11), 1-7.

Nguyen, S. P., & Gordon, C. L. (2020). The relationship between gratitude and happiness in young children. *Journal of Happiness Studies, 21,* 2773-2787.

Pedersen, E., & Lieberman, D. (2017). *How gratitude helps your friendships grow.* Greater Good magazine. https://greatergood.berkeley.edu/article/item/how_gratitude_helps_your_friendships_grow

Polak, E. L., & McCullough, M. E. (2006). Is gratitude an alternative to materialism? *Journal of Happiness Studies, 7*(3), 343–360.

Seligman, M., Steen, T., Park, N., & Peterson, C. (2005). Positive psychology progress: Empirical validation of interventions. *American Psychologist, 60*(5), 410.

Siegel, D. J. (2013). *Brainstorm: The power and purpose of the teenage brain.* TarcherPerigee.

Siegel, D. J. (2017). *The 'yes-brain' approach to parenting and life.* U. S. News website, https://health.usnews.com/wellness/for-parents/articles/2017-11-29/the-yes-brain-approach-to-parenting-and-life

Siegel, D. J., & Bryson, T. P. (2018). *The yes brain: How to cultivate courage, curiosity, and resilience in your child.* Bantam.

Siegel, D. J. (2020). *Mindsight.* https://drdansiegel.com/mindsight/

Siegel, D. J., (2021). *An interview with Dr. Dan Siegel.* PsychAlive website. https://www.psychalive.org/what-is-mindsight-an-interview-with-dr-dan-siegel/

Singer, T. (2016). *Gratitude: "A vaccine against impulsiveness."* News@Northeastern. https://news.northeastern.edu/2016/04/14/gratitude-a-vaccine-against-impulsiveness/

Witliet, C. V., Richie, F., Luna, L. R., & Van Tongeren, D. R. (2019). Gratitude predicts hope and happiness: A two-study assessment of traits and states. *The Journal of Positive Psychology, 14*(3), 271-282.

Wood, A. M., Joseph, S., & Maltby, J. (2009). Gratitude predicts psychological well-being above the Big Five Facets. *Personality and Individual Differences, 46*(4), 443-447.

Woods, T. W. (2016). *Beyond good manners: How to raise a sophisticated child.* First Impression Publishing.

Zahn, R., Moll, J., Paiva, M., Garrido, G., Krueger, F., Huey, E. D., & Grafman, J. (2009). The neural basis of human social values: Evidence from functional MRI. *Cerebral Cortex, 19*(2), 276-83.

Zak, P. J. (2017a). The neuroscience of trust. *Harvard Business Review, Jan-Feb,* 84-90.

Zak, P. J. (2017b). *The trust factor: The science of creating high-performance companies.* AMACOM.

Second Pillar—Relationships ━━━━━━━━━━━━━━

Alexander, K., Entwisle, D., & Horsey, C. (1997). From first grade forward: Early foundations of high school dropout. *Sociology of Education, 70,* 87-107. http://dx.doi.org/10.2307/2673158

Baker, J. A. (2006). Contributions of teacher-child relationships to positive school adjustment during elementary school. *Journal of School Psychology, 44*(3), 211-229.

Baker, J. A., Grant, S., & Morlock, L. (2008). The teacher-student relationship as a developmental context for children with internalizing or externalizing behavior problems. *School Psychology Quarterly, 23*(1), 3-15.

Bandura, A. (1997). *Self-efficacy: The exercise of control.* W Freeman/Times Books/ Henry Holt & Co.

Barth, R.S. (2006) Improving relationships within the schoolhouse. *Educational Leadership, 63*(6), 8-13.

Berman, S. (1997). *SUNY series, democracy and education. Children's social consciousness and the development of social responsibility.* State University of New York Press.

Bierman, K. L. (2004). *Peer rejection: Developmental processes and intervention strategies.* Guildford.

Birch, S.H., & Ladd, G. W (1998). Children's interpersonal behaviors and the teacher-child relationship. *Developmental Psychology, 34*, 934–946.

Blum, R. W. (2005). A case for school connectedness. *Educational Leadership, 62*(7), 16-20.

Boynton, M., & Boynton, C. (2005). *Educator's guide to preventing and solving discipline problems.* Association for Supervision and Curriculum Development.

Brownell, M. T., & Skrtic, T. (2002). *Assuring an adequate supply of well-qualified teachers to improve the educational outcomes of students with disabilities.* Written testimony submitted to the President's Commission on Special Education.

Bryk, A. S., & Schneider, B. (2003). Trust in schools: A core resource for reform. *Educational Leadership, 60*(6), 40-45.

Buhs, E. S., Ladd, G. W., & Herald-Brown, S. L. (2010). Victimization and exclusion: Links to peer rejection, classroom engagement, and achievement. In S. R. Jimerson, S. M. Swearer, & D. L. Espelage (Eds.), *Handbook of bullying in schools: An international perspective* (pp. 163–172). Routledge/Taylor & Francis Group.

Caprara, G. V., Barbaranelli, C., Borgogni, L., & Steca, P. (2003). Efficacy beliefs as determinates of teachers' job satisfaction. *Journal of Educational Psychology, 95*(4), 821-832.

Caprara, G. V., Barbaranelli, C., Steca, P., & Malone, P.S. (2006). Teachers' self-efficacy beliefs as determinates of job satisfaction and students' academic achievement: A study at the school level. *Journal of School Psychology, 44*(6), 473-490).

Chiu, M. M., Chow, B., McBride, C., & Mol, S. T. (2016). Students' sense of belonging at school in 41 countries: Cross-cultural variability. *Journal of Cross-Cultural Psychology, 47*(2), 175–196.

Comer, J. P., Haynes, N. M., Joyner, E. T., & Ben-Avie, M. (1996). *Rallying the whole village: The Comer process for reforming education.* Teachers College Press.

Day, C., & Gu, Q. (2014). *Resilient teachers, resilient schools. Building and sustaining quality in testing times.* Routledge.

Deci, E. L., & Ryan, R. M. (2014). Autonomy and need satisfaction in close relationships: Relationships motivation theory. In N. Weinstein (Ed.), *Human motivation and interpersonal relationships: Theory, research, and applications* (pp. 53-73). Springer.

Decker, D.M., Dona, D.P., Christenson, S. L. (2007). Behaviorally at-risk African American students: The importance of student-teacher relationships for student outcomes. *Journal of School Psychology, 45*, 83–109.

Elledge, L. C., Elledge, A. R., Newgent, R.A., and Cavell, T.A. (2016). Social Risk and peer victimization in elementary school children: The protective role of teacher-student relationships. *Journal of Abnormal Child Psychology, 44*(4), 691-703.

Friedman, I. (1991). High- and low-burnout schools: School culture aspects of teacher burnout. *Journal of Educational Research, 85*(5), 541-570.

Furrer, C., & Skinner, E. (2003). Sense of relatedness as a factor in children's academic engagement and performance. *Journal of Educational Psychology, 95*(1), 148–162.

Garris, A. (2017). *The effect of school social environment on student success.* Classroom. https://classroom.synonym.com/

Giles, D. (2011). Relationships always matter: Findings from a phenomenological research inquiry. *Australian Journal of Teacher Education, 36*(6), 80-91.

Goleman, D. (2000). Emotional intelligence: Issues in paradigm building. In C. Cherniss & D. Goleman (Eds.), *The emotionally intelligent workplace* (pp. 13-26). Jossey-Bass.

Goleman, D. (2006) *Emotional intelligence: Why it can matter more than IQ.* Bantam.

Goleman, D. (2019). *Daniel Goldman's five components of emotional intelligence.* https://web.sonoma.edu/users/s/swijtink/teaching/philosophy_101/paper1/goleman.htm

Goleman, D., Boyatzis, R., & McKee, A. (2002). *Primal leadership: Realizing the power of emotional intelligence.* Harvard Business Review Press.

Goleman, D., Boyatzis, R., & McKee, A. (2013). Primal leadership: The hidden driver of great performance. *Harvard Business Review.* https://hbr.org/2001/12/primal-leadership-the-hidden-driver-of-great-performance

Hagenauer, G., Hascher, T., Volet, S. E. (2015). Teacher emotions in the classroom: Associations with students' engagement, classroom discipline and the interpersonal teacher-student relationship. *European Journal of Psychology of Education 30*, 385-403.

Hamre, B.K., & Pianta, R. C. (2001). Early teacher–child relationships and the trajectory of children's school outcomes through eighth grade. *Child Development. 72*, 625–638.

Hartman, S. (2019). *A Texas bus driver spreads love with no expectation for reward. He got one anyway.* CBS Evening News. https://www.cbsnews.com/news/curtis-jenkins-bus-driver-at-lake-highlands-elementary-in-dallas-texas-rewarded-for-lifelong-giving-2019-12-27/

Headden, S., & McKay, S. (2015). *Motivation matters: How new research can help teachers and boost student engagement.* Carnegie Foundation for the Advancement of Teaching.

Howells, K. (2013) *Enhancing teacher relationships and effectiveness through the practice of gratitude.* Teachers Matter. http://www.kerryhowells.com/wp-content/uploads/2013/11/58-Enhancing-teacher-relationships-and-effectiveness-through-the-practice-of-gratitude.pdf

Hughes, J. N., Cavell, T. A., & Willson, V. (2001). Further support for the developmental significance of the quality of the teacher-student relationship. *Journal of School Psychology, 39*(4), 289-301.

Kamath, S. (2019). *Cultivating self-awareness to move learning forward.* Education Dive, https://www.educationdive.com/spons/cultivating-self-awareness-to-move-learning-forward/565498/

Kauffman, J. M., & Wong, K. L. (1991). Effective teachers of students with behavioral disorders: Are generic teaching skills enough? *Behavioral Disorders, 16*(3), 225–237.

Kemple, K. M., & Hartle, L. C. (1997). Getting along: How teachers can support children's peer relationships. *Early Childhood Education Journal, 24*(3), 139-146.

Knapp, M. S., Copland, M. A., Honig, M. I., Plecki, M. L., & Portin, B. S. (2010). *Learning-focused leadership and leadership support: Meaning and practice in urban systems.* University of Washington.

Konishi, C., Hymal, S., Zumbo, B. D., & Zhen, L. (2010) Do school bullying and student-teacher relationships matter for academic achievement? A multilevel analysis. *Canadian Journal of School Psychology 25*(1), 19-39.

Konishi, C., & Wong, T. (2018). Relationships and school success: From a social-emotional learning perspective. In B. Bernal-Morales (Ed.), *Health and academic achievement* (pp. 103-122). Books on Demand.

Kuhl, P. (2018). *The social classroom.* Edutopia. https://www.edutopia.org/video/social-classroom

Kuruvilla, C. (2018). School bus driver who went viral hopes act of kindness will inspire others. *Huffpost.* https://www.huffpost.com/entry/texas-bus-driver-curtis-jenkins-christmas-gifts_n_5c262f34e4b08aaf7a8fd557

Ladd, G. W. (1999). Peer relationships and social competence during early and middle childhood. *Annual Review of Psychology 50*, 333–359.

Ladd, G. W. (2005). Making friends and becoming accepted in peer groups. In G. W. Ladd (Ed.), *Children's Peer Relationships and Social Competence: A Century of Progress* (pp. 89-112). Yale University Press.

Ladd, G. W., Birch, S.H., & Buhs, E. S. (1999). Children's social and scholastic lives in kindergarten: Related spheres of influence? *Child Development, 70,* 1373–1400.

Lasater, K. (2016). School leader relationships: The need for explicit training on rapport, trust, and communication. *Journal of School Administration Research and Development 1*(2), 19-26.

Leadbeater, C (2008) It's all about relationships. *Educational Leadership 66*(3). http://www.ascd.org/publications/educational-leadership/nov08/vol66/num03/It%27s-All-About-Relationships.aspx

Louis, K. S, (2007). Trust and improvement in schools. *Journal of Educational Change, 8,* 1-24.

Louis, K. S., Leithwood, K., Wahlstrom, K., & Anderson, S. (2010). *Learning from leadership project: Investigating the links to improved student learning.* University of Minnesota.

Martin, A., & Collie, R. (2016). The role of teacher-student relationships in unlocking students' academic potential: Exploring motivation, engagement, resilience, adaptability, goals, and instruction. In K.R. Wentzel & G. Ramani (Eds.), *Handbook of social influences in school contexts: Social-emotional, motivation, and cognitive outcomes in school contexts* (pp. 158-177). Routledge.

Marzano, R. J., Marzano, J. S., & Pickering, D. J. (2003). *Classroom management that works.* Association for Supervision and Curriculum Development.

Ming-tak, H. (2008). Promoting positive peer relationships. In H. Ming-tak & L. Wai-shing (Eds.), *Classroom Management: Creating a Positive Learning Environment* (pp. 129-148). Hong Kong University Press.

Moses, L. (2019*). How trusting relationships advance school culture and influence student achievement.* ASCDINService. https://inservice.ascd.org/how-trusting-relationships-advance-school-culture-and-influence-student-achievement/

Murray, C., & Malmgren, K. (2005). Implementing a teacher-student relationship program in a high-poverty urban school: Effects on social, emotional, and academic adjustment and lessons learned. *Journal of School Psychology 43*(2), 137-152.

National Policy Board for Educational Administration (NPBEA). (2015). *Professional Standards for Educational Leaders*. NPBEA. https://www.npbea.org/wp-content/uploads/2017/06/Professional-Standards-for-Educational-Leaders_2015.pdf

Nishioka, V. (2019). *Positive and caring relationships with teachers are critical to student success*. Education Northwest. https://educationnorthwest.org/northwest-matters/positive-and-caring-relationships-teachers-are-critical-student-success

Northouse, P. G. (2015). *Introduction to leadership (3rd ed.)*. SAGE.

O'Connor, E., Dearing, E., & Collins, B. A. (2011). Teacher-child relationship and behavior problem trajectories in elementary school. *American Educational Research Journal 48*(1), 120-162.

Orth, U., Robins, R.W., & Widaman, K. F. (2012). Life-span development of self-esteem and its effects on important life outcomes. *Journal of Personality and Social Psychology, 102*(6), 1271-1288.

Pettigrew, Thomas F. (1988). Intergroup contact theory. *Annual Review of Psychology, 49*(1), 65-85.

Pettigrew, T. F., & Tropp, L. R. (2008). How does intergroup contact reduce prejudice? Meta-analytic tests of three mediators. *European Journal of Social Psychology, 38*(6), 922—934.

Piaget, J. (1932). *The moral judgment of the child.* Kegan, Paul, Trench, Trubner, & Co.

Pianta, R. C., & Stuhlman, M. W. (2004). Teacher-child relationships and children's success in the first years of school. *School Psychology Review, 33*(3), 444–458.

Price, H. (2012). Principal-teacher interactions: How affective relationships shape principal and teacher attitudes. *Educational Administration Quarterly, 48*(1), 39-85.

Quin, D. (2016). Longitudinal and contextual associations between teacher-student relationships and student engagement: A systematic review. *Review of Educational Research, 87*(2), 345-387.

Richardson, T. G., & Shupe, M. J. (2003). The importance of teacher self-awareness in working with students with emotional and behavioral disorders, *Teaching Exceptional Children*, 36(2), 8-13.

Ridley, D. S., Schutz, P. A., Glanz, R. S., & Weinstein, C. E. (1992). Self-regulated learning: The interactive influence of metacognitive awareness and goal setting. *The Journal of Experimental Education, 60*, 293-306.

Rimm-Kaufman, S., & Sandilos (2011). *Improving students' relationships with teachers to provide essential supports for learning.* American Psychological Association. https://www.apa.org/education/k12/relationships

Roffey, S. (2012). Pupil wellbeing-teacher wellbeing: Two sides of the same coin? *Educational and Child Psychology 29*(4), 8-17.

Rohrbeck, C. (2003). Peer relationships, childhood. In T. P. Gollatta (Ed.), *Encyclopedia of primary prevention and health promotion* (pp. 804-808). 10.1007/978-1-4615-0195-4_117

Rohrbeck, C. A., & Gray, L. S. (2014). Peer relationships: Promoting positive peer relationships during childhood. In T. Gullotta & M. Bloom (Eds.). *Encyclopedia of Preventive and Community Psychology* (2nd Ed., pp. 828-836). Springer SBM. http://dx.doi.org/10.1007/978-1-4614-5999-6_137

Rubin, K. H., Coplan, R. J., Bowker, J. C. (2009). Social withdrawal in childhood. *Annual Review of Psychology 60*(1), 141-171.

Rubin, K. H., Coplan, R., Chen, X., Buskirk, A. A., & Wojslawowicz, J. C. (2005). Peer relationships in childhood. In M.H. Bornstein & M.E. Lamb (Eds.), *Developmental science: An advanced textbook* (pp. 469-512). Lawrence Erlbaum Publishers.

Rudasill, K.M., Reio, T.G., Jr., Stipanovic, N., & Taylor, J.E. (2010). A longitudinal study of student-teacher relationship quality, difficult temperament, and risky behavior from childhood to early adolescence. *Journal of School Psychology, 48*(5), 389-412.

Ryan, R. M., & Deci, E. L. (2000). Self-determination theory and the facilitation of intrinsic motivation, social development, and well-being. *American Psychologist, 56,* 68-78.

Ryan, R. M., Stiller, J. D., & Lynch, J.H. (1994). Representations of relationships to teachers, parents, and friends as predictors of academic motivation and self-esteem. *The Journal of Early Adolescence, 14*(2), 226-249.

Shelton, J. (2018). *The brain science is in: Students' Emotional Needs Matter: What the neuro-, cognitive, and behavioral research says about social-emotional learning.* Education Week. https://www.edweek.org/leadership/ opinion-the-brain-science-is-in-students-emotional-needs-matter/2018/04

Silver, D., Berckemeyer, J., & Baenen, J. (2014). *Deliberate optimism: Reclaiming the joy in education.* Corwin.

Silver, R. B., Measelle, J. R., Armstrong, J. M., & Essex, M. J. (2005). Trajectories of classroom externalizing behavior: Contributions of child characteristics, family characteristics, and the teacher-child relationship during the school transition. *Journal of School Psychology 43*, 39-60.

Silvia, P. J., & O'Brien, M. E. (2004). Self-awareness and constructive functioning: Revisiting "the human dilemma." *Journal of Social and Clinical Psychology, 23*, 475-489.

Sparks, S.D. (2019). Why teacher-student relationships matter. *Education Week, 38*(25), 8.

Steinberg, L., & Monahan, K. C. (2007). Age differences in resistance to peer influence. *Developmental Psychology, 43*(6), 1531-1543.

Storey, K., Slaby, R., Adler, M., Minotti, J., & Katz, R. (2013). *The eyes on bullying toolkit.* Education Development Center, Inc. http://www.promoteprevent.org/sites/www.promoteprevent.org/files/ resources/Eyes%20on%20Bullying%20Toolkit%202013.pdf

Sullivan, H. S. (1953). *The interpersonal theory of psychiatry.* Norton.

Sutton, A. (2016). Measuring the effects of self-awareness. *European Journal of Psychology, 12*(4), 645-658.

Sutton, A., Williams, H. M., & Allinson, C. W. (2015). A longitudinal, mixed-method evaluation of self-awareness training in the workplace. *European Journal of Training and Development, 39*, 610-627.

U. S. Department of Education. (2016 December *Student reports of bullying: Results from the 2015 school crime supplement to the national crime victimization survey.* https://nces.ed.gov/pubs2017/2017015.pdf

Weber, C., & Scott, S. (2013). Principles for principal preparation. In C. L. Slater & S. W. Nelson (Eds.), *Understanding the principalship: An international guide to principal preparation* (Vol. 19, pp. 95-125). Emerald Group Publishing.

Wentzel, K. R., & Caldwell, K. (1997). Friendships, peer acceptance and group membership: Relations to academic achievement in middle school. *Child Development, 68*(6), 1198-1209.

Ybing, L., Lynch, A. D., Kalvin, C, Liu, J., & Lerner, J. (2011). Peer relationships as a context for the development of school engagement. *International Journal of Behavioral Development, 35*(4), 329-342.

Zee, M., & Koomen, H. M. (2016). Teacher self-efficacy and its effects on classroom processes, student academic adjustment, and teacher well-being: A synthesis of 40 years of research. *Review of Educational Research, 86*(4), 981-1015.

Third Pillar—Expectations

Agarwal, P. (2020). *What neuroimaging can tell us about our unconscious biases.* Scientific American. https://blogs.scientificamerican.com/observations/what-neuroimaging-can-tell-us-about-our-unconscious-biases/

Asendorpf, J. B., Banse, R., & Mucke, D. (2002). Double dissociation between implicit and explicit personality self-concept: The case of shy behavior. *Journal of Personality and Social Psychology, 83*(2), 380-393.

Bamburg, J. (1994). *Raising expectations to improve student learning.* North Central Regional Educational Laboratory. ERIC Number ED378290

Berman, S. (1997). *SUNY series, democracy and education. Children's social consciousness and the development of social responsibility.* State University of New York Press.

Bierman, K. L. (2004). *Peer rejection: Developmental processes and intervention strategies.* Guildford.

Bloom, D., Peters, T., Margolin, M., & Fragnoli, K. (2013). Are my students like me? The path to color-blindness and White racial identity development. *Education and Urban Society, 47*(5), 555-575.

Boser, U., Wilhelm, M., & Hanna, R. (2014). *The power of the Pygmalion Effect, Teachers' expectations strongly predict college completion.* Center for

American Progress. https://www.americanprogress.org/issues/education-k-12/reports/2014/10/06/96806/the-power-of-the-pygmalion-effect/

Brophy, J. E. (1983). Research on the self-fulfilling prophecy and teacher expectations. *Journal of Educational Psychology, 75*(5), 631-661.

Brophy, J. E., & Good, T. L. (1970). Teachers' communication of differential expectations for children's classroom performance: Some behavioral data. *Journal of Educational Psychology, 61*(5), 365-374.

Brophy, J. E., & Good, T. L. (1974). *Teacher-student relationships: Causes and consequences.* Holt, Rinehart, and Winston.

Busch, B. (2017). *Research every teacher should know: Setting expectations.* The Guardian. https://www.theguardian.com/teacher-network/2017/nov/10/what-every-teacher-should-know-about-expectations

Center for American Progress (October, 2014). *The power of the Pygmalion Effect.* National Center for Education Statistics. https://www.americanprogress.org/issues/education-k-12/reports/2014/10/06/96806/the-power-of-the-pygmalion-effect/

Cheng, D. A. (2017). Teacher racial composition and exclusion rates among Black or African American students. *Education and Urban Society.* https://journals.sagepub.com/doi/abs/10.1177/0013124517748724

Cherng, H. S. (2017). If they think I can: Teacher bias and minority student expectations and achievement. *Social Science Research, 66, 170-186.*

Dasgupta, N. (2013). Implicit attitudes and beliefs adapt to situations: A decade of research on the malleability of implicit prejudice, stereotypes, and the self-concept. *Advances in Experimental Psychology, 47,* 233-279.

deBoer, H., Bosker, R., & van der Werf, M. (2010) Sustainability of teacher expectation bias effects on long-term student performance. *Journal of Educational Psychology 102*(1), 168-179.

de Boer, H., Timmermans, A. C., & van der Werf, M. P. (2018) The effects of teacher expectation interventions on teachers' expectations and student achievement: Narrative review and meta-analysis. *Educational Research and Evaluation 24*(3-5), 180-200.

Devine, P. G., Forscher, P. S., Austin, A. J., & Cox, W. T. (2012). Long-term reduction in implicit race bias: A prejudice habit-breaking intervention. *Journal of Experimental Social Psychology, 48*(6), 1267-1278.

Dusek, J. B., & Joseph, G. (1983). The bases of teacher expectations: A meta-analysis. *Journal of Educational Psychology, 75*(3), 327–346.

Facing History and Ourselves (2021). *Confirmation and other biases.* https://www.facinghistory.org/resource-library/facing-ferguson-news-literacy-digital-age/confirmation-and-other-biases

FitzGerald, C., Martin, A., Berner, D., & Hurst, S. (May, 2019). Interventions designed to reduce implicit prejudices and implicit stereotypes in real world contexts: A systematic review. *BMC Psychology.* https://doi.org/10.1186/s40359-019-0299-7

Glock, S. (2016). Does ethnicity matter? The impact of stereotypical expectations on in-service teachers' judgments of students. *Social Psychology of Education, 19,* 493-509.

Glock, S., & Krolak-Schwerdt, S. (2013). Does nationality matter? The impact of stereotypical expectations on student teachers' judgments. *Social Psychology of Education, 16*(1), 111-113.

Gershenson, S., Holt, S. B., & Papageorge, N. W. (2016). Who believes in me? The effect of student-teacher demographic match on teacher expectations. *Economics of Education Review, 52*, 209-224.

Gonder, P. O. (1991). *Caught in the middle; How to unleash the potential of average students.* American Association of School Administrators.

Hinnant, J. B., O'Brien, M., & Ghazarian, S. R. (2009). The longitudinal relations of teacher expectations to achievement in the early school years. *Journal of Educational Psychology, 101*(3), 662-670.

Hughes, J. M., Gleason, K. A., & Zhang, D. (2005). Relationship influences on teachers' perceptions of academic competence in academically at-risk minority and majority first grade students. *Journal of School Psychology, 43*(4), 303-320.

Jamil., F. M. (2013). *Understanding teacher effectiveness: Theory and measurement of teacher skills, knowledge, and beliefs* (Doctoral dissertation). University of Virginia, Ann Arbor. https://search.proquest.com/docview/1445390422?accountid=14681

Jamil, F. M., Ross, A. L., & Hamres, B. K. (2018). Exploring longitudinal changes in teacher expectancy effects on children's mathematics achievement. *Journal for Research in Mathematics Education, 49*(1),

Johnston, O., Wildy, H., & Shand, J. (2019). A decade of teacher expectations research 2008-2018. *Australian Journal of Education, 63*(1), 44-73.
Johnston, J. (2017). Teacher expectations and the Black-White scholastic achievement gap. *Intuition: The BYU Undergraduate Journal in Psychology 12*(2), 83-93.

Jussim, L., Eccles, J., & Madon, S. (1996). Social perception, social stereotypes, and teacher expectations: Accuracy and the quest for the powerful self-fulfilling prophecy. In M. P. Zanna (Ed.), *Advances in experimental social psychology* (Vol. 28, pp. 281-388). Academic Press.

Lexico (2021). *Expectation.* https://www.lexico.com/en/definition/expectation

Lombardi, J. D. (2016). *The deficit model is harming your students.* Edutopia. https://www.edutopia.org/blog/deficit-model-is-harming-students-janice-lombardi

Losen, D. J., Sun, W., & Keith, M. A. (March, 2017). *Suspended education in Massachusetts: Using days of lost instruction due to suspension to evaluate our schools.* The Civil Rights Project. https://civilrightsproject.ucla.edu/resources/projects/center-for-civil-rights-remedies/school-to-prison-folder/summary-reports/suspended-education-in-massachusetts-using-days-of-lost-instruction-due-to-suspension-to-evaluate-our-schools

Luskin, B. (2016). MRIs reveal unconscious bias in the brain. *Psychology Today.* https://www.psychologytoday.com/us/blog/the-media-psychology-effect/201604/mris-reveal-unconscious-bias-in-the-brain

Lynch, M. (May, 2019). *How teacher expectations influence student performance.* The Edvocate. https://www.theedadvocate.org/how-teacher-expectations-influence-student-performance/

The Master Teacher (October, 2015). Know what happens when you lower expectations. https://masterteacher.net/know-what-happens- when-you-lower-expectations/

Merriam-Webster (2021). *Expect.* https://www.merriam-webster.com/dictionary/expect

McKown, C., & Weinstein, R. S. (2008). Teacher expectations, classroom context, and the achievement gap. *Journal of School Psychology, 46*(3), 235-261.

Mistry, R. S., White, E. S., Benner, A., & Huynh, V. W. (2009). A longitudinal study of the simultaneous influence of mothers' and teachers' educational expectations on low-income youth's academic achievement. *Journal of Youth and Adolescence, 39*(6), 826-838.

Nelson, L. (August, 2015). *Racism in the classroom: The "soft bigotry of low expectations" is just regular bigotry.* Vox. https://www.vox.com/policy-and-politics/2015/8/19/9178573/teacher-students-race-study

Nordell, J. (May, 2017). Is this how discrimination ends? *The Atlantic.* https://www.theatlantic.com/science/archive/2017/05/unconscious-bias-training/525405/

Nordell, J. (2021). *The end of bias: A beginning: The science and practice of overcoming unconscious bias.* Macmillan.

Nordell, J. (2021). *The end of bias: How we change our minds.* Granta Publications.

Papageorge, N., & Gershenson, S. (2016). *Do teacher expectations matter?* Brookings Institution. https://www.brookings.edu/blog/brown-center-chalkboard/2016/09/16/do-teacher-expectations-matter/

Papageorge, N. W., & Kang, K. (2020). Teacher expectations matter. *Review of Economics and Statistics, 102*(2), 234-25.

Peterson, E. R., Rubie-Davies, C. M., Osborne, D., & Sibley, C. G. (2016). Teachers' explicit expectations and implicit prejudiced attitudes to educational achievement: Relations with student achievement and the ethnic achievement gap. *Learning and Instruction 42*, 123-140.

Pettigrew, T. F., & Tropp, L. R. (2008). How does intergroup contact reduce prejudice? Meta-analytic tests of three mediators. *European Journal of Social Psychology, 38*(6), 922—934.

Psychology Today (2021). *Bias.* https://www.psychologytoday.com/us/basics/bias

Raffini, J. (1993). *Winners without losers: Structures and strategies for increasing student motivation to learn.* Allyn and Bacon.

Rosenthal, R., & Jacobson, L. (1968). *Pygmalion in the classroom: Teacher expectation and pupils' intellectual development.* Holt, Rinehart and Winston.

Rubie-Davies, C. M. (2006). Teacher expectations and student self-perceptions: Exploring relationships. *Psychology in the Schools, 43,* 537–552.

Rubie-Davies, M. (2007). Classroom interactions: Exploring the practices of high- and low-expectation teachers. *British Journal of Educational Psychology 77*(2), 289-306.

Rubie-Davies, C. M. (2008). Teacher beliefs and expectations: Relationships with student learning. In C. M. Rubie-Davies & C. Rawlinson (Eds.), *Challenging thinking about teaching and learning* (pp. 25–39). Nova.

Rubie-Davies, C. M. (2009). Teacher expectations and labeling. *International Handbook of Research on Teachers and Teaching, 695-707.*

Rubie-Davies, C. M. (2010). Teacher expectations and perceptions of student attributes: Is there a relationship? *British Journal of Educational Psychology, 80*(1), 121-135.

Rubie-Davies, C. (July, 2015a). *The teacher expectation project.* Society for Personality and Social Psychology. http://www.spsp.org/news-center/blog/the-teacher-expectation-project#gsc.tab=0

Rubie-Davies, C. (2015b) *Becoming a high expectation teacher: Raising the bar.* Routledge.

Rubie-Davies, C. M., Hattie, J., & Hamilton, R. (2006). Expecting the best for students: Teacher expectations and academic outcomes. *British Journal of Educational Psychology, 76*(3), 429-444.

Rubie-Davies, C. M., Peterson, E. R., Sibley, C. G., & Rosenthal, R. (2015). A teacher expectation intervention: Modelling the practices of high expectation teachers. *Contemporary Educational Psychology, 40,* 72–85.

Rubie-Davies, C. M., & Rosenthal, R. (2016). Intervening in teachers' expectations: A random effects meta-analytic approach to examining the effectiveness of an intervention. *Learning and Individual Differences. 50,* 83-92.

Speybroeck, S., Kuppens, S., Van Damme, J., Van Petegem, P., Lamote, C., Boonen, T., & de Vilde, J. (2012). The role of teachers' expectations in the association between children's SES and performance in kindergarten: A moderated mediation analysis. *PLOS One, 7*(4).

Starck, J. G., Riddle, T., Sinclair, S., & Warikoo, N. (2020). Teachers are people too: Examining the racial bias of teachers compared to other American adults. *Educational Researcher, 49*(4), 273-284.

Sorhagen, N. S. (2013). Early teacher expectations disproportionately affect poor children's high school performance. *Journal of Educational Psychology, 105*(2), 465-477.

Tenenbaum, H., & Ruck, M. (2007). Are teachers' expectations different for racial minority than for European American students? A meta-analysis. *Journal of Educational Psychology, 99*(2), 253-273.

Weinstein, R., Gregory, A., & Stambler, M. (2004). Intractable self-fulfilling prophecies: Fifty years after Brown v. Board of Education. *American Psychologist, 59,* 511-520.

Fourth Pillar—Achievement

Akey, T. M. (2006). *School context, student attitudes and behavior, and academic achievement: An exploratory analysis.* MDRC. https://files.eric.ed.gov/fulltext/ED489760.pdf

Ames, C. (1992). Classrooms: Goals, structures, and student motivation. *Journal of Educational Psychology, 84,* 261-271.

Anderman, L. H. (2003). Academic and social perceptions as predictors of change in middle school students' sense of school belonging. *The Journal of Experimental Education, 72,* 5-22.

Annenberg Learner. (2020). *Neuroscience & the classroom: Making connections.* https://www.learner.org/series/neuroscience-in-the-classroom/building-new-neural-networks/

APA (American Psychological Association). (2003). *Believing you can get smarter makes you smarter.* American Psychological Association. https://www.apa.org/research/action/smarter

APA (American Psychological Association). (2006). *Stereotype threat widens achievement gap.* https://www.apa.org/research/action/stereotype

APA (American Psychological Association). (2009). *School Connectedness.* https://www.apa.org/pi/lgbt/programs/safe-supportive/school-connectedness

Aronson, J., Fried, C. B., & Good, C. (2002). Reducing the effects of stereotype threat on African American college students by shaping theories of intelligence. *Journal of Experimental Social Psychology, 38*(2), 113-125.

Blackwell, L., Dweck, C., & Trzesniewski, K. (2007). Implicit theories of intelligence predict achievement across the adolescent transition: A longitudinal study and an intervention. *Child Development, 78*(1), 246-263.

Boser, U., Wilhelm, M., & Hanna, R. (2014). *The power of the Pygmalion Effect: Teachers' expectations strongly predict college completion.* Center for American Progress. https://www.americanprogress.org/issues/education-k-12/reports/2014/10/06/96806/the-power-of-the-pygmalion-effect/

Black, P., & Wiliam, D. (2010, September). Inside the black box: Raising standards through classroom assessment. *Phi Delta Kappan*, 139-148.

Blum, R. W., McNeely, C. A., & Rinehart, P. M. (2002). *Improving the odds: The untapped power of schools to improve the health of teens.* Center for Adolescent Health and Development, University of Minnesota. http://www.sfu.ca/cfrj/fulltext/blum.pdf

Brown, B.L. (1999). *Vocational certificates and college degrees.* (ERIC Digest No. 212). ERIC Clearinghouse on Adult, Career, and Vocational Education. https://files.eric.ed.gov/fulltext/ED434248.pdf

Bryk, A., and Schneider, B. (2002). *Trust in schools: A core resource of improvement.* Russell Sage Foundation.

Caine, R. N., & Caine, G. (2014). *12 brain/mind natural learning principles.* Natural Learning Research Institute. https://www.nlri.org/wp-content/uploads/2014/04/12-B_M-NLPs_CM.pdf

Caprara, G. V., Barbaranelli, C., Pastorelli, C., Bandura, A., & Zimbardo, P. G. (2000). Prosocial foundations of children's academic achievement. *Psychological Science, 11*, 302–306.

CDC (National Center for Chronic Disease Prevention and Health Promotion). (2009). *Health and academic achievement.* https://www.cdc.gov/healthyyouth/health_and_academics/pdf/health-academic-achievement.pdf

Cicchetti, D., & Toth, S. L. (1998). The development of depression in children and adolescents. *American Psychology. 53*(2), 221-241.

Cook, J. E., Purdie-Vaughns, V., Garcia, J., & Cohen, G. L. (2012). Chronic threat and contingent belonging: Protective benefits of values affirmation on identity development. *Journal of Personality and Social Psychology, 102*(3), 479–496.

Dean, C. B., Hubbell, E. R., Pitler, H., & Stone, B. (2012). *Classroom instruction that works: Research-based strategies for increasing student achievement* (2nd ed.). Association for Curriculum Supervision and Development.

Deci, E. L., & Ryan, R. M. (2012). Motivation, personality, and development within embedded social contexts: An overview of self-determination theory. In R. M. Ryan (Ed.), *The Oxford handbook of human motivation* (pp. 85-110). Oxford University Press.

Downey, M. (2019). New study: Achievement gap persistent and resistant to reform. *The Atlanta Journal-Constitution.* https://www.ajc.com/blog/get-schooled/new-study-achievement-gap-persistent-and-resistant-reform/fLVGOjK8kSc2pFuCCDkq1J/

Dweck, C. S. (2007). *Mindset: The new psychology of success.* Ballantine.

Dweck, C. S. (2017). *Mindset: Changing the way you think to fulfill your potential.* Random House Publishing Group.

Dweck, C. S., Walton, G. M., & Cohen, G. L. (2014). *Academic tenacity: Mindsets and skills that promote long-term learning.* Bill and Melinda Gates Foundation. https://ed.stanford.edu/sites/default/files/manual/dweck-walton-cohen-2014.pdf

Eby, K. (2019). *The essential guide to writing SMART goals.* Smartsheet.com. https://www.smartsheet.com/blog/essential-guide-writing-smart-goals

Eccles, J. S., & Wigfield, A. (1995). In the mind of the actor: The structure of adolescents' achievement task values and expectancy-related beliefs. *Personality and Social Psychology Bulletin, 21*, 215–225.

EL Education (2016). *How schools can improve student achievement: A summary of research regarding strategies and conditions.* ELED-HowSchoolsCan ImproveStudentAchievement-0216-2.pdf

Fergus, E. (2016). *Solving disproportionality and achieving equity: A leader's guide to using data to change hearts and minds.* Corwin.

Fergus, E. (2017). *Solving disproportionality and achieving equity: A leader's guide to using data to change hearts and minds.* ERIC ED573400 abstract. https://eric.ed.gov/?id=ED573400

Fernald, A., Marchman, V. A., & Weisleder, A. (2013). SES differences in language processing skill and vocabulary are evident at 18 months. *Developmental Science, 16*(2), 234-248.

Filozof, E. M., Albertin, H. K., Jones, C. R., Sterne, S. S., Myers, L., & McDermott, R. J. (2009). Relationship of adolescent self-esteem to selected academic variables. *Journal of School Health, 68*(2), 68-72.

Fleetwood, C., & Shelley, K. (2000). The outlook for college graduates, 1998-2008: A balancing act. *Occupational Outlook Quarterly, Fall,* 3-9.

Frazier, L. (2019). Study shows link between early education and future career success. *Forbes.* https://www.forbes.com/sites/forbes-personal-shopper/2021/03/23/best-gaming-laptops/?sh=38c1a57b48b4

Franzel, A. C., Pekrun, R., & Goetz, T. (2007). Perceived learning environment and students' emotional experiences: A multilevel analysis of mathematics classrooms. *Learning and Instruction, 17*(5), 478-493.

Furrer, C., & Skinner, E. (2003). Sense of relatedness as a factor in children's academic engagement and performance. *Journal of Educational Psychology, 95,* 148-162.

Furrer, C.J., Skinner, E.A., & Pitzer, J.R. (2014). The influence of teacher and peer relationships on students' classroom engagement and everyday motivational resilience. *National Society for the Study of Education, 113,* 101-123.

Gutman, L.M., Sameroff, A., & Eccles, J.S. (2002). The academic achievement of African American students during early adolescence: An examination of multiple risk, promotive, and protective factors. *American Journal of Community Psychology, 30,* 401-428.

Hallikari, T., Nevgi, A., & Komulainen, E. (2007). Academic self-beliefs and prior knowledge as predictors of student achievement in mathematics: A structural model. *Educational Psychology (28)*1), 59-71.

Hanover Research (2017). *School-based strategies for narrowing the achievement gap.* www.hanoverresearch.com.

Hanushek E. A., Peterson, P. E., Tapley, L. M., Woessmann, L. (2019). The achievement gap fails to close. *Education Next (19)*3, 1-9.

Hart, B., & Risley, T. R. (2003). The early catastrophe. The 30 million word gap. *American Educator, 27*(1), 4-9.

Harackiewicz, J. M., Barron, K. E., Carter, S. M., Lehto, A. T., & Elliott, A. J. (1997). Predictors and consequences of achievement goals in the college classroom: Maintaining interest and making the grade. *Journal of Personality and Social Psychology, 73*(6), 1284–1295.

Hattie, J. (2008). *Visible learning: A synthesis of over 800 meta-analyses relating to achievement.* Routledge.

Hattie, J. (2012). *Visible learning for teachers.* Routledge.

Hattie, J. (2018). *Hattie's 2018 updated list of factors related to student achievement: 252 influences and effect sizes.* Visible Learning. https://visible-learning.org/hattie-ranking-influences-effect-sizes-learning-achievement/

Hattie, J. (2021). *Visible learning: What works best for learning.* Visible Learning. https://visible-learning.org/

Haughey, D. (2014). *A brief history of SMART goals.* Project SMART. https://www.projectsmart.co.uk/brief-history-of-smart-goals.php

Hearn, J. C. (2006). *Student success: What research suggests for policy and practice.* National Postsecondary Education Cooperative. https://nces.ed.gov/npec/pdf/synth_Hearn.pdf

Howard, G. (2002). School improvement for all: Reflections on the achievement gap. *Journal of School Improvement, 3*(1), 11-17.

Howard, G. (2004). *We can't lead where we can't go: An educator's guide to equity.* Corwin.

Jordan, M. (2017). *Michael Jordan Competitor mentality. How important is practice?* YouTube. https://www.youtube.com/watch?v=hXdj8scRdFE

Kasen, S., Cohen, P., & Brook, J. S. (1998). Adolescent school experiences and dropout, adolescent pregnancy, and young adult deviant behavior. *Journal of Adolescent Research, 13*(1), 49–72.

Kaufer, D. (2011). *Neuroscience and how students learn.* Berkeley Graduate Student Instructor Teaching and Resource Center. https://gsi.berkeley.edu/gsi-guide-contents/learning-theory-research/neuroscience/

Kuncel, N., Hezlett, S. A., & Ones, D. S. (2004). Academic performance, career potential, creativity, and job performance: Can one construct them all? *Journal of Personality and Social Psychology 86*(1), 148-161.

Learning Point (2004). *Improving student achievement and teacher effectiveness through scientifically-based practices.* North Central Regional Educational Laboratory. https://files.eric.ed.gov/fulltext/ED518744.pdf

Leithwood, K., Louis, K. S., Anderson, S., & Wahlstrom, K. (2004). *How leadership influences student learning. Review of research.* The Wallace Foundation. https://www.wallacefoundation.org/knowledge-center/documents/how-leadership-influences-student-learning.pdf

Lexico (2020). *Achievement.* https://www.lexico.com/en/definition/achievement

Liem, J. H., Dillon, C., & Gore, S. (2001). *Mental health consequences associated with dropping out of high school.* Eric Document ED457502. https://files.eric.ed.gov/fulltext/ED457502.pdf

Louis, K. S., Leithwood, K., Wahlstrom, K. L., & Anderson, S. E. (2010). *Learning from leadership: Investigating the links to improved student learning.* The Wallace Foundation. https://www.wallacefoundation.org/knowledge-center/pages/investigating-the-links-to-improved-student-learning.aspx

Martin, A.J., & Collie, R.J. (2016). The role of teacher-student relationships in unlocking students' academic potential: Exploring motivation, engagement, resilience, adaptability, goals, and instruction. In K.R. Wentzel & G. Ramani (Eds.), *Handbook of social influences on social-emotional, motivation, and cognitive outcomes in school contexts* (pp. 158-177). Routledge.

Martin, A.J., & Dowson, M. (2009). Interpersonal relationships, motivation, engagement, and achievement: Yields for theory, current issues, and practice. *Review of Educational Research, 79,* 327-365.

Mcneely, C., Nonnemaker, J. M., & Blum, R. (2002). Promoting school connectedness: Evidence from the National Longitudinal Study of Adolescent Health. *Journal of School Health, 72*(4), 138-146.

Mooney, T. (2018). *Why we say "Opportunity Gap" instead of "Achievement Gap."* Teach for America. https://www.teachforamerica.org/stories/why-we-say-opportunity-gap-instead-of-achievement-gap

National Alliance of Business, Inc. (1998). *The multifaceted returns to education.* Workforce Economic Trends [Abstract]. ERIC Document Reproduction Service No. ED419983.

NAESP (National Association of Secondary Principals). (2013*). From the Editor: Redefining the achievement gap.* https://www.naesp.org/principal-mayjune-2013-achievement-gap/editor-redefining-achievement-gap

National Center for Education Statistics. (2001). Chapter 5: Outcomes of Education. *Digest of Education Statistics* (pp. 443-460). https://nces.ed.gov/pubs2002/2002130.pdf

National Center on Safe Supportive Learning Environments (2020). *Protective factors.* https://safesupportivelearning.ed.gov/training-technical-assistance/education-level/early-learning/protective-factors

Nicholls, J. G. (1984). Achievement motivation: Conceptions of ability, subjective experience, task choice, and performance. *Psychological Review, 91*(3), 328–346.

O'Neill, J. (2003). SMART Goals connect a school. *Classroom Leadership (6)*6.
Pink, D. (2011). *Drive: The surprising truth about what motivates us.* Riverhead Books.

Reardon, S. F. (2016). School segregation and racial academic achievement gaps. *The Russell Sage Foundation Journal of the Social Sciences (2)*5, 34-57.

Rentner D., & Kober, N. (2001). *Higher learning-higher earnings: What you need to know about college and careers.* American Youth Policy Forum. Center on Education Policy. https://files.eric.ed.gov/fulltext/ED458440.pdf

Roeser, R. W., Midgley, C., & Urdan, T. C. (1996). Perceptions of the school psychological environment and early adolescents' psychological and behavioral functioning in school: The mediating role of goals and belonging. *Journal of Educational Psychology, 88*(3), 408—422.

Rubie-Davies, C. M., Peterson, E. R., Sibley, C. G., & Rosenthal, R. (2015). A teacher expectation intervention: Modelling the practices of high expectation teachers. *Contemporary Educational Psychology, 40*, 72–85.

Rubie-Davies, C. M., & Rosenthal, R. (2016). Intervening in teachers' expectations: A random effects meta-analytic approach to examining the effectiveness of an intervention. *Learning and Individual Differences. 50,* 83-92.

Safer, N., & Fleischman, S. (2005). Research matters: How student progress monitoring improves instruction. *Educational Leadership (62)*5, 81-83.

Saphier, J. (2016). *High expectations teaching: How we persuade students to believe and act on "smart is something you can get."* Corwin.

Shenk, D. (2013). *Intelligence is not static. It's a set of skills that we acquire.* Bigthink. https://bigthink.com/in-their-own-words/intelligence-is-not-static-its-a-set-of-skills-that-we-acquire

Steele, C. M. (1997). A threat in the air: How stereotypes shape intellectual identity and performance. *American Psychologist, 52*(6), 613-629.

Steele, C. M. (2010). *Whistling Vivaldi: How stereotypes affect us and what we can do.* W.W. Norton and Co.

Steele, C. M., & Aronson, J. (1995). Stereotype threat and intellectual test performance of African Americans. *Journal of Personality and Social Psychology, 69*(5), 797-811.

Steele, C., Spencer, S., & Aronson, J. (2002). Contending with group image: The psychology of stereotype and social identity threat. In M. P. Zanna (Ed.). *Advances in experimental social psychology* (Vol. 34, pp. 379–440). Academic Press.

Snow, K. (2013, October). *New research on early disparities: Focus on vocabulary and language processing.* NAEYC Blog. https://www.naeyc.org/blogs/gclarke/2013/10/new-research-early-disparities-focus-vocabulary-and-language-processing

Tucker, C. (2013-2014), Five musts for mastery. *Educational Leadership (71)*4, 56-60.

United States. (1983). *A nation at risk: The imperative for educational reform*. National Commission on Excellence in Education. https://www2.ed.gov/pubs/NatAtRisk/risk.html

Wallace (2020). *Learning from leadership: Investigating the links to improved student learning, Report*. Wallace Foundation Knowledge Center. https://www.wallacefoundation.org/knowledge-center/pages/investigating-the-links-to-improved-student-learning.aspx

Walton, G. M., & Cohen, G. L. (2011). A brief social belonging intervention improves academic and health outcomes for minority students. *Science 331* (6023), 1447-1451.

Wentzel, K.R. (2010). Students' relationships with teachers. In J. L. Meece & J.S. Eccles (Eds). *Handbook of research on schools, schooling, and human development* (pp. 75-91). Routledge.

Wexler, N. (2019, March). The achievement gap hasn't budged in 50 years. What next? *Forbes*. https://www.forbes.com/sites/nataliewexler/2019/03/17/the-achievement-gap-hasnt-budged-in-50-years-nowwhat/?sh=7c6870ce4d90

Willis, Judy. (2012, July). *A neurologist makes the case for teaching teachers about the brain*. Edutopia. https://www.edutopia.org/blog/neuroscience-higher-ed-judy-willis

Yin, Y., Shavelson, R., Ruiz-Primo, M. A., Brandon, P., & Furtak, E. (2008). On the impact of formative assessment on student motivation, achievement, and conceptual change. *Applied Measurement in Education, 21*(4), 335-359.

Fifth Pillar—Tenacity

Anderson, J. (2018). *Mindsets matter—but that's only half the story*. Mindful by Design. https://mindfulbydesign.com/mindsets-matter-thats-half-story/

Anderson, J. (2018b). *Putting growth back into Growth Mindset*. Mindful by Design. https://mindfulbydesign.com/putting-growth-back-into-growth-mindset/

Bandura, A. (1997). *Self-efficacy: The exercise of control*. W. H. Freeman.

Barseghian, T. (2013). *How to foster grit, tenacity, and perseverance: An educator's guide.* MindShift. https://www.kqed.org/mindshift/27212/how-to-foster-grit-tenacity-and-perseverance-an-educators-guide

Bashant, J. (2014). Developing grit in our students. *Journal for Leadership and Instruction.*

Blackwell, L., Trzesniewski, K., & Dweck, C. S. (2007). Implicit theories of intelligence predict achievement across an adolescent transition: A longitudinal study and an intervention. *Child Development, 78,* 246–263.

CASEL (2020a). *Niemi: CASEL is updating the most widely recognized definition of social-emotional learning. Here's Why.* https://www.the74million.org/article/niemi-casel-is-updating-the-most-widely-recognized-definition-of-social-emotional-learning-heres-why/

CASEL (2020b). *What are the core competence areas and where are they promoted?* https://casel.org/what-is-sel/

CDC (Centers for Disease Control and Prevention). (2009). *School connectedness: Strategies for increasing protective factors among youth.* U.S. Department of Health and Human Services. https://www.cdc.gov/healthyyouth/protective/pdf/connectedness.pdf

Cohen, G. L., & Garcia, J. (2008). Identity, belonging, and achievement: A model intervention, and implications. *Current Directions in Psychological Science, 17,* 365-369.

Cohen, G. L., & Sherman, D. K. (2014). The psychology of change: Self-affirmation and social psychological affirmation. *Annual Review of Psychology.* https://www.semanticscholar.org/paper/The-psychology-of-change%3A-self-affirmation-and-Cohen-Sherman/bc1fad3a8d927848aad76b3ee8482378eeb1ae76?p2df

Cook, J. E., Purdie-Vaughns, V., Garcia, J., & Cohen, G. L. (2012). Chronic threat and contingent belonging: Protective benefits of values affirmation on identity development. *Journal of Personality and Social Psychology, 102*(3), 479-496.

Damon, W. (2008). *The path to purpose: Helping our children find the calling in life.* The Free Press.

Denoël, E., Dorn, E. Goodman, A. Hiltunen, J., Krawitz, & Mourshed, M. (2017). *Drivers of student performance: Insights from Europe.* McKinsey & Company.

Duckworth, A. L. (2001). The significance of self-control. *Proceedings of the National Academy of Science, 108*(7), 2639-2640.

Duckworth, A. L. (2018). *Grit: The power of passion and perseverance.* Scribner.

Duckworth, A. L., & Kern, M. L. (2011). A meta-analysis of the convergent validity of self-control measures. *Journal of Research in Personality, 45*(3), 259-268.

Duckworth, A.L., Peterson, C., Matthews, M. D., & Kelly, D. R. (2007). Grit: Perseverance and passion for long-term goals. *Journal of Personality and Social Psychology, 92*(6), 1087-1101.

Duckworth, A. L., & Seligman, M. (2005). Self-discipline outdoes IQ in predicting academic performance of adolescents. *Psychological Science, 16*(12),939-944.

Dweck, C. S. (2007). The perils and promises of praise. *Educational Leadership, (65)*2, 34-39.

Dweck, C. S. (2017a). *Growth mindset is on a firm foundation, but we're still building the house.* Mindset Scholars Network Blog. https://studentexperiencenetwork.org/growth-mindset-firm-foundation-still-building-house/

Dweck, C.S. (2017b). *Mindset: The new psychology of success.* Ballantine Books.

Dweck, C. S., Walton, G. M., & Cohen, G. L. (2014). *Academic tenacity: Mindsets and skills that promote long-term learning.* Bill and Melinda Gates Foundation. https://ed.stanford.edu/sites/default/files/manual/dweck-walton-cohen-2014.pdf

Eby, K. (2019). *The essential guide to writing SMART goals.* Smartsheet.com. https://www.smartsheet.com/blog/essential-guide-writing-smart-goals

Eccles, J. S., Wigfield, A., & Schiefele, U. (1998). Motivation to succeed. In N. Eisenberg (Ed.), *Handbook of child psychology: Social, emotional, and personality development* (5th ed., pp. 1017-1095). Wiley.

Education Northwest (2015). *What we are learning about the academic tenacity of our youngest learners.* https://educationnorthwest.org/news/what-we-are-learning-about-academic-tenacity-our-youngest-learners

Elmore, Tim. (2014a, June). Seven Ideas to Build Perseverance in Students, Part One. *Huffpost.* https://www.huffpost.com/entry/seven-ideas-to-build-pers_b_5175097

Elmore, Tim. (2014b, June). Seven Ideas to Build Perseverance in Students, Part 2. *Huffpost.* https://www.huffpost.com/entry/seven-ideas-to-build-perseverance_b_5232312

Farrington, C., Nagaoka, J., Keys, T. S., Johnson, D. W., Roderick, M., Allensworth, E., & Beechum, N. W. (2012). *Teaching adolescents to become learners: The role of noncognitive factors in shaping school performance.* University of Chicago Consortium on School Research. https://consortium.uchicago.edu/publications/teaching-adolescents-become-learners-role-noncognitive-factors-shaping-school

Furrer, C., & Skinner, E. (2003). Sense of relatedness as a factor in children's academic engagement and performance. Journal of *Educational Psychology, 95,* 148–162.

Good, C., Aronson, J., & Inzlicht, M. (2003). Improving adolescents' standardized test performance: An intervention to reduce the effects of stereotype threat. *Journal of Applied Developmental Psychology, 24,* 645–662.

Goodenow, C. (1992). Strengthening the links between educational psychology and the study of social contexts. *Educational Psychologist, 27,* 177–196.

Haughey, D. (2014). *A brief history of SMART goals.* Project SMART. https://www.projectsmart.co.uk/brief-history-of-smart-goals.php

Headden, S., & McKay, S. (2015). *Motivation matters.* Carnegie Foundation for the Advancement of Teaching. https://www.carnegiefoundation.org/resources/publications/motivation-matters-how-new-research-can-help-teachers-boost-student-engagement/

Kaplan, A., & Flum, H. (2009). Motivation and identity: The relations of action and development in educational contexts—An introduction to the special issue. *Educational Psychologist, 44,* 73–77.

Kaufman, S. B. (2014). *Why academic tenacity matters.* Scientific American.com. https://blogs.scientificamerican.com/beautiful-minds/why-academic-tenacity-matters/

Korpershoek, H., Canrinus, E. T., Fokkens-Bruinsma, M., & deBoer, H. (2020). The relationships between school belonging and students' social, motivational, social-emotional, behavioural, and academic outcomes in secondary education: A meta-analytic review. *Research Papers in Education, 35*(6).

Lemberger, M. E., & Clemens, E. V. (2012). Connectedness and self-regulation as constructs of the student success skills program in inner-city African American elementary school students. *Journal of Counseling & Development, (90),* 4, 450-458.

Lexico. (2021). *Grit.* https://www.lexico.com/en/definition/grit

Lucas, B., & Spencer, E. (2018). Teaching tenacity. *Creative Teaching and Learning 8*(1), 8-14.

McKnight, P. E., & Kashdan, T. B. (2009). Purpose in life as a system that creates and sustains health and well-being: An integrative, testable theory. *Review of General Psychology, 13,* 242–251.

Merriam-Webster, 2021a. *Tenacity.* https://www.merriam-webster.com/dictionary/courage

Merriam-Webster, 2021b. *Persistence.* https://www.merriam-webster.com/dictionary/persistence

Merriam-Webster, 2021c. *Perseverance.* https://www.merriam-webster.com/dictionary/perseverance

Merriam-Webster, 2021d. *Determination.* https://www.merriam-webster.com/dictionary/determination
Merriam-Webster, 2021e. *Mettle.* https://www.merriam-webster.com/dictionary/mettle

Merriam-Webster, 2021f. *Grit.* https://www.merriam-webster.com/dictionary/grit

Merriam-Webster, 2021g. *Courage.* https://www.merriam-webster.com/dictionary/courage

Merriam-Webster, 2021h. *Resilience.* https://www.merriam-webster.com/dictionary/resilience

Merriam-Webster, 2021f. *Grit.* https://www.merriam-webster.com/dictionary/grit

MindTools. (2021). *SMART Goals: How to make your goals achievable.* https://www.mindtools.com/pages/article/smart-goals.htm

O'Neill, J. (2003). *SMART Goals connect a school.* ASCD. http://www.ascd.org/publications/classroom-leadership/mar2003/SMART-Goals-Connect-a-School.aspx

Oyserman, D., Gant, L., & Ager, J. (1995). A socially contextualized model of African American identity: Possible selves and school persistence. *Journal of Personality and Social Psychology, 69*, 1216–1232.

Perkins-Gough, Deborah. (2013). The significance of grit: A conversation with Angela Lee Duckworth. *Educational Leadership, 71*(1), 14-20.

Sansone, R. S., & Sansone, L. A. (2010). Gratitude and well being: The benefits of appreciation. *Psychiatry, (7)*11, 18-22.

SRI International (2018). *Promoting grit, tenacity, and perseverance: Critical factors for success in the 21st century.* SRI International. https://www.sri.com/work/publications/promoting-grit-tenacity-and-perseverance-critical-factors-success-21st-century

Tung, L. (2019). *Your brain on gratitude: How a neuroscientist used his research to heal from grief.* PBS News. https://whyy.org/segments/your-brain-on-gratitude-how-a-neuroscientist-used-his-research-to-heal-from-grief/

Villares, E., Lemberger, M., Brigman, G., & Webb, L. (2011). Student success skills: An evidence-based school counseling program grounded in humanistic theory. *Journal of Humanistic Counseling, 50,* 42-55.

Walton, G. M., & Cohen, G. L. (2007) A question of belonging: Race, social fit, and achievement. *Journal of personality and Social Psychology, (91)*2, 82-96.

Walton, G. M., & Cohen, G. L. (2011). A brief social-belonging intervention improves academic and health outcomes among minority students. *Science, 331,* 1447-1451.

West, M. R. (2016). *Should non-cognitive skills be included in school account-ability systems?* Brookings Institute. https://www.brookings.edu/research/should-non-cognitive-skills-be-included-in-school-accountability-systems-preliminary-evidence-from-californias-core-districts/

Wingspread. (2004). *Wingspread Declaration: A national strategy for im-proving school connectedness.* https://www.pcsb.org/cms/lib/FL01903687/Centricity/Domain/202/national_strategy.pdf

Witvliet, C. V., Richie, F. J., Luna, L. M., & Van Tongeren, D. R. (2019). Gratitude predicts hope and happiness: A two-study assessment of traits and states, *The Journal of Positive Psychology, 14*(3), 271-282.

About The Author

Dr. Andy Parker, a native Mississippian and outspoken advocate for public education, is an energetic, motivational leader and speaker who has been teaching students, leading schools and districts, and coaching school leaders for over three decades. In 2008, he created his G.R.E.A.T. Leadership Philosophy™ that he applies to his work and life. His background as a high school English teacher and his passion for leadership and supporting those in leadership roles propelled him to write this book, *Building Brilliant Schools: What GREAT Leaders Do Differently.* Implementing his GREAT Leadership Philosophy in the role as a high school principal, Dr. Andy and his team accomplished these GREAT results:

- The school's rating moved from underperforming to high performing.
- Coaches and students secured 7 state championships in five years, up from 1 in the school's history.
- The school's dismal drop-out rate - one of the highest in Mississippi - dropped to one of the lowest in the state, coupled with one of the highest completion rates!
- His drive and inspiration compelled senior classes to jump from receiving under $700,000 in scholarship offerings to over $5 million.

- Dr. Andy's team reduced physical altercations to almost 0 during his five-year tenure as principal.

An energizing, humorous, and frank speaker on issues surrounding education, Dr. Andy is an avid lover of animals, and he knows that life is too short for bad coffee and cheap wine.

For more information about Dr. Andy or to book him for your next conference or training event and explore how he works with schools and those who lead them, please visit his website:

www.drandyparker.com

Additional Materials
& Resources

**Access your Additional Materials & Resources
referenced throughout this book at
https://drandyparker.com/bookbonus**

Made in the USA
Coppell, TX
20 March 2023

14490056R00184